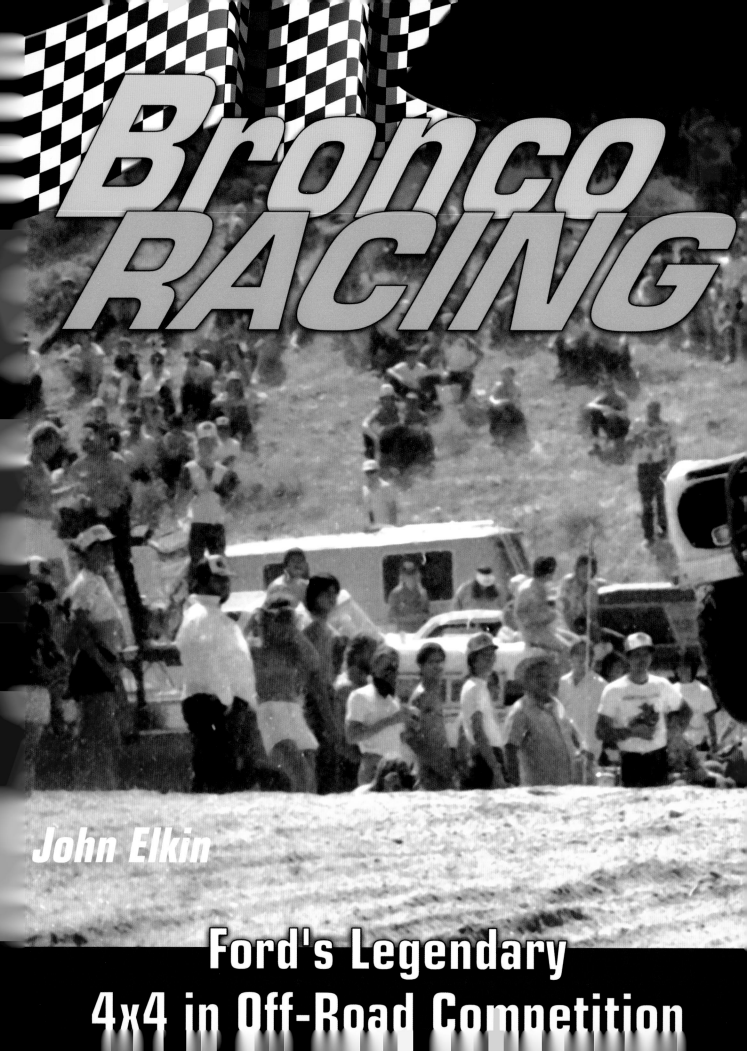

Bronco RACING

John Elkin

Ford's Legendary
4x4 in Off-Road Competition

CarTech®

CarTech®

CarTech®, Inc.
6118 Main Street
North Branch, MN 55056
Phone: 651-277-1200 or 800-551-4754
Fax: 651-277-1203
www.cartechbooks.com

Edit by Wes Eisenschenk
Layout by Monica Seiberlich

ISBN 978-1-61325-596-4
Item No. CT678

Library of Congress Cataloging-in-Publication Data Available

Written, edited, designed, and printed in the U.S.A.
10 9 8 7 6 5 4 3 2 1

DISTRIBUTION BY:

Europe
PGUK
63 Hatton Garden
London EC1N 8LE, England
Phone: 020 7061 1980 • Fax: 020 7242 3725
www.pguk.co.uk

Australia
Renniks Publications Ltd.
3/37-39 Green Street
Banksmeadow, NSW 2109, Australia
Phone: 2 9695 7055 • Fax: 2 9695 7355
www.renniks.com

Canada
Login Canada
300 Saulteaux Crescent
Winnipeg, MB, R3J 3T2 Canada
Phone: 800 665 1148 • Fax: 800 665 0103
www.lb.ca

TABLE OF CONTENTS

DEDICATION

To my wife, Mary, and my son, Robby,
who were my support team during a crazy year and a half.

ACKNOWLEDGMENTS

I never thought that I would write a book. I always considered myself a magazine writer, reporting on events, testing vehicles, interviewing the interesting, and digging up news. It took one fateful trip to the Specialty Equipment Manufacturers Association (SEMA) Show in 2019 to change all that.

Had I known at the time that I would be writing a book during a global pandemic, I may have reconsidered the notion. But honestly, who plans the upcoming year and thinks, "Well, I'll do everything I plan unless a global pandemic pops up." Although, the situation presented one positive aspect: when calling a source, odds were good that they were home and eager to talk to another human being.

Every writer needs a support group to push him or her during the dark times when the words do not come as easily as you would like. This book would not have been possible without my quarantine support group: my wonderful wife, Mary; and my teenage son, Robert. They supported me by being at my side when I needed them most and, more importantly, left me alone when I was "in the zone." They also knew when to get me away from the computer.

My professional support group is equally important: Wes Eisenschenk, my editor at CarTech Books. His guidance and help with connections were instrumental in putting this whole project together. His patience when things went sideways a few times was much appreciated.

Thanks to my writing brother from another mother: Jeff Zurschmeide. He convinced me that I could do this project. On many occasions, Jeff has been a wonderful cheerleader, sounding board, editor, and generator of vital support.

A special thanks to Robert Holcomb of Terra Design Photography, who donated hours of his time tuning and tweaking the photos in this book. Through Robert, I was granted access to The Historic Trust of Vancouver, which provided unlimited access to its advanced scanning equipment.

Thanks to Todd Zuercher, who wrote *Ford Bronco: A History of the Ford's Legendary 4x4* for CarTech Books. Todd answered hundreds of emails and sent me valuable information. He was supportive of my parallel project from the start. I could never completely pay him back for his help, but I will try.

Thanks to Willie Stroppe for his time behind the wheel of a Bronco and memories of his father, Bill. He provided me with a copy of the book *Boss: The Bill Stroppe Story* by Tom Madigan when mine went missing. Willie notched some impressive wins and recounted those stories for me.

I would love to take credit for all 50,000-plus words in this book, but I cannot. Quotes and reference material were freely given by people who understand the need to record the history of the Ford Bronco in off-road racing. People including Rod Koch, whose books *7 Years from Start to Finish—The Baja 1000 –The Early Years* and *When the Green Flag Drops* were so beautifully written and full of information about off-road racing in the 1968–1975 period. Thanks to Marty Fiolka, who supplied me with his history book on the 1,000-mile off-road race *1000 Miles to Glory: The History of the Baja 1000*.

So many wonderful websites and forums contributed to the research for this book. A special thanks to Curtis Guise for race-dezert.com, whose forum members were a fountain of knowledge and stories. Thanks to Andrew Norton for bajabronco.com, which is a wealth of information about Stroppe-era Broncos. Andrew also answered about a million emails from me. Thanks to Boyd Jaynes, a fierce competitor and journalist who fills devilhorsemotorsports.com with great information and photographs.

The men and woman who raced Broncos were so giving of their time. Steve Kelley, who spent a bit of time in a Bronco and is a heck of an off-road racer, helped get me in contact with Larry Minor. Larry Minor gave me many hours of his valuable time and was available at all hours. He donated personal family photos and detailed memories because he was there from the beginning.

Dick Landfield was especially helpful from his memories of his first race in a Bronco to helping grow this sport from his Ford dealership. Dick provided me detailed information about how he conceived the idea to combine teams to make the Ford Roughriders a force in off-road racing in the 1990s.

Gale Pike and the entire Pike Family gave freely of their time and memories of racing a Bronco from 1974–1989. Rest in peace, Gale.

Other hearty competitors contributed to this book. John Baker is long removed from racing but still has the competitive fire. However, he channels it into his real-estate business these days. Jim Loomis and Carl Jackson, two of Bill Stroppe's go-to drivers were wonderful sources of information and photos. Don Barlow, the driver of the *Crazy Horse* Bronco, helped with great stories and photos from his private collection. Thanks to Don and Ken Moss for photos and taking much of their personal time to answer every single inquiry of mine in exquisite detail.

Shelby Hall was awesome at filling in some blanks about Rod Hall that had slipped my memory as well as her time driving in a vintage Bronco at NORRA events. She supplied valuable information and photos from her participation in the Bronco R and Bronco Sport projects.

Thanks to "Baja" Bill Puentes, whose stepfather Lou Puentes took him along to Stroppe's Signal Hill shop and to the races. Bill's passion for Baja California is infectious; it equals his passion to make off-road racing as safe as possible. Bill coined the term "Bajaholic" for those addicted to Baja California.

Thanks to Ivan Stewart for taking time to remember his two events in the *Crazy Horse* Bronco. Ivan filled me in on some great facts and memories. Thanks to Cal Wells for his valuable time answering questions and verifying photos. Thanks to Kim, Lance, and Becky Kovel for their help in keeping Kirk Kovel's memory alive long after his tragic loss. They contributed stories, photos, and inspiration.

Ed Gudenkauf restores historic Broncos and keeps tabs on the ownership chain of famous rigs. His photos and knowledge were a welcome and much-needed addition to my expanding knowledge of all things Bronco. Ed is the current owner of the *Crazy Horse* and other notable Broncos.

A special thanks to the late, great Bobby Unser, and Al Senior, who had a few turns at the wheel of some Stroppe-prepared Broncos. Bobby's wife, Lisa, was especially helpful in getting me connected to the two brothers, who combined have seven Indy 500 wins. In off-road racing, book or not, that is an accomplishment worth noting. Next time you are in Albuquerque, New Mexico, the Unser family museum is a must visit for any fan of racing.

The Off-Road Motorsports Hall of Fame was a great resource during the research for this book. Barbara Rainey gave her time to help me get access to materials and people. The company website, ormhof.org, is a great resource for information about the sport.

Many thanks to Jim Ober of Trackside Photo. He was there from the earliest days of off-road racing until 2015. His collection is amazing. It can be found at tracksidephoto.com and is like walking through the entire history of the sport. Other photographic triumphs are directly due to Jim Delamarter, who oversees the collection of Parnelli Jones; Ed Justice, who administers the Justice Archive; Boyd Jaynes; Justin W. Coffee; and others who had photos to include. Look for their names in the photo credits.

A special thanks to the Petersen Archive and the *MotorTrend* group for contributing essential photographs. Thank you to Matt Paige, the director of *MotorTrend* group's publishing systems, who pushed the requests through the corporate labyrinth.

Finally, thank you to the Bronco and off-road racing community that has embraced this project. Fewer communities are more helpful and inclusive than racers, no matter what kind of racing. Thanks to the fans who keep the Bronco in their hearts and minds long after production ended. It is these people who nudged Ford into bringing the Bronco back into production. Long may it race, recreationally off-road, and safely transport the next generation of Bronco fans.

FOREWORD

by Larry Minor

From the first time I had the opportunity to strap in behind the wheel of a Ford Bronco, I knew it was going to be a game changer. It was 1966, and the off-road world was growing exponentially—both in numbers of enthusiasts but more importantly in the design and use of the vehicles. Any number of grassroots builders were already modifying vehicles for off-road use. However, having Ford, a major manufacturer, jump into the off-road world was a monumental shift in the landscape.

Growing up as a farmer, I had been playing in the dirt my whole life. It was a good life though, and one in which I learned the value of hard work and the importance of keeping my word. I had the good fortune of coming of age at a time when our area was the very epicenter of hot rodding and the postwar car culture. For me, the intersection of my farm life and my ever-growing interest in horsepower was realized through my active membership in the Hemet Jeep Club.

I was 16 years old, and all my friends were members of the club. We would spend every Thanksgiving at the Glamis Sand Dunes. We would spend weekends at Afton Canyon or any one of the great off-road destinations. We were the biggest and most active club around. My friends and I were the youngest members. The senior members would refer to us as the "hot rod kids" because they said we had more horsepower than horse-sense.

It should come as no surprise then that when Ford came looking for accomplished enthusiasts, it contacted the Hemet Jeep Club. The Bronco was in the final stages of real-world testing and on the verge of being released. I was among the first people to get to see and drive one. We met at Afton Canyon, where Ford not only wanted us to drive them but also wanted us to help film a commercial.

I was honored to be taking the new Bronco out for a run. My first impression of the Bronco was that with the longer wheelbase and coil spring suspension, it was a much more comfortable ride than other off-road vehicles I had driven. I was impressed with the overall performance and had great fun. It was clear that when released, the Bronco would hit the ground running.

Off-road racing received a big shot in the arm when Ed Pearlman announced that he and his group, the National Off-Road Racing Association (NORRA), was going to host the Mexican 1000. My good friend Rodney Hall and I decided we were going to compete with our race Jeep. For context, neither Rod nor I had been any further south into Baja California than Tijuana, Mexico. We had no

idea what to expect. We packed the Jeep with two spare tires, an ice chest, a tool chest, and other essential items and headed down there.

We had one goal in mind: to win . . . or at least finish. We also wanted to beat Ray Harvick and Bill Stroppe. I had known Ray Harvick from my summers down by the beach where we harvested potatoes together in the San Pasqual Valley. You can read about what happened in the race in Chapter 5.

Not long after the race, Bill Stroppe contacted Rodney and I and invited us to race for him in 1968. I said yes right away, but Rodney wanted to stay with Jeep.

My first race for Stroppe was the Mint 400. Stroppe did not have my Bronco done, so I rode with my brother-in-law, Jim Loomis, and we won. I took my mechanic, Jack Bayer, with me once my Bronco was done, and we won the Stardust 7-11 and the NORRA Mexican 1000—all with a V-8 engine, stick shift, and manual steering. The year 1968 was very good.

Ford was impressed with our victories, and I was invited to the end-of-the-year race banquet that they threw in Michigan. I will never forget standing in that room. Everyone was there: A. J. Foyt, the Unsers, Junior Johnson, etc. It was a virtual who's who of the racing world. It was humbling for this small-town farm boy to be there with those people who were not only accomplished racers but also my heroes. After 1968, I was recognized as Off-Road Driver of the Year by *Four Wheeler* magazine to cap an amazing year.

Rodney Hall tried to beat me all year long, but he couldn't do it. By now, Rodney wanted to drive a Bronco, but Stroppe did not have one for him yet, so he teamed up with me. For 1969, Bill Stroppe built me a new Bronco. It had a Boss 302 V-8 engine, automatic transmission, and a better suspension. This was also the first Bronco racer in which Stroppe installed power steering. At the next Mexican 1000, Rodney and I won it overall and even beat the motorcycles.

I always wanted a faster racer, so in 1970, when Parnelli built *Big Oly*, I was able to drive the *Pony* with sponsorship from Minolta cameras. Parnelli is a truly talented driver and really tough to beat. In 1971, when we got back to the Mexican 1000, he won in 14-1/2 hours, but we were a really close second—only 25 minutes behind him. Parnelli taught me a lot, and we became good friends.

The Bronco served me well for many years. I am blessed to have had an adventurous and truly wonderful 80-plus years on this earth. My years of racing Broncos with Stroppe and Ford and competing with all of the great drivers and crew members who were there every step of the way will always be among the best times of my life.

The Bronco changed the whole landscape of off-road racing. The Ford four-wheel-drive program showed that you could take a production vehicle and be competitive. Ford went all out to win. It knew how to put all the right personnel in place. We may have been a bunch of dirt racers, but they treated us as professionals. They promoted a winning mindset for sure, and for this small-town boy to be able to follow his passion and fulfill his dreams, it has been a true honor.

"Luck lives at the intersection of hard work and opportunity," they say, and lucky me was at the right place at the right time when it came to fulfilling my off-road dreams. I hope that you enjoy reading this book and learning about what it was like to be there at the time.

Just to let you know, I am not done with off-roading yet. I have a new orange Bronco on order, and I am looking forward to seeing everyone in Death Valley!

Larry Minor
Member of the Off-Road Motorsports
and Drag Racing Halls of Fame

FOREWORD

by Todd Zuercher

Dirt, sand, rocks, cacti, silt, and mud. To these ingredients add a throaty V-8 engine and a rough-and-tumble off-road rig and you've created the concoction known as an off-road racer. Ford knew this recipe would be a key to the success of its new off-roader, the Ford Bronco, when it was introduced in 1965. In very short order, the Bronco proved itself in competition.

As a result, the Bronco, arguably more than any other sport-utility vehicle (SUV), counts its rich competitive history in the deserts of the American Southwest and Baja California as an integral and necessary part of its story and its lore among enthusiasts. The immaculately prepped and painted Broncos in the Stroppe fleet in the late 1960s and early 1970s left an indelible mark in the minds of those people that saw them firsthand. It did the same for the thousands more who followed their exploits in books, magazines, and television programs. The men who piloted those ponies, including Parnelli Jones, Rod Hall, Larry Minor, James Garner, Ray Harvick, and Bill Rush, became heroes and household names to legions of contemporary admirers and the generations of fans that have followed. In the pages of this book, the stories and accomplishments of those giants, along with many others, come alive in great detail.

Broncos continued their travels on the rutted racecourses through the years until the next era of Bronco domination that occurred with the Ford Rough Riders off-road racing team. Through the efforts of Dick Landfield and others, this modern-era "super team" brought together an impressive phalanx of the Blue Oval's finest at the time, including the mighty Bronco from Enduro Racing that was piloted by Dave Ashley and Dave Smith. The driving skills of Ashley and Smith along with the

2010, each year's race has included a variety of Broncos in multiple classes. The NORRA has allowed those of us with limited resources to live the dream of racing our favorite thoroughbreds in the beautiful and rugged Baja backcountry where our heroes raced 50 years ago.

As we begin another decade, the Ford Bronco R continues the long legacy of Ford Broncos battling the Baja. The introduction of the new Bronco promises a new chapter of Bronco desert racing in the years ahead. The future is bright!

All of these stories and so much more are contained in this book! Drawing upon extensive interviews with those who were there and plenty of behind-the-scenes research, veteran off-road racing journalist John Elkin tells the story of Broncos in off-road racing that has never before been told in such detail or entirety. You'll enjoy learning many new stories with details told in John's familiar and folksy style. This book not only covers details and specifications of the Broncos themselves but also the stories about the drivers—a cast of characters as diverse as life itself.

It's an honor for me to write a foreword for this book. I know we'll all enjoy it!

Todd Zuercher
Author of *Ford Bronco: A History of Ford's Legendary 4x4*

Bronco's capabilities ensured that it was virtually unbeatable in Class 3 (short-wheelbase 4x4) for nearly half a decade.

The advent of a new century brought the Moss brothers from Sacramento, California, to the desert behind the wheel of their faithful 1979 Bronco. In the following years, these "everyman" racers have compiled the most impressive record of all Bronco racers (over 50 wins), a voluminous amount of Baja 500 and Baja 1000 wins, and many Class 3 championships. With their racing careers now at the 20-year mark, they're not done yet.

The second decade of the 2000s ushered in a renewed interest in racing vintage vehicles in Mexico, and the NORRA Mexican 1000 was born. Since the first race in

INTRODUCTION

With goggles in place and helmets securely fastened, a hearty Bronco team forges into the desert landscape. Those early days in the sport of off-road racing were truly adventures akin to covered wagons setting off in search of someplace better. (Photo Courtesy MotorTrend and Petersen Museum Archive)

Imagine it is 1967 and you are sitting at the start line of the first Mexican 1000 in the middle of Tijuana, Mexico. Aside from the paved road to Ensenada and 30 miles after, everything is a mystery. In front of you is 1,000 miles of unknown. Parked around you are 67 other entries hoping to be the first to La Paz. Hours, maybe several days of constant driving over some very inhospitable terrain is ahead. No GPS, no satellite phone, no chase helicopter, no chase crew. The guy or gal next to you has a map of Baja that he or she found at the Automobile Club and a compass. In the back of your rig is a pup tent—just in case. There are some spare parts, tools, some cans of oil, maybe a bag of sandwiches, and a couple of gallons of water.

This is off-road racing at the very beginning, and you are there with no idea of what is going to happen. Sure, you have a plan for the race, but you will quickly find out that the desert eats those for lunch. Whatever lies ahead will be a great adventure. The flagman raises and then drops the green flag with a flourish, the gas pedal gets mashed to the floor, and all of Baja Norte

and Sur lie ahead of you. Somewhere in the distance is La Paz. Just keep it pointed southeast.

These are the people who wrote the book on how to tackle Baja without any of the guidance technology that we enjoy today. They wrote it on their own through trial and error in a variety of vehicles that proved either worthy or woefully inadequate after just a few hundred miles. It did not take long before it became clear that Baja was special, and it called for a sturdy base platform to handle the rigors of the desert trails.

We are talking about off-road racing in its infancy and a Baja peninsula that was like stepping back 40 years in time in some parts and 100 years in others. Short wheelbases, limited suspension travel, bare-minimum safety equipment, and some backyard ingenuity made up most of the entry lists. The early days of off-road racing called for a hearty sense of adventure and a press-on regardless attitude. If you could start with a tougher platform, you were more likely to see La Paz about 27, 30, or 48 hours after leaving Tijuana or Ensenada.

Meet the Bronco

The Ford Bronco was the magic carpet that a lot of adventurous souls invested their money into in a bid to outrun everything else. It competed down the Baja peninsula, in the unforgiving Nevada desert, the Mojave Desert around Barstow, California, the dry washes outside Riverside, California, and the ever-changing conditions around Parker, Arizona. Later, the Bronco saw competition in the United States Midwest and Canada.

As much as the machine is the star here, it was people channeling their inner pioneering spirit who steered, developed, and poured their blood, sweat, tears, and money into those machines. In the end, because of this relationship between people and the machine, the Bronco was the clear-cut favorite over Jeep and International.

Ford Motor Company knew it had to design a better four-wheel-drive vehicle platform than Jeep and International offered. It had to be more innovative to make a more capable performer. Anyone with an early Jeep or International will tell you that the truck was tough, but so was the ride. The Bronco fulfilled the need for a more innovative suspension. The advanced design came along at the perfect time.

The People and the Machine

The purpose of writing this book is to highlight not only the machine but also the people and the effort that it took to bring the racing version of the Bronco to life. The Bronco caught on with teams of all types at different financial levels from the mighty Stroppe Holman-Moody factory-backed effort and dealership owners to a man who moved to California from the Midwest, where he planned to use his Bronco to plow snow but instead went racing and went on to be a factory-backed driver.

This book contains legendary tales of battles waged at the earliest events in Southern California, Nevada, Arizona, and Baja California with Parnelli Jones and Mickey Thompson banging wheels, dodging cacti, and passing and re-passing each other for 150 miles. More tales include Larry Minor and Rod Hall slaughtering the competition on two and four wheels to take an overall win in a four-wheel-drive class Bronco, which is still a record at the writing of this book.

In the rough-and-tumble world of off-road racing, you cannot go back and examine the roots of the sport as well as its rise in popularity without taking into consideration the role that the Ford Bronco played. Ford has

This is a typical early Bronco setup for the rigors of off-road racing. Note the multiple shock absorbers above the front tire, the heavy-gauge metal tubing to form the roll cage to protect the driver and codriver, and the extra driving lights attached to the top of the windshield frame. The larger tires allowed for better floatation on loose surfaces such as sand and silt. Private teams, such as Viva Broncos, put a lot of faith in the durability of the Ford Bronco to get to the finish of each race. (Photo Courtesy Kurt Strecker)

With the short wheelbase and the larger tires, a Bronco launches into the air with just the slightest provocation. It was fun.

designed and built vehicles with an eye toward competition as a cog in its marketing effort. That tradition began with none other than Henry Ford himself in 1901, when he successfully raced and won with a 26-hp automobile of his design.

Throughout Ford's history, racing was at times a primary method of marketing. "Win on Sunday, Sell on Monday" was a battle cry by which many company advertising men lived. From the dirt tracks of early NASCAR to the Indianapolis Motor Speedway and the world of Formula One, Ford was there. In the dry riverbed outside Riverside, California, where off-road racing truly started to evolve, Ford used the occasion to introduce the Bronco. In 1963, with the emergence of people besting each other with timed endurance runs down the Baja California peninsula, a proper race was organized in 1967, and Ford was there.

The Bronco was purpose-built to be a tough rig. The suspension was built to take on the toughest roads whether they were made from rocks, mud, sand, or rutted dirt. The interior lacked creature comforts to emphasize the toughness of the vehicle. This, along with a proven dependable drivetrain, made it a logical choice to tackle the race down the Baja Peninsula. Starting with a stout platform from which to build their racers was what put Ford on par with Jeep and International.

The Stroppe Team

In the capable hands of Bill Stroppe and his talented crew, which teamed with Ford's powerhouse racing arm

Holman-Moody, the team built Ford's fleet of Broncos and F-Series pickups to tackle the race. Stroppe took what he learned in those early events and modified the Bronco to handle the rigors of the deserts of the Southwest United States and Mexico's Baja Peninsula.

Since there was not a strong aftermarket for off-road parts at that time, it was left to early off-roaders to fabricate, weld, jury rig, and generally make do with what was available at the time. Companies that were aware of what was happening in the off-road world jumped at having their names on the sides of cars, trucks, and motorcycles to alert the public that their products could survive the harsh desert conditions. Therefore, their products could probably handle your every driving demand. Filter companies, tire manufacturers, auxiliary lighting manufacturers, motor oil companies, and spark plug makers were but a few of the visionaries that saw what was coming.

The Bronco was not only used in the rough-and-tumble world of off-road racing. Believe it or not, for a short time, a Funny Car Bronco drag raced. A few Broncos competed in rally events in the United States, the Paris to Dakar Rally, and a myriad of sand drag competitions, mud races, tough truck events, and even some land speed records.

The Bronco Returns

There has been a recent resurgence of the original Bronco in off-road racing as vintage off-road racing has become popular. It is giving these retired racers a place to reclaim the desert as their own.

The reintroduction of a whole new Bronco with a retro bodystyle close to its ancestors was announced by Ford in 2019 with models available in 2021. Ford, excited to get the Bronco back out in the desert, made a 2019 Baja race its first event back. Ford teamed with the Desert Assassins off-road racing team to introduce the new bodystyle. With the announcement of the return of the Bronco in both production and racing, it seems that the Bronco story as a family SUV and a racing machine will continue.

Whether you are discovering the Bronco for the first time or reliving memories, there is something in this book for everyone who loves racing in the dirt.

CHAPTER 1

THE GENESIS OF THE BRONCO

I n 1962, the Ford Motor Company took notice that the Jeep CJ-5 and the International Harvester Scout 800 were getting the lion's share of the recreational off-road vehicle market. More people were exploring the mountains and deserts, towing recreational vehicles, and looking for an option to the standard family station wagon. While pickup trucks had limited seating, a utilitarian vehicle had room for the kids, the family dog, and cargo.

There were other reasons to design such a vehicle: fleet sales. Ford envisioned several entities utilizing such a vehicle: the U.S. Forest Service, U.S. Postal Service, local law enforcement in the desert and forested or mountainous areas, search-and-rescue crews, surveyors breaking new ground for highways, and utility companies with water and power lines running across inhospitable land.

In researching the needs of the prospective Bronco buyer, many consumers of the International 800 and Jeep vehicles were looking for something that their World War II–era Jeeps could not provide: stability at modern highway speeds, a smoother ride, and better protection from the elements. An overwhelming percentage of those polled registered a distain for fancy frills, communicating to Ford to keep the interior spartan and utilitarian.

In designing the Bronco, a group of engineers studied the competition to achieve the goals set out by prospective buyers. In designing the suspension for the best overall compromise in highway and off-road handling, engineers agreed on a 92-inch wheelbase. This provided improved approach, departure, and ramp break-over angles. The ramp break-over angle was determined to be most important to those who were surveyed by Ford after internal testing. In addition, Ford engineers carefully considered the various interactions of wheelbase, track width, and wheel turn angle to meet the Bronco's design goals of maneuverability, ride comfort, and stability.

Whether it was intentional or not, Ford designing the Bronco so well for the consumer also made it an amazing platform to be a desert racing machine. A longer

ABOVE: The Advanced Styling department made considerable gains with its clay models from November 27, 1963, through July 14, 1964. By late fall 1964, working prototypes were being tested in preparation for the 1966 model year. (Photos Courtesy Ford Motor Company)

This was the target at which Ford aimed its biggest guns: the Jeep M38-A1, which was later known as the CJ5. The International Scout 800 was a target as well, but Jeep had the lion's share of the recreational off-road market. (Photo Courtesy Jeff Zurschmeide)

The early Bronco half cab was the second-most-popular configuration. First was the hardtop version. You can see the care Ford engineers took in getting maximum clearance for the front and rear of the Bronco. (Photo Courtesy Andrew Norton)

It may be spartan or utilitarian, but prospective Bronco owners were not looking for frivolous interiors. This has tough written all over it. Controls for lights, wipers, and a heater make up the bulk of the controls. (Photo Courtesy Andrew Norton)

There's not much to look at on the passenger side. You could fiddle with the heater controls or look through the map compartment (I would not dare call it a glove box). (Photo Courtesy Andrew Norton)

Ford Engineer Paul Axelrad is often credited as being the "Father of the Bronco." He stands strategically positioned between a Bronco and a bronco in the fall of 1964 in Kingman, Arizona. This prototype Bronco was used and abused in a 1966 commercial. It was launched repeatedly over embankments and plowed through streams. (Paul Axelrad Photo, Photo Courtesy Ken Axelrad)

wheelbase equals a smoother ride. Better approach and departure angles mean you can hit holes and washouts harder without damage to the bumpers, rocker panels, or quarter panels.

Donald N. Frey, Ford's product manager in 1963, was deeply involved in the mammoth task of getting a new vehicle (the Mustang) to market in only 18 months. He worked closely with Lee Iacocca, Ford's vice president and general manager, to bring the Bronco to

market to accomplish this task. Frey brought in Paul Axelrad, an engineer of note at Ford. Frey set Axelrad to work on the chassis design and early clay modeling of this new project vehicle. It was Axelrad's job to build from the ground up something with a tough-looking stance that was stylish for the time: an off-road-capable vehicle that would stand up to everything that the Jeep and International could and more.

The Mustang was a great success for Iacocca and his team. While Ford worked to refine and accessorize the two-door coupe to make it more of a performance car than a "secretary's car," the Bronco was taking shape in the background.

Before long, test mules were being driven at the Ford Proving Grounds in Romeo, Michigan. These stripped-down versions of the production Bronco helped lay the groundwork to build a tough platform that could handle rough duty and yet be practical on the highways and streets, which was something the International and Jeep struggled with. These mules also went to Arizona and other destinations in the West with a Jeep and an International to gauge how they operated compared to the competition. However, these mule's duty to Ford was far from over.

Looking Back:
The Start of Off-Road

When off-road enthusiasts gather in groups, the inevitable conversation turns to asking where off-road exploration started. One could argue that the early pioneers in their wagons headed to California and Oregon started it all. Others may argue that the early transcontinental and point-to-point races were the start when men such as Barney Oldfield underwent tackling the American landscape at speed. Then, there are those who talk about the Jeeps and World War II.

The answer to the question is, as far as this author is concerned, that they are all correct. Granted, the early pioneers were undergoing an ordeal in pursuit of a better life, and the soldiers of World War II were simply trying to stay alive. Those early instances of off-road necessity were the nucleus of off-road recreation. Human beings are born to explore from the moment we pick up a new item

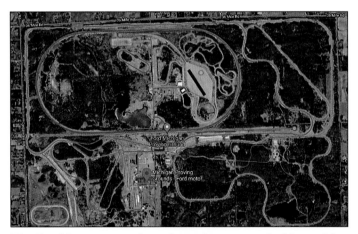

The Ford Bronco may have been born on a drafting table, but this is where it grew up. Eight test mules lived here at the Ford Michigan Proving Grounds in Romeo. This is where test drivers put the new platform through its paces. (Photo Courtesy Google Maps)

The barren landscape of Nevada can look a lot like the moon. Although the moon is only slightly more inhospitable, both have their challenges. At the 1973 Mint 400, a young Cal Wells (a future car builder for Toyota Motorsports) wheels his homebuilt Bronco down the road. Riding shotgun is Ralph Kosmides, who went on to be a successful businessman and championship-winning rally driver. (Photo Courtesy MotorTrend and Petersen Museum Archive)

The Broncos were durable to the point where a driver would not even think twice about launching them into the air. (Photo Courtesy MotorTrend and Petersen Museum Archive)

in our crib to examine to the freedom that a bicycle provided (as long as we were home by sundown lest we face the wrath of Mom). Going off-road is simply built into our DNA strands no matter our race, creed, or color.

We as humans are considered pack creatures. As much as we enjoy some time alone, we inevitably join together in a group in pursuit of recreation. To this end, off-roaders, when encountering each other on the trail, are always helpful and friendly because we have found someone who is like minded. This is the basis from which automobile clubs were formed, in particular off-road clubs, which are sometimes designated by the vehicle manufacturer, region, or having two or four wheels.

As humans, racing is the natural by-product of our desire to be competitive. Growing up, we raced bicycles or on foot. We crowded around a radio or a television on Memorial Day weekend to catch who won the Indianapolis 500. Our childhoods were measured by the fastest and smartest.

The Ford Bronco represented every one of these human desires wrapped up into one neat package. In the Bronco, we could get away and be alone. We could travel in a pack with our clubs to seek adventure. We could race if we wanted. While all of that was being accomplished,

we were wrapped around by a supe-
riorly engineered product that rode
better, went faster, and still provided
a level of comfort we were used
to. Ford filled that gap and made
off-roading a little more civilized.

Then, in the latter end of the
1960s, children growing up could
marvel at the models of *Big Oly* on
the shelves of their local retailer,
paper their walls with posters, and let
their imaginations loose with Johnny
Lightning miniature die-cast cars of
many off-road machines. These kids,
the ones who did not have the internet or a computer growing up, would
seek adventures just like their heroes,
such as Parnelli Jones.

Once educated and off in the
working world, a human needs a
release, a way to leave the stresses

In the early days of off-road racing, Carl Jackson and Jim Fricker make their way down the Baja Peninsula at the 1972 NORRA Mexican 1000. (Photo Courtesy Carl Jackson)

of the modern-day world behind. A great many of these
people did just that by seeking the adventure of treading
where most could or would not. My own father found
his stress relief by taking his family to Death Valley and
exploring the Old West, while teaching his sons about
respecting the land and leaving history undisturbed.
Some take it a step further and go racing.

Every one of us who has strapped into an off-road
machine to beat the competition has a similar story that
harkens back to these roots. Slaves to our own DNA, some
of us just want to satisfy that need a little faster than
everyone else. Racing is a natural progression of who we
are, and I believe it pays homage to those pioneers, cross
country racers, and military veterans. The fact that the
Ford Bronco was the chariot for modern day pioneers
and racers is just the cherry on top.

Off-Road Racing

After World War II, a flood of military-issue Jeep vehicles was auctioned off across the country. Former soldiers
who knew the capabilities of the little machine immediately bought them to use for exploring.

In 1948, in a low desert community called Hemet
in Southern California, a group of 70 families formerly
known as the Hemet Cavalcaders reorganized into the
Hemet Jeep Club. Their events on the De Anza Trail,
Afton Canyon, and the annual sand drag event drew
more than 400 entries in the early 1960s.

Whether it was something in the water in Hemet or
maybe how tightly knit the Jeep Club members were,
Hemet churned out off-road racing stars like Hostess

turns out Twinkies. Larry Minor, Rod Hall, Ray Harvick,
Carl Jackson, Jim Loomis, and Jim Fricker were just some
of those who found success in the Bronco and beyond.

In 1962, Hollywood stuntman Bud Ekins was
approached by Honda to prove the durability and reliability of its motorcycles by making a timed speed run
950 miles down the Baja Peninsula from Tijuana to La

These are Hemet's winningest off-road racers: Rod Hall and Jim Fricker. Hall is a former president of the Hemet Jeep Club. Fricker was the codriver of choice for a lot of good drivers. They won together for more than 30 years. (Photo Courtesy Trackside Photo)

To trace back to the true beginnings of the desire to conquer the Baja Peninsula, you need to go back to 1962. Honda sent Dave Ekins (left) and Bill Robertson Jr. (right) on a 952.7-mile journey to La Paz. It took 40 hours, but the benchmark was set, and the first footstep on the path to the first Mexican 1000 was unknowingly taken. (Walt Fulton Sr. Photo/Photo Courtesy the Dave Ekins Family)

Paz. Bud had contractual obligations to Triumph at the time, so he approached his brother Dave to head up the riding. A search for a second rider turned up Billy Robertson Jr., the son of a North Hollywood Honda dealership owner who had off-road experience.

The method of timing was crude but official as Ekins and Robertson sent telegrams from the start at the Western Union office in Tijuana, and then from the Western Union office in La Paz to get an official elapsed time. This first known attempt came in at just under 40 hours.

A slew of attempts followed on two and four wheels, and the elapsed time crept lower and lower. Each attempt gained more notoriety in the press and in the off-road community at large.

National Four-Wheel-Drive Grand Prix

In 1965, Brian Chuchua, a young Southern California Jeep dealership owner, organized an event called the National Four-Wheel-Drive Grand Prix near Riverside, California, in the Santa Ana Wash. Chuchua set up the event so spectators could see the event. The racecourse

ran about a mile over natural terrain in a figure eight. The event had an elimination format until a winner was determined. Entrants each ran identical twin loops, and the first competitor back to the start was the winner.

The 1965 event brought out around 100 entrants with some not-yet historical names dotting the entry list: Vic Hickey, Rod Hall, Dick Cepek, Ray Harvick, Ed Pearlman, Bill Stroppe, and Larry Minor would all become future stars in the off-road industry. The National Four-Wheel Drive Grand Prix continued until 1972.

Ed Pearlman Has a Gem of an Idea: NORRA

An enterprising man named Ed Pearlman who had run those early Grand Prix events figured that the Baja Peninsula, a place he knew well, was primed for an organized and sanctioned race. In 1967, the Mexican 1000 was born after Ed took part in a record attempt with two Chevrolet-powered Toyota Land Cruisers.

Ed was no stranger to organizing. Back in his military days on the island of Guam, he staged impromptu Jeep races. After his service, he purchased a military Jeep and began scouting around Baja. Along with his partner, Don Francisco, a plan to run the length of the peninsula was hatched, and word got around about this crazy adventure. Ed and Don formally marketed themselves as the National Off-Road Racing Association (NORRA), and a new type of racing was born.

It was not just as easy as gathering entries at a start location and waving a green flag. There were logistical issues to tackle with fuel as the main issue. NORRA arranged for crews willing to take their own vehicles ahead of the race date filled with gasoline and some spare parts for teams. These crews also doubled as a checkpoint. Timing parameters were established as well as checkpoint procedures. It was a mammoth undertaking considering the primitive nature of the Baja peninsula.

Perlman and Francisco put out a general-information booklet to answer the questions that potential entries might have. The booklets were handed out to every off-road shop and taken to club events. (Photo Courtesy NORRA Photo Archives)

The founding fathers of NORRA, Don Francisco (left) and Ed Pearlman (right), were the right men at the right time. Ed had the vision while attending the National Four-Wheel-Drive Grand Prix, and Don Francisco just happened to be in the right place at the right time to help get it all started. (Photo Courtesy NORRA Photo Archives)

Up-and-coming companies, such as K Bar S, took advantage of its racing successes and that of its customers. Parts built by people who knew how to race in Baja were highly sought after. (Photo Courtesy Ed Gudenkauf)

Sixty-eight hearty teams in four classes lined up to race the first Mexican 1000 in every conceivable vehicle you can imagine—and some you might not. Stock vehicles, modified vehicles, homebuilt vehicles, sedans, trucks, and motorcycles were split into four different classes by their capability.

First Mexican 1000 Classes	
Class I	Production two-wheel-drive vehicles
Class II	Production four-wheel-drive vehicles and dune buggies
Class III	Non-production vehicles (homebuilt)
Class IV	Production motorcycles

The Race to be Proven "Baja Tough"

Many manufacturers saw this challenge as a way to prove that their product was tougher than the desert. By inspecting their parts after a race, smart manufacturers used the information gleaned from 1,000 miles of the roughest terrain to make improvements.

Today, manufacturers do the same. The same went for tire companies, such as Goodyear, BFGoodrich, Western Auto, Cooper, Sears, and many others, as they sent their best tires to try and tame the Baja. Through manufacturer support and the examination of their parts after the race, everyday vehicles were made tougher, brighter, and more dependable thanks to those early pioneers in off-road racing.

Tire companies were very quick to get their products proven in Baja. If their rubber could tame the unknown wilderness of Baja California, that related to sales. (Photo Courtesy Ed Gudenkauf)

A favorite HDRA event was the Barstow Fireworks 250 run on the Fourth of July weekend. The heat of the desert had Walt Lott starting the race in the late afternoon, so racers got some relief once the sun went down. Gale Pike catches some air off the rough Mojave terrain.

Catching on Like Wildfire

Each year, entry lists grew larger with more and more adventurous souls looking to tame the Baja Peninsula. Events grew north of the border as well with a 500-mile NORRA event near Parker, Arizona, and the Stardust 7-11 out of Las Vegas (run only once), which was followed by what you might call the Super Bowl of off-road racing in America: the Mint 400. More areas for events opened for

The NORRA Baja 500 became popular quickly. It had all the fun of racing in Baja without the added expense of hauling your team back from La Paz. John Baker lights up a warm June evening with his driving lights. (Photo Courtesy Trackside Photo)

racing in Barstow, California, through the Stoddard and Lucerne valleys. Events in Baja increased as well with the birth of the NORRA 500 in 1969.

With the expansion of the sport came a proliferation of sanctioning bodies that were trying to find the success that NORRA was starting to garner. The Southern Nevada Off Road Racing Enthusiasts (SNORE) group began overseeing events out of Las Vegas and Laughlin, Nevada. The Mint 400 self-sanctioned itself as an independent event well into the 1980s. Former SNORE Member and President Walt Lott began his own series called Walt's Racing Association (WRA), which quickly turned into the High Desert Racing Association (HDRA), which was for many years considered to be the foremost strictly United States series. HDRA did not operate outside the American Southwest.

Many other organizations formed all over the American Southwest, the Pacific Northwest, Canada, and the American Midwest with events ranging from short-course-style events to flat-out runs across prairie lands and mountains. However, the Mexico and the southwestern U.S. events drew the bulk of the manufacturer interest. Media coverage increased as documentaries were produced and films were made. Then, ABC's *Wide World of Sports* came in 1968 and brought Jim McKay and the splendor and challenge of the Baja peninsula to millions of people's homes. ABC Sports returned to cover the race several times.

As the sport grew, innovative people found ways to increase their vehicle's speed over rough terrain. A big engine was not the answer to a successful off-road race car. You had to beat the terrain first with the toughest

In the midwestern United States, off-road racing took on a slightly different look. The majority of racing was done on short courses in a wheel-to-wheel format. These racers were built lighter and did not have to carry codrivers or spare parts. The Bronco of Milan Mazanec leads Jack Flannery into a tight turn. (Photo Courtesy Milan Mazanec)

tires, the best shock absorbers, the most wheel travel, and precise preparation. Many racers met the end of their event prematurely. Many of these failures can be traced back to their shops and garages during preparation. It was something the early Bill Stroppe–built Ford Bronco

Fillmore Ford Dealer Coco Corral was an early supporter of off-road racing. His support brought such names into the sport as Don Barlow and boosted Ivan Stewart on his way to Toyota stardom. Coco and his wife, Charlotte, stayed involved in the sport for several decades. (Photo Courtesy MotorTrend and Petersen Museum Archive)

This a high-tech trophy truck that eats up 3-foot holes in the desert today. It is not uncommon to see figures of more than 1,100 hp with wheel travel of 36 inches. (Photo Courtesy Trackside Photo)

Bill Stroppe (left) and Parnelli Jones (right) are pictured at the finish of the 1973 Mint 400, which was their only Mint 400 win together. There were not many people tougher or smarter than Bill Stroppe. His attention to detail and crafty race strategies were a large part of the Ford Bronco's success. (Photo Courtesy Trackside Photo)

teams knew about from years of preparing all kinds of racing machines. That work ethic garnered those teams much success. Others quickly caught on as well.

Today, the sport has machines that cost more than a half million dollars to build, leading the way on four wheels with 36 inches of wheel travel. Those early intrepid racers in the beginning were lucky to have six inches of wheel travel. However, the sport has never forgotten the backbone that built off-road racing. There are plenty of classes of vehicles in which the average person can afford to compete and win without spending six figures and having to pay for more wheel travel than a yard stick and 900-hp engines.

Meet Bill Stroppe

Bill Stroppe is largely considered to be the father of the desert racing Bronco. He is the man who Ford trusted to bring home wins. Bill had a long history with Ford before the Bronco.

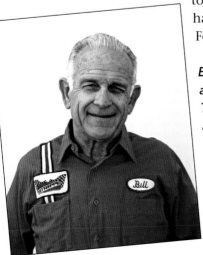

Bill Stroppe poses for a Ford publicity photo. These usually were added into press kits and sent to magazines and newspapers. Occasionally, one would get autographed for a fan. (Photo Courtesy Trackside Photo)

He began racing in midgets and then speed runs on the dry lakes of Southern California. As an enterprising young man with great mechanical aptitude, he worked his way up from being a mechanic at Art Hall Lincoln-Mercury to form his own shop to handle Lincoln-Mercury's West Coast racing endeavors by 1950.

Stroppe was noticed initially after impressing Ford at the prestigious 1947 Henry Ford Memorial Detroit International Boat Races. Using a flathead 6-cylinder engine that Stroppe's friend and partner Clay Smith had built, they dominated in the 225-ci displacement class. The element that caught Ford's attention was that engine was on the chopping block because of crankshaft and vibration issues over 4,500 rpm. Smith, a master engine builder, went through the engine and found the answers to the oil starvation and balance issues on the crankshaft.

Benson Ford, which oversaw the Lincoln-Mercury line, was impressed with Stroppe and Smith, so they were offered jobs right away in Detroit. Stroppe initially wanted to take the offer. Clay Smith reminded Bill that Southern California was where their customers were as well as their friends. He reminded Stroppe about having to uproot their families and deal with Michigan winters.

Stroppe and Smith counteroffered with running the West Coast racing operations for Lincoln and Mercury. They would also handle special operations and maintain the fleet of cars for the media to test. Clay Smith would handle engine duties, and Stroppe would build the cars, which was a combination that worked miracles for the fledgling company.

Bill Stroppe began by handling the entries for the Mobilgas Economy Runs in the early 1950s and then went on to success at the La Carrera Road Races in Mexico, winning outright and taking the top three places in 1952 and 1953. Prior to the 1955 event, the Mexican government shut down the race for economic and safety reasons.

In 1954, Clay Smith was killed at a AAA National Championship 100-mile race in Du Quoin, Illinois, when Roger Ward and Chuck Stevenson came together on the 83rd lap, sending Ward's car into the infield and a crowd of people, which instantly killed Smith and injured eight other people. Smith was the mechanic on Stevenson's car. The loss of Clay Smith was a huge blow.

Stroppe continued to handle the press fleet and racing operations on his own after the untimely death of Smith. The next year, Stroppe switched to Mercury and handled its stock car racing operations on the West Coast with the United States Auto Club (USAC) until 1964, when the company pulled out of stock car racing. After that, the Stroppe team worked on police packages for Mercury, had some dealings in the GT40 cars that went to the 24

Hours of Le Mans, and handled Mercury's efforts at the Pikes Peak International Hillclimb.

Bronco Prototypes Go Racing

The Bronco test mules that were mentioned earlier had sat in the test track infield when Ford decided it was time to market the Bronco by proving its capabilities in the American Southwest. Ford summoned Stroppe to come pick them up and make them into racers.

Bill and his son Willie, who was a junior high school student at the time, traveled east with their car hauler and picked up the eight Bronco mules. Four had front-end damage and four had rear-end damage. Once back in Signal Hill at the shop, the Stroppe team cobbled them together into four complete Broncos.

In those early days with the racers built, the main source of off-road competition included club events, such as Jamborees. Stroppe took the Bronco to club events in California, Arizona, and Colorado with drivers such as Ray Harvick, himself, and Charles Alvarez. Thus began what became an amazing stretch of victories for the Stroppe team.

Bill Stroppe unfortunately passed away due to complications from a fall in 1995. In the capable hands of Bill's son Willie, the winning tradition continued for many more years.

This unique Bronco ran on propane. Bill Stroppe was a proponent of propane and has used it in several different kinds of racing. The gasoline-powered Bronco drivers would tease that the only thing that should run on propane is a stove. Thus, this Bronco was named the Baja Stove. *(Photo Courtesy MotorTrend and Petersen Museum Archive)*

CHAPTER 2

THE BRONCO SEES COMPETITION

With Bill Stroppe heading the racing program, the former Bronco mules were getting into the final stages of design, building, and preparation. It was time to get the Broncos dirty.

In 1965, if you wanted to race your new four-wheel-drive vehicle, your choices were mostly four-wheel-drive club events. Some, such as the Hemet Jeep Club, allowed non-Jeep vehicles to join. The club's Afton Canyon Jeep Junket was just such an event, and it featured upward of 400 entries. Afton Canyon is in the upper Mojave Desert near Barstow, California.

A win at Afton Canyon added to your standing in the off-road community. In 1965, the Junket featured 398 entries over a variety of events. The obstacle course was the featured event, and it featured a timed run over a set course.

Stroppe took his Broncos to Afton Canyon in 1966 to challenge the Hemet Jeep Club elite. He came away with a first and third place in the hill-climb event as well as a second place in the obstacle course behind the Jeep of up-and-coming driver Rod Hall.

1967: The Inaugural NORRA Mexican 1000

As the Beatles basked in the glow of their ground-breaking Sgt. Pepper's Lonely Hearts Club Band album and Vince Lombardi and the Green Bay Packers enjoyed being the first Super Bowl champions, there was a new motorsport evolving. In Southern California, the formation of NORRA was underway. Plans were grandiose and the timeline was short, but these determined men and women made it happen.

Stroppe was no stranger to Mexico, having raced the Pan America Road Races from 1950 to 1954, but that was on the mainland and on paved roads. Baja California, while a part of Mexico, is its own kind of place. Stroppe had some Baja experience when General Motors had him prepare some trucks for an attempt at the Baja record. Unfortunately, the attempt was fraught with problems and did not break the record.

Entry fees were set at $250 (raised to $375 as the event neared) per vehicle and included full insurance coverage, fuel at the checkpoints, accommodations for

ABOVE: A solitary Bronco thunders down the desolate Baja peninsula. For the last few years of the 1960s, Broncos ruled Baja. (Photo Courtesy MotorTrend and Petersen Museum Archive)

The National Four-Wheel-Drive Grand Prix

Brian Chuchua, a Jeep dealership owner from Southern California, was busy preparing for his National Four-Wheel-Drive Grand Prix event to take place in a dry riverbed near Riverside. Chuchua also owned a Jeep dealership in Anaheim, California, and was well-known as being an avid competitor in club events. His event was stacked full of soon-to-be legendary names, including Rod Hall, Larry Minor, Bill Stroppe, Ed Pearlman, and Dick Cepek, running Jeep and International vehicles. Including Chuchua, these six men eventually became members of the Off-Road Motorsports Hall of Fame.

Headed into Brian Chuchua's National Four-Wheel-Drive Grand Prix from March 4–6, 1966, five Broncos were entered. Ray Harvick, Jim Loomis, and Paul Jones were among the drivers. One Bronco was a 6-cylinder, and the others where the new 289-ci V-8. Stroppe was not intimidated by the competition in Riverside that day in 1966, and he knew that he provided the best possible preparation for his team and that Ford had designed a superior machine to the Jeep and International. With that, the Stroppe team battled the competition.

Harvick won overall Top Eliminator with the 6-cylinder Bronco, and Jim Loomis was fastest of the 8-cylinder vehicles. Only Jim Loomis had any kind of problem.

"On an early run my seat back broke," Loomis said. "I pulled in the pit, and Stroppe grabbed a metal fence post from nearby and the welder. In a few minutes, he had fabricated a support for my broken seat. [They were the] most beautiful welds you ever saw out there in a riverbed."

After the inaugural Riverside event, Stroppe returned to the site a few weeks later to introduce the press to the new Bronco. The event was a tremendous success with the members of the media. Stroppe and Ford had the Bronco starting off on the right foot with race wins and positive press reviews of the stock units.

In the 1967 race, Paul Jackson of Hemet won the race—shifting without a clutch in his Jeep. His reward for winning Top Eliminator? A Ford Bronco.

The National Four-Wheel-Drive Grand Prix continued until 1972 with Broncos populating the field year over year.

Larry Minor gives the crowd something to cheer about at an early National Four-Wheel-Drive Grand Prix. Brian Chuchua's idea of involving large crowds in off-road racing worked well, as several thousand showed up in just the first year. The Ford versus Jeep battles were fiercely fought through the final Grand Prix in 1972. (Photo Courtesy Larry Minor)

1965-1972: The Beginning of Off-Road Racing Competitions

Top: *Running in a sandy river bottom meant that there was no shortage of places to get stuck. Even the Bronco could fall victim to the nearly bottomless sand. Jack Bayer digs furiously to free the Bronco from its predicament. (Photo Courtesy Larry Minor)* **Center Left:** *During a promotional shoot for Petersen Publishing, the Bronco of Jim Loomis found the limits of the Bronco's front axle. This was photographed on the course for the 1968 National Four-Wheel-Drive Grand Prix. (Photo Courtesy MotorTrend and Petersen Museum Archive)* **Center Middle:** *The National Four-Wheel-Drive Grand Prix was run in a dry riverbed. This made for a sandy, bumpy course that tested the suspensions of the day. The Bronco and its superior design made it an instant favorite for such events. (Photo Courtesy MotorTrend and Petersen Museum Archive)* **Center Right:** *This 1968 photo shows that Bill Stroppe was building as safe a racer as possible with the technology of the day. By today's standards, it looks mostly unsafe with its lack of diagonal support bars and corner gussets. (Photo Courtesy MotorTrend and Petersen Museum Archive)* **Bottom Left:** *The dry riverbed made for many interesting natural terrain obstacles in its 1-mile course. This 1968 photo shows that driving suits were still optional. (Photo Courtesy MotorTrend and Petersen Museum Archive)*

two in La Paz for three days and two nights, and tickets to the awards banquet on November 4. A total of $20,000 in prize money was offered across four classes.

On October 31, 1967, 68 teams gathered 20 miles south of San Diego, California, at the Plaza del Toro (bull-fighting ring) in Tijuana, Baja California, Mexico. The inaugural NORRA Mexican 1000 was about to start. The finish line was in La Paz, about 850 to 950 miles to the southeast depending on your navigational abilities. Finishing depended on your driving skills and prepara-

Awaiting the start of the 1967 NORRA Mexican 1000, Dick Russell (in the passenger's seat) and Cliff Brien were expected to back up Ray Harvick and Bill Stroppe. The plan did not work out, as the pair broke an axle early in the race. (Photo Courtesy MotorTrend *and Petersen Museum Archive)*

The Stroppe team for the 1967 NORRA Mexican 1000 was (left to right) Cliff Brien, Dick Russell, Bill Stroppe, and Ray Harvick. The Bronco in this photo went on to win the 1968 Mint 400, Stardust 7-11, and Mexican 1000 with Larry Minor driving. (Photo Courtesy MotorTrend *and Petersen Museum Archive)*

In 1967, before the start of the first NORRA Mexican 1000, Ray Harvick (in the driver's seat) chats with Larry Minor. They met again in a silt bed south of El Arco with race-changing consequences. (Photo Courtesy Motor-Trend *and Petersen Museum Archive)*

At the first Mexican 1000, teams took a rally style road section transit from the Bull Ring in Tijuana to Ensenada, where the racing would start in earnest. Cliff Brien and Dick Russell are lined up awaiting the start of the race that began a new era in off-road competition. (Photo Courtesy MotorTrend *and Petersen Museum Archive)*

tion. Of those 68 starters, only 31 were listed as official finishers within the official 48-hour time limit.

Bill Stroppe entered two Broncos in the event: one for himself and Ray Harvick and another for Dick Russell (Stroppe's master fabricator) and Cliff Brien. The Jeep guys were gunning for the Broncos from the start. Whether it was brand loyalty or fear of being beaten by a newcomer, both the Stroppe Broncos had targets on their taillights.

Among the entries was the independent entry of Vic Abruzzese and Irv Hanks in what became known as the *Banquet Bronco*. Abruzzese was focused on the promised banquet that was advertised to happen in La Paz after the race. He had his Bronco lettered as the *Banquet Bronco* and even had himself and Hanks in tuxedos for the race, complete with top hats and tails.

Bill Stroppe was learning the off-road game quickly, which was evident in his prep work on the Broncos. Wider wheels, high floatation tires, multiple shocks per wheel, off-road lighting, and engine modifications were done between the Riverside events and this first attempt at the NORRA Mexican 1000. With sponsorship from *Car Craft* magazine and Bardahl oil additives, the team felt confident and looked professional.

The Adventure Begins

Harvick and Stroppe were out front early, having their way with the handful of Jeeps and Internationals. Rod Hall and Larry Minor could not believe the lead that the Bronco had built. According to a checkpoint worker, the lead was almost two hours by El Arco, which was the halfway point.

The late Ray Harvick remembered the 1967 Mexican 1000 in a 2006 video with an amusing fact. Bill Stroppe looked for any competitive advantage he could find. To this end, he decided that stopping to pee would cost too much time, so he installed what Harvick referred to as a "piss tube."

Harvick had been driving for about 13 hours straight. He told Stroppe he needed a rest, so they switched seats. Not even 30 minutes later, Stroppe rolled the Bronco onto its roof. A friendly driver in a buggy stopped and pulled them back onto their wheels. While the Bronco was resting on its roof, some battery acid leaked onto the "piss tube" and made a hole. After they were going down the road a little farther, they had to pee. As Ray said many times, "I don't have to tell you the rest."

At some point around San Ignacio, the Bronco got turned around and was headed the wrong way. Worse, they also got stuck in a silt bed and lost some more time. Turned around now and trying to catch up to the field, another rollover slowed the team. During one of their inverted adventures, sand got inside the timing cover. Only 50 miles from La Paz, the timing chain broke. By the time they limped into La Paz, the official time limit for the race had expired. They made it to the finish but were not recorded as official finishers.

Vic Abruzzese and Irv Hanks finished down the order and got the banquet they were promised. The other Bronco of Dick Russell and Cliff Brien did not finish, either. The reason has been lost to time, as have many great adventure stories from this era. As Larry Minor told me several times, "If we knew we were making history at the time, we would have paid more attention. We were just racing."

A beaten and battered Ford Bronco arrives in La Paz several hours past the official finisher time limit. You can see the damage from several rollovers and the very tired face of Ray Harvick showing the fatigue that comes with 40-plus hours of driving in Baja California. (Photo Courtesy Motor- Trend and Petersen Museum Archive)

Big Game Hunting with Bill Stroppe

Late in 1967, anyone in Los Angeles who was anyone in the automotive field would be at Ray Brock's house for his Christmas party. Brock, a World War II U.S. Navy veteran and car enthusiast, started working at Petersen Publishing in 1951. He worked his way up to become editor of two of its hottest magazines: *Hot Rod* and *Motor Trend*. Eventually, he oversaw the entire Petersen empire.

A few months before this party, Ray and fellow hot-rodder Ak Miller took a stock Ford Ranchero and won the Production car class at the Mexican 1000. Thus, there was bench racing of a new kind going on. Stroppe, full

Rod Hall and Larry Minor's First Mexican 1000

To properly put this accomplishment in perspective, you need to know Larry Minor and Rod Hall's history. In 1967, they were just two guys from Hemet who spent their days working hard and then playing hard on weekends with their 4x4 vehicles.

Larry and Rod had heard about the first Mexican 1000, and they sat down, had a meeting, and decided to race in it. They prepped a Jeep as well as they could, not fully understanding what was ahead. They installed a tool chest and an ice chest and decided that they would need six new tires and wheels to make it to La Paz. Neither of them was adept at procuring sponsors at that time, so Rod and Larry convinced their wives to visit Dick Cepek, who recently began selling tires out of a rented space behind a hair salon.

The ladies were successful in procuring what they needed in exchange for some room on the front fenders for Cepek, who himself was about to have his life changed by the boom in off-road competition.

Neither Larry nor Rod had been beyond Tijuana, Mexico, in their lives. Here they were though, lined up with 67 other teams all hoping to see La Paz about 800 miles to the south. Only 31 of those teams would.

Larry and Rod planned to alternate driving when the terrain suited one or the other's driving style. Larry liked going fast, and Rod liked the rougher, more technical roads.

Looking over the competition, the pair decided that they had two goals. First, of course, was to finish the race. Second, being confirmed Jeep guys, there was no way they wanted to lose to a Ford Bronco. There was already a healthy rivalry between the Jeeps and Stroppe's Broncos from Brian Chuchua's Riverside Grand Prix races that started in 1966.

In a March 2020 interview, Larry Minor recalled that first Mexican 1000.

"So, the race started, [and] gosh that was a long race!" he said. "We saw the sun come up twice. So, people are passing us, we are passing people on the side of the road broke down. We get down to El Arco, that was about the halfway point in the race about

midnight, and Rod asks the checkpoint guy, 'How far is that Bronco ahead of us?' He says it was two hours ahead of us. 'Holy crap,' we said. 'How are we going to catch that Bronco?'

"So, Rodney and I decided, 'Let's go racing like we do.' We took the ice chest out, the tool chest out, and left them with the checkpoint crew. We air our tires down like we would running an obstacle race, and we took off and drove the crap out of that Jeep.

"Just as the sun come up, we are in the silt beds down around San Ignacio, and we're just heading south in these deep ruts. All we know is La Paz is south, and a cheap compass was all we had to go by. So, we're going along, and here come Stroppe and Harvick going the wrong way, so we wave them down to talk.

"That was really the first time I met Bill Stroppe. I had known Ray Harvick a long time because he was from the beach area, and we went down there to street race all the time.

"So, Stroppe said, 'You guys are going the wrong way.'

"And we said we weren't. *This* is south.

"Stroppe said something about a magnetic field interfering with the compasses.

"I said, 'I don't know about you Bill, but we're going to keep going this way.'

"So, we went and took off and left them. What we didn't know when we left them was that the ruts they were in were really deep and when they went to take off, they high centered and got stuck."

It was not until well after Larry and Rod arrived in La Paz that Stroppe and Harvick finally finished. It was then when Larry heard the rest of the story. Bill and Ray had to wait until someone came along to pull them out of the silty ruts.

The Bronco, with Stroppe driving, took off looking to catch the Jeep, and with over-exuberant driving rolled and crashed the Bronco about four to six times. Different people have different numbers. The exact number depends on whom you asked. Minor was impressed that the Bronco was able to take that kind of abuse and still finish (although not officially within the prescribed time limit).

of ideas after his experiences in Baja, had a plan to nab a big-name driver to drive one of the Broncos. When you are shooting for a big name, you might as well start at the top. Stroppe wanted Parnelli Jones.

As the moment seemed right talking about off-roading with a big crowd around, Stroppe pounced. He asked Parnelli about joining the team for the upcoming Mint 400 race. Parnelli graciously declined, stating that he had enough of inhaling pounds of dust and bouncing around the dirt in Midgets and Sprints. Stroppe figured he would say that and took a swipe at Parnelli's machismo. According to Stroppe himself in his 1986 biography, he said, "Maybe off-road was too tough? Maybe Parnelli wasn't up to the task? His arms are a little weak. How about it? Admit it, Parnelli!"

Challenging Parnelli was going to get you one of two things: a great driver in your machine or a punch in the nose. Stroppe had a great driver in his machine!

At the first Del Webb Mint 400, the efficiency of a Stroppe pit crew is shown in action. Many years of fielding the La Carrera and Lincoln and Mercury stock cars gave the team a definite advantage over early desert-racing teams. (Photo Courtesy MotorTrend and Petersen Museum Archive)

1968: The Inaugural Mint 400

In this first annual edition of the soon-to-be-classic desert race, a nearly 400-mile lap was laid out up to the former mining town of Beatty and back to the Mint Hotel in downtown Las Vegas. An astounding 101 hearty teams entered the race to vie for a share of the $15,000 guaranteed purse before contingency prizes that pushed the total closer to $30,000. Only 32 of those teams made it back to finish the race.

This was the off-road debut of Parnelli Jones paired with Ray Harvick whom Stroppe believed would be a good driving coach. Harvick and Jones came from the same kind of background: the dirt tracks of the West Coast. Both were hard chargers, but in off-road events Harvick learned that off-road racing was a different beast. You had to learn to slow down to go fast.

A relaxed Parnelli Jones behind the wheel awaits the start of his first foray into off-road racing. Next to him is Ray Harvick, who was considered at the time to be Stroppe's No. 1 driver. Bill Stroppe thought Harvick could help show Parnelli how to drive an off-road race. He was wrong. (Photo Courtesy MotorTrend and Petersen Museum Archive)

Parnelli Jones versus Nevada

Parnelli and Ray lined up at the start next to a motorcycle competitor. This was before common sense prevailed and motorcycles started a few hours before the four-wheeled vehicles. It was safer for the riders who had far less protection. Parnelli dumped the clutch and left that motorcycle behind as he thundered away down the racetrack toward the open desert.

Parnelli was hard on it, as you would expect, and headed for the first dirt turn out of the speedway grounds. Harvick noticed the speed Jones was carrying and figured this was going to be a short day. There was no way that they were making it around the corner. Jones, using his years of dirt track experience, threw the Bronco sideways, stomped on the gas, and headed out into the Nevada desert in a cloud of dust.

At the start line for the 1968 Mint 400, the Broncos of Parnelli Jones and Jim Loomis wait to get out in the desert. Jones's Bronco (No. 15) had a 302-ci V-8, while Loomis and Minor's Bronco had a straight-6 engine. (Photo Courtesy MotorTrend and Petersen Museum Archive)

Parnelli was charging hard, and Harvick was yelling that he was tearing the Bronco apart and had to slow down. Parnelli Jones, at this time in his driving career, did not know the meaning of the words "slow down" and kept his pace. Passing cars and charging hard, they missed a turn in the dust and started up into a box canyon—one with no exit. At the end of the road, with cars piling up behind them, Parnelli got on the radio and called for Stroppe, who had run for their team airplane. From the air, Stroppe radioed directions to get them back to the proper road.

Once out of the box canyon, Parnelli was back to flat-out driving. Harvick went back to yelling and swearing at Jones to slow down. While flat-out across the floor of a valley about 50 miles from the start, Parnelli Jones was introduced to the "wash out." It was wide and deep and no place to be running flat-out, but he was. The hit was tremendous, blowing the two front tires and cauliflowering the wheels all the way around the brake drums. It took a blow torch to free the bent wheels.

While it, in fact, was a short day, Parnelli was hooked on desert racing, and Ray Harvick swore to never ride with him again.

Loomis and Minor usher in the Stroppe Era

Soon after that 1967 NORRA Mexican 1000, Larry Minor received a call from Bill Stroppe offering to build him a Bronco to race in 1968.

"Rodney and I saw each other almost every day," Minor said. "I would stop by his gas station to get gas, or we would go out and have a beer—stuff like that. I told him Stroppe wants us to drive a Bronco next year. Rodney said he didn't want to drive one; he was a Jeep guy, and he thought a guy could get killed in one of those things."

Minor went to drive for Stroppe with no hard feelings from Rod, who started driving for Brian Chuchua with another Hemet Jeep Club member, Carl Jackson. Larry continued,

"I went down to Stroppe's, and he said, 'I'll build you a Bronco, whatever one you want, we can build up a brand new one,' Minor said.

"That Bronco that him and Harvick were racing was sitting in the corner just beat up and crashed, so I said I want that one right there. As many times as they wrecked it and crashed it, it still finished. I knew that it would not break down on me. The Bronco wouldn't be rebuilt in time for the race, so Stroppe switched to Plan B."

Bill Stroppe set him up to co-drive with Jim Loomis in his 6-cylinder Bronco. Parnelli, the only other Stroppe entry, had a V-8 in his.

Neither Jim Loomis nor Minor had the time to pre-run the long loop, so they set off blindly into the desert from in front of the Mint Hotel & Casino.

"Man, it was rough, real rough, mostly rock," Minor said. "We only had maybe 8 inches of wheel travel back then. It was a good thing we were young because that race beat us up good."

The lack of familiarity with the course caused the pair to get lost when the sun set. The course was not well marked, and stories came back after the event of teams who simply stopped until the sun came back up.

"At times there was no trail at all, but we wouldn't quit," Minor said. "We must have got lost a dozen times.

"We did not get one flat tire. Amazing because of all the rocks. I think it was because we had that 6-cylinder engine in there. We didn't have the power to hurt the Bronco."

Jim Loomis and Larry Minor won for the Stroppe team, taking the four-wheel-drive class win in 16 hours, 36 minutes, and 54 seconds.

1968 NORRA Stardust 7-11: The Only One

The NORRA Stardust 7-11 was presented by the famous hotel and casino of the same name. Originally, Pearlman and NORRA were in talks with the Mint Hotel to sanction their 400-mile race. The two could not come to terms financially, so NORRA went looking for a new hotel. The Stardust chose an off-road race to bring attention to racers and spectators who would come to south-

At the start of the 1968 Stardust 7-11, Vic Abruzzese (right) and Irv Hanks (left) were running the **Banquet Bronco** *for the second time. This was before Vic started to modify it from its mostly stock configuration. The guys donned tuxedos again, just as they had at the inaugural Mexican 1000. (Photo Courtesy* **MotorTrend** *and Petersen Museum Archive)*

ern Nevada and off-road, take advantage of the Las Vegas nightlife after a quick shower to scrub off the Nevada dust, and party with the likes of fellow competitors Steve McQueen, James Garner, and Dick Smothers. It was sort of a desert adventure with the prairie dogs and tortoises by day and the Rat Pack at night kind of thing. The Stardust was already well established to sports car racers. The raceway was home to Can-Am series road races, NHRA drag races, and in 1968 held a 150-mile race for the USAC Champ Cars (Indy Cars). On the weekend of June 11–14, 1968, it served as the start and finish line for a desert race. Sadly, the racetrack had a short life (from 1965–1971) before being developed into homes in what is now Spring Valley, Nevada.

Awaiting the 137 teams for a $25,000 purse was two 355-mile loops of everything Nevada can throw at you to rattle even the best-prepared machines apart. Baja is tough, but so is Nevada—each in their own way. Think of Baja and Nevada as muggers. Baja kindly walks up to you and asks for all your belongings, leaving you feeling violated because you were robbed. Nevada sneaks up behind you with a tire iron, beats you senseless, and takes all of your belongings. Not content with that, Nevada also takes your clothes, any gold teeth, and shaves you bald for fun.

The Stroppe team numbered five Broncos entered in the event.

This was Larry Minor's first event for Stroppe as the driver of record. With Loomis piloting another Bronco, Minor decided to take his sand drag engine builder, Jack Bayer, along for the ride. Minor figured he was an okay mechanic, but Bayer was better and faster. Being the second race in a row out of Las Vegas and close to the same course as the Mint race, Minor had a better idea of what to expect this time around.

Stroppe Team Notches Win No. 1 in the Desert

Larry Minor and Jack Bayer, the seasoned pros that they were, had their Bronco flying. They avoided getting lost, and even though it took 27 hours and 14 minutes to complete those two long laps, they brought the Stroppe team Bronco home as the first four-wheeled vehicle. They were second overall about two hours behind the winning motorcycle of Larry Berquist and Gary Preston aboard a 305cc Honda. The race was so tough that only 30 vehicles finished.

The team of Jim Loomis and Bud Wright was one of those finishers, but it was not easy. It might sound great to say that they got fourth place in their class, but the fact they finished was the real accomplishment. The race had a 40-hour time limit to be considered an official finisher. Jim and Bud rolled back into the Stardust Speedway after 39 hours and 40 minutes.

The majority of time lost was in a silt bed outside the little town of Pahrump. The Bronco became mired in the

The Bronco pictured here at the 1968 Stardust 7-11 race was the same Bronco that Bill Stroppe and Ray Harvick drove in the 1967 NORRA Mexican 1000. Unfortunately, they did not finish within the official time limit. Fortunately, Larry Minor and Jack Bayer (pictured here) won the 7-11. (Photo Courtesy Larry Minor)

With a big lead after the first lap, Stroppe decided to take the time to do a complete service on Larry Minor and Jack Bayer's Bronco. The Stardust 7-11 turned out to be one of the most challenging off-road races ever run. (Photo Courtesy MotorTrend and Petersen Museum Archive)

Ford's winning entries pose the day after the 1968 Stardust 7-11 race: Larry Minor (left) was the race winner, Jim Loomis and Bud Wright (center) stand near their Bronco, and the driver on the right is unknown. (Photo Courtesy Larry Minor)

powdery silt, and Wright and Loomis started digging. It took a long time to get the Bronco to the point where they thought they could get it out, and Loomis went to start the engine. Dead battery. Circling the area was Bill Stroppe in a small plane. Loomis radioed to the plane that he needed a battery, and off toward Las Vegas the plane went.

Almost two hours later, the plane was back with a fresh battery. The problem was that there was no place to land in a silt bed. However, silt is a very soft substance, and it was thought that if the plane could fly over the deepest part and drop the battery, the silt would cushion the landing. It worked! It was not the end of their problems, but it was the one that lost them the most time.

The 1968 NORRA Mexican 1000

The second annual running of the Baja Peninsula attracted a much larger entry, as 243 started the race. Everything was bigger about this running of the Mexican 1000, not just the entry numbers. There was television coverage by ABC's *Wide World of Sports* with Jim McKay interviewing drivers and legendary moviemaker Bruce Brown shooting film.

As word got around the racing world about this crazy run down Mexico's long peninsula, more notable drivers were showing up. Besides Parnelli Jones, you had sports car and circle track stars, such as Bob Bondurant, Roger McCluskey, Swede Savage, Dan Gurney, Sam Posey, and Peter Brock, and drag racing star Don Prudhomme. Celebrities competed as well, including James Garner, Steve

Ray Harvick, pictured here at the 1968 Mexican 1000, partnered with Marvin Carroll for the race. Harvick was with Stroppe from the beginning of the Bronco program. Harvick is driving the Bronco that Dick Russell broke at the 1967 Mexican 1000. (Photo Courtesy MotorTrend and Petersen Museum Archive)

Actor and racer James Garner took the Bill Stroppe-prepared Bronco in 1968 through technical inspection himself. Garner took to racing while filming the 1966 movie Grand Prix, *where he did some of his own driving. Garner and Scooter Patrick had a respectable fourth-place finish in their first attempt on the Baja Peninsula. (Photo Courtesy MotorTrend and Petersen Museum Archive)*

McQueen, Pat Wayne (John Wayne's son), and Michael Nesmith. Nesmith, while never in a Bronco, was a serious off-road racer well into the mid-1980s.

Larry Minor and Jack Bayer drew the number 3, which cut down the amount of dust they would have to drive through. James Garner and Scooter Patrick started 59th, Ray Harvick was 63rd, Parnelli Jones was 83rd, and the team of Dick Kennedy and Larry Mathes started 210th but was not recorded as a finisher.

Unlike in 1967, this time, teams were doing pre-running before the event to find the fastest way to La Paz. Remember, back in the early days, you just had to find the checkpoints. It did not matter how you got there. One of the areas that caused teams problems was the trails from Punta Prieta to El Rosarito. The "road" (if you could call it that) went right through some of the deepest silt beds that could get a vehicle stuck for hours.

This time, Parnelli Jones took the time to pre-run the course extensively with his teammates and the Boss himself, Bill Stroppe. Stroppe figured that maybe he had the ability to reign in some of Parnelli's enthusiasm and show him how to slow down enough to finish. It was a tall order, but really, who else could do it but the Boss? The slower pace of pre-running also gave Jones a lifelong appreciation for the peninsula and its people who stayed with him long after his days as an off-road racer were over.

Larry Minor and Jack Bayer make last minute adjustments before starting the 1968 NORRA Mexican 1000. The No. 3 starting spot translated into only having to pass two racers they had clear air all the way to La Paz. (Photo Courtesy MotorTrend and Petersen Museum Archive)

Rod Hall chased his old teammate all the way down the peninsula for second place. Hall teamed with Carl Jackson in the Chuchua's Jeep, both of whom by the end of the year were driving for Stroppe in Broncos. (Photo Courtesy MotorTrend and Petersen Museum Archive)

This very-stock-looking Bronco was run by John and Johnny Crean at the 1968 NORRA Mexican 1000. The team persevered for almost 36 hours to reach La Paz in 10th place. Crean was the founder of the Fleetwood motor home company. An avid off roader, Crean, raced dune buggies as well as this Bronco. (Photo Courtesy MotorTrend *and Petersen Museum Archive)*

You can almost read the expression on Rod Hall's face as he just heard he was 90 minutes behind his old friend at the finish. (Photo Courtesy MotorTrend *and Petersen Museum Archive)*

With all eyes on the Stroppe team, its eyes were on the Jeep No. 27 of Rod Hall and Carl Jackson. Here were two men who knew how to finish a race, and like Minor and Hall together, their driving styles complemented each other.

Brian Chuchua did not remember if it was himself or his team manager, Cam Warren, who believed he had a route over to the west coast of the peninsula where his Jeeps could really move down the beaches and avoid the dreaded silt beds. During the race, Rod and Carl found the marked turnoff and headed west while most everyone kept southeast and took their chances. The road to the beach was horribly rough and longer than anyone thought, but there were no silt beds. The extra miles and the rougher-than-expected roads cost the team about 1-1/2 hours. Minor and Bayer beat them to La Paz by 1 hour and 32 minutes.

"We shared the driving, [and] Rod did about 75 percent of it that race," Carl Jackson said. "Later, we ran into a truck driver who drives up and down Baja delivering to ranches. He said the loop we took from Punta Prieta to the beach usually takes him three days."

Hard lessons are learned on the Baja Peninsula.

The morning of the race was glorious: blue skies and perfect weather. Parnelli felt very prepared and looked

Baja California can be a big, lonely place. There are hundreds of miles of road just like this stretching from horizon to horizon. (Photo Courtesy Mark Atherton)

forward to running up front. The green flag fell, and he and Stroppe made the most of the paved portion through Santo Tomas, passing a lot of cars. At the first checkpoint in Camalu, timing showed that Parnelli had the lead, but it was short-lived because not far after that, the Bronco broke a spindle and wheel. That ended their first Baja foray together, but there were more.

Larry Minor again teamed with the engine builder of his sand drag cars, Jack Bayer.

"He was a really good mechanic—a wiry, tough guy, small guy. He could do anything," Larry said. "I think that's how we won so many races. If we had a problem, he could get out and fix it in a hurry."

Minor and Bayer kept the pace up all day and night long, and as the sun came up in La Paz, they were the first four-wheeled vehicle. Only 30 minutes separated the winning motorcycle of Larry Berquist and Gary Preston from the Bronco. Minor started planning out a strategy to win the next Mexican 1000 and beat everyone to La Paz on two *and* four wheels.

For Rod Hall and Carl Jackson, the 1968 NORRA Mexican 1000 was a mission to beat the Broncos—especially Larry and Jack's Bronco. Rod and Carl now ran Chuchua's Jeep Commander with an automatic transmission and V-6 engine. You can call it a friendly rivalry, but these Hemet Jeep Club members wanted bragging rights at the next years' worth of meetings.

Ray Harvick was a distant third, placing nearly 3½ hours behind the Jeep. James Garner and Scooter Patrick brought home a solid fourth-place finish 40 minutes later.

Things were coming together for the Stroppe team. Through Bill's detailed preparation, execution of the race plan, and the driving talent, the Ford Bronco was a winner. And for Ford, winning meant sales.

The 1969 Mint 400

In only its second year, the Mint 400 ran on Monday and Tuesday (March 24 and 25) and produced 188 entries and some big changes. The start/finish area was moved to the Mint Gun Club in Tule Springs, which was a rocky, silty area of the desert northwest of Las Vegas. Instead of one long lap, a 50-mile loop was laid out, and each entry did eight laps (four on each of the two days), and repairs were allowed overnight.

The loop format was friendlier for spectators, as every few hours fans could see their favorite driver come by. The new format was also friendlier for the 256 members of the press who came out to record the madness in the desert. For competitors, the format was nice, but the $30,000 prize purse was the reason they were there. Adjusted for inflation, $30,000 in 1969 is equal to about $217,000.

The money was good, and the entry list was deep with every big name in the sport's early days. In the four-wheel-drive class, there were 32 entries. By the end of the two days, only seven of those finished the eight laps. The first two finishers were Jeeps, and American Motors immediately placed big advertisements in major publications about how it kicked Bronco, International, and Toyota tail all over the Nevada desert.

After 26 hours and 53 minutes, a weary, dirty, and tired James Garner and Scooter Patrick arrive at the finish of the 1968 NORRA Mexican 1000. Just 40 minutes behind third place, it was an excellent debut for the team. (Photo Courtesy MotorTrend *and Petersen Museum Archive)*

The best-dressed man in off-road racing, Vic Abruzzese, and his clean-air breathing system take on the Nevada desert in the 1969 Mint 400. Abruzzese was an avid supporter of the sport for 10 years with a rotating cast of codrivers going with him on his adventures. (Photo Courtesy MotorTrend *and Petersen Museum Archive)*

Larry Minor and James Garner

In a phone conversation with Larry Minor in April 2020, I asked him if anything humorous ever happened in a Bronco, and he immediately began telling this story.

"One of funniest things that ever happened in a Bronco was with Jim Garner," Minor said. "He had a Bronco, I don't recall what year, maybe 1968 after the Mexican 1000. He asked me once, 'Larry, when do you put your Bronco into four-wheel-drive?'

"'As soon as I hit the dirt,' I said.

"'Man, I put my Bronco into four-wheel-drive, and I can't keep it in a straight line," he responded. 'It goes everywhere.'

"After the Mexican 1000, there was a race in Ocotillo Wells, [which was] about a 150-mile race, and Jim asked me to drive his Bronco at this race. Well, it was all dirt, so I started in four-wheel drive, and I couldn't keep that thing straight. About halfway through the race, I could tell that there had to be a difference in the gear ratios between the front and back gears. Later, we took it apart and found that one end was a 4.56 gear ratio and the other was a 3.90 gear ratio. In fact, during that race, we threw a driveline climbing a hill, and

James Garner is world renown for his acting skills, but many people do not know that he was a talented racer. He may not be the best mechanic, but lucky for James, he is with Larry Minor. (Photo Courtesy MotorTrend and Petersen Museum Archive)

at the top of that hill was a brand-new Bronco. We talked him out of the driveline and told him to come by the Stroppe pit and said we would give him a brand new one.

"We didn't win that one, I think we came third, but that was the funniest thing trying to figure out why this Bronco wouldn't go straight. I can't believe the transfer case survived that long."

At Parnelli Jones's urging, the Unser brothers (Bobby and Al) were provided a Bronco from the Stroppe stable. In 1969, the Unser name was at the forefront of up-and-coming drivers destined to win Indianapolis. Hailing from Albuquerque, New Mexico, they were not strangers to the desert, although neither had raced in one. They had paid their dues driving Pikes Peak, midgets, sprints, and stock cars. This was their first attempt at taking on the Nevada desert.

In a phone conversation with Bobby Unser, he remembered that it was "very unsuccessful." According

Here you get a better look at the filtration system Abruzzese manufactured. Modeled after a motorcycle filter, Vic used foam to filter out fine particles. (Photo Courtesy MotorTrend and Petersen Museum Archive)

Larry Minor and Jack Bayer are at the finish line in La Paz after 21 hours and 11 minutes of driving. They were second only by half an hour to the first motorcycle and an 1-1/2 hours ahead the next four-wheeled vehicle. This fueled Minor to work with Bill Stroppe on a plan to overhaul the whole event in 1969. (Photo Courtesy MotorTrend and Petersen Museum Archive)

to his brother, Al, who was in the Bronco riding with him, "I kept yelling at him to slow down, but he didn't, and he rolled us."

Bobby remembered he could not stay for the second day because he had a tire testing date in Indianapolis. Instead of putting someone else in with Al, Stroppe had a different idea.

"I got rolled over on the first day, and then Bobby had to leave," Al said. "So, the second day, Bill Stroppe didn't want to run with Parnelli, so I hopped in with him, and I got rolled again. Parnelli and I were racing and along came a dune buggy that ran us off the road. Well, Parnelli wasn't happy about that. He had a bit of a temper and took off after him. We caught up and passed some dune buggies until we found the one that looked like the guy who ran us off the road. Parnelli took off across the open desert to try and close in on him, but there was this big ditch, and we crashed into it and rolled the Bronco over—my second [time] of the weekend."

"Some folks helped roll us back on the wheels, and it wasn't hurt too bad," Al continued. "So, we continued on, but it was a rough day. We had a total of four flats that day, and when we came into the finish, that Bronco was only on two tires because we had two more flats just before the end."

Both of the Unser brothers stated throughout my conversations with them that they really enjoyed off-road racing and wished they could have done more. One would guess that winning seven Indianapolis 500 races between them keeps a driver busy.

Sadly, it was four more rough years at the Mint before a Bronco would win again.

At the 1969 Mint 400, Larry Minor and Jack Bayer were flying in the Bronco and took the four-wheel-drive class win. (Photo Courtesy MotorTrend and Petersen Museum Archive)

The late racing legend Bobby Unser is seen here with his brother Al at the 1969 Mint 400. Bobby had a short day, rolling the Bronco and his brother at least once. Al remained for the second day and rode with Parnelli Jones, his boss, who also rolled him over. Al returned to off-road many times over the years despite his initial weekend experience. (Photo Courtesy Trackside Photo)

The Mint 400 brings big spectator numbers. It was not uncommon to be in the middle of the desert and come across an encampment of excited fans. (Photo Courtesy Mark Atherton)

1969 NORRA Baja 500

After the humiliation of the Mint 400 result, Stroppe was eager to redeem himself and Ford. The NORRA Baja 500 was next on the schedule, but Stroppe sent a light crew and entry. He was looking to double down on the Mexican 1000 for his revenge on Jeep.

This was a brand-new event. With the Mexican 1000 becoming such a notable event in just two years, the call for more racing in Baja spawned a loop event that

At the 1969 Mint 400, Parnelli Jones was driving too hard and was beating up poor Bill Stroppe. In the second half of the race, Stroppe stepped out of the Bronco and put poor Al Unser Sr. in with him. Parnelli then proceeded to beat up his Indy Car driver as well. (Photo Courtesy MotorTrend and Petersen Museum Archive)

started and finished in Ensenada. Leaving Ensenada, the course took you south and west to the Pacific Ocean, east across the peninsula, and then north along the Gulf of California to San Felipe before heading west and north back to Ensenada. This same course was used from 1969 through 1972.

The race featured 149 entries at the start, and each had a 30-hour time limit to get back to Ensenada. Par-

At the end of the 1969 Mint 400, Parnelli Jones and Al Unser Sr. show the damage from their rollover. They were chasing down a driver who ran them off the road. (Photo Courtesy MotorTrend and Petersen Museum Archive)

Parnelli Jones (left), Miss Mint 400, and Al Unser Sr. (right) pose at the finish of the 1969 Mint 400. (Photo Courtesy MotorTrend and Petersen Museum Archive)

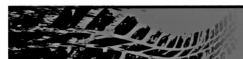

Dick Landfield and Irv Hanks

The Southern California Ford dealership owner started his very first off-road race in a Bronco with Irv Hanks, who was an established Bronco racer. It was at the 1969 NORRA Baja 500, where his first adventure in the desert turned into a prolonged rescue effort.

Racing in Baja is never what you would consider easy. However, some areas are tougher than others. One such area of carnage lies south of San Felipe; it is called the Three Sisters (where three rocky mountain trails need to be crossed).

In the middle of the Three Sisters, the Bronco lost a rear wheel bearing, allowing the axle assembly to slide out. Several attempts were made to rig a fix, but each lasted maybe 5 miles. Eventually, they resorted to using their leather belts to act as a bearing of sorts. That only lasted 3 miles. Eventually, the Bronco ground to a halt and was not going any further.

Dick agreed to hitchhike into Gonzaga Bay to try and find parts. Dick left Irv with some water, Spam, salami, and honey, and headed down the road with the international sign for needing a ride (his thumb was out). Dick caught a civilian ride south to Gonzaga Bay, where he found no parts. He did, however, find a drunk

crop duster pilot who flew him on a harrowing ride to Mexicali. Once safely on the ground, Dick walked across the border and hitchhiked to a Ford dealer in El Centro, California.

After buying the needed parts to repair Irv's Bronco, Dick also purchased a used Ford F-150 so that he could get back to his castaway teammate who by now had to be tired of Spam, salami, and honey. He also figured that he was getting low on water. Back across the border and south on Mexico Highway 5, Landfield picked his way over the rough road to find the Bronco and a surprisingly happy Irv Hanks.

The terrain between San Felipe and Gonzaga Bay was inhospitable, but it could also be busy. People were stopping to check on the stranded racer and leaving him with water, food, candy, and beer . . . a lot of beer. A bored and inebriated Hanks had spent his time sitting on the ground, surrounded by piles of food, and building little mazes. Irv had spent his time in the dirt and watching captured ants travel through his elaborate mazes.

The men repaired the Bronco and eased down the road headed back to civilization with more food than they started out with and a story for the ages.

nelli Jones was back in a Bronco that Stroppe had been working on specially for him (the *Colt*). A racer such as Parnelli only knew one way to drive at that time: hard on the gas. It was great on short dirt tracks and at Indianapolis but not so great in Baja to this point. Every attempt so far ended with flattened wheels or a broken front differential or something else that could not take Jones's pace. Larry Minor was back with Jack Bayer riding shotgun.

What exactly happened on race day seems to be lost to the sands of time. Maybe it is one event that all the surviving competitors would like to forget. Either way, Jeep swept the top three spots in four-wheel-drive class. Victor Abruzzese finished but was way down in the order. All in all, it was one to forget for the Blue Oval.

James Duff

One Bronco legend had a particularly rough start to his racing career at this race. James Duff was a mechanic at a Los Angeles–area Ford dealership. As part of his daily routine, he bought parts to upgrade Broncos for the dealership to sell. In his daily dealings with Bill Stroppe

and Dick Landfield at Fairway Ford, he was convinced to strip his new Bronco and build a racer out of it.

Duff's biography on his website recalled the short race.

"His codriver took the first leg of the 1969 Baja 500, and at over 100 mph, they came upon a hay truck stalled in the middle of the road! Avoiding it proved challenging, as the front-end bushings had disappeared. They caught the edge of the pavement, dove into the ditch, and did 3-1/2 rolls end over end, corner to corner. Their race was over before Duffy even got behind the wheel."

That rough start started a small aftermarket parts empire, as Duff Tuff parts soon found their way onto all kinds of Broncos from racers to dune runners. The company is still active today run by family, and it all started with a stalled hay truck in the wrong place.

The 1969 NORRA Mexican 1000

By 1969, the NORRA Mexican 1000 was a big deal. In Ensenada, 247 entries lined up for a shot at the peninsula. The ABC *Wide World of Sports* coverage the year

AFTER BAJA 500 CRASH JUNE 13

James Duff had a rough start to his off-road racing career, crashing in a big way at the NORRA Baja 500. That crash inspired Duff to start marketing better, stronger parts for all kinds of Bronco owners. He built a company based on it that is still going strong today. (Photo Courtesy James Duff Inc.)

Here's a shot of most of the Stroppe team in the impound yard on the morning of the 1969 NORRA Mexican 1000. At the end of the line, you can see the Pony getting attention. Larry and Rod's Bronco is next to it. (Photo Courtesy MotorTrend and Petersen Museum Archive)

before along with coverage by every major car magazine brought the challenge of Baja to more and more adventuresome individuals. Some of those were famous folks, such as actors James Garner and Steve McQueen. World Rally Champion Eric Carlsson and Indy 500 winner Parnelli Jones were also there.

Work on the new two-wheel-drive competition Bronco (the *Pony*) was not complete for the race, so the heavily modified *Colt* four-wheel-drive Bronco was entered for Jones and Stroppe.

To propagate the number of Broncos entered in a race, Stroppe helped independent teams with technical information and discounts on parts. Among those teams were James Duff's Bronco, Richard and Steve Smith, Dan Eames and Els Lown, and others. Although they looked like a part of the team (except Duff), these were independently owned Broncos, and, as such, Bill Stroppe had no final say about how they were prepared.

Bill Stroppe, ever the strategist, put together a comprehensive pre-run plan for Larry, Rod, Parnelli Jones, and Walker Evans (running a F-150 pickup). The three ran the length of the peninsula prior to the race, looking for more shortcuts and even smoother roads. Again,

Larry Minor and Rod Hall scream along a flat piece of road en route to their historic 1969 Mexican 1000 win. (Photo Courtesy Larry Minor)

in the early NORRA days, there was no marked racecourse. All you had to do was to be timed through the checkpoints along the way. It did not matter what route you took to get there. After arriving in La Paz, the three teams turned around and retraced their route back north, double-checking for any advantages.

After the big crash at the Baja 500 earlier in the year, James Duff returned to the 1969 Mexican 1000 with his Bronco looking as immaculate as it had before the crash. Unfortunately, the Bronco did not make it to La Paz. (Photo Courtesy James Duff Inc.)

Larry Minor and Rod Hall are shown en route to victory in the 1969 Mexican 1000. (Photo Courtesy MotorTrend and Petersen Museum Archive)

Just prior to the start of the 1969 NORRA Mexican 1000, some staged photos were taken while Larry Minor was testing the Bronco for the upcoming race. (Photo Courtesy Larry Minor)

Tragedy

Stroppe took pride in the "Smith Boys" entry. Richard Smith owned and built his Bronco for the 1969 race. Racing with him was Steve Smith. The boys were not related but were longtime friends. Steve was the son of Stroppe's original partner, Clay Smith, who was tragically killed by an out-of-control sprint car years earlier. The Smith Boys came off the start line with youthful 20-something-year-old exuberance. Flying down the road, they passed Hall and Minor in the pits after the first checkpoint. On the fast road to Camalu, the boys were pushing too hard in the dust. Attempting to pass an open-wheeled car, their front tire caught the rear tire of the open-wheel car, which flipped the Bronco into the air and it landed hard on the roof.

Richard Smith had not opted for a sheet metal roof over the driver and codriver like the factory racers. This fatal mistake allowed their heads to contact the ground when the flipping Bronco landed upside down on the side of the road. Richard died instantly on scene, and Steve was in bad shape and transported to medical facilities. Steve died on the operating table not long after.

Minor and Hall Shine

"That was the only thing that went wrong for us the whole way," Larry said. "[At] Every checkpoint, we would come in and put more water in the radiator, just fill it up and keep going. One thing was that we didn't drive over our heads. We both drove what we thought we could handle and what the car could take. There were always people going faster than us. They would pass us on the road, and a few miles later, they would be stuck in a ditch or upside down or with the hood up, and we'd pass them."

Rodney and Larry arrived first in La Paz, 48 minutes ahead of the winning Husqvarna motorcycle of J.N. Rob-

erts and Gunnar Nilsson. The goal was achieved by beating the motorcycles to La Paz. It would be the last time in more than 50 years that a four-wheel-drive vehicle would beat the entire field on a peninsula run. It says a lot about the kind of person who tackled Baja in those days as well as the level of preparation that Bill Stroppe himself oversaw in his shop and in planning out the race.

Rod Hall brings the Bronco across the finish line in La Paz, Baja Sur, 20 hours and 48 minutes after leaving Ensenada. Although they won overall, it was not a new record for the race. That was set in 1968 and still belonged to the motorcycles by 10 minutes. (Photo Courtesy MotorTrend and Petersen Museum Archive)

Larry Minor and Rod Hall

For 51 years, Larry Minor and Rod Hall have stood atop the Baja record books for a supreme achievement. In 1969, they took the overall win in a four-wheel-drive vehicle. That means not just the four-wheeled vehicles, they beat the motorcycles too!

Technology has a way of advancing over time, and at the time this book was published, their record still stands. The quickly advancing technology of long-travel four-wheel drive in today's trophy trucks may see the record fall very soon.

Larry Minor and Rod Hall took the Stroppe Holman-Moody-prepared Ford Bronco the length of the Baja Peninsula in 20 hours 48 minutes and 10 seconds, which was the fastest time set that year by any competitor.

That achievement, however, was years in the making. It goes way back to the early days in the off-road mecca of Hemet, California.

Larry Minor

Larry Minor is the son of a potato farmer, who, starting in 1943, used the rich soil of the San Jacinto Valley and the agreeable Southern California climate to

Things are looking clean, so this must be early in the race. Larry Minor is at the wheel as Rod Hall watches for landmarks and obstacles. (Photo Courtesy MotorTrend and Petersen Museum Archive)

After the races in 1968 and early 1969, Bill Stroppe had learned so much about the Bronco and the demands of off-road racing that he started a new build for Larry Minor and Rod Hall. Here, you can see a bit of what goes on under the skin of a race Bronco from this era. Extra bracing, more tubing to build the suspension off of, and a safer roll cage. The Bronco under construction went on to win the 1969 NORRA Mexican 1000 and win overall. (Photos Courtesy Larry Minor)

build a year-round potato farm. Working hard on the farm tends to make young men want to play as hard as they work, and in Hemet, that usually involved something with an engine and a dirt road.

Larry was dating the daughter of the owner of the Loomis Turkey Ranch when he met one of the employees, a guy named Rodney Hall. They both had an interest in off-roading so, as guys do, they bonded over things mechanical and started building Jeep vehicles.

In 1959, returning from a trip to the Glamis Sand Dunes, Larry had an engine failure. They looked for more power for their toys, and small-block Chevrolet engines are cheap. This was the beginning of a long line of Jeeps with Chevrolet V-8 engine conversions from small-blocks to 409-ci W motors. This helped Larry build a reputation as a sand drag competitor in his powerful Jeeps.

In 1962, he and Rod joined the Hemet Jeep Club and started doing a lot of four wheeling and competing in various Jeep club obstacle-course races. In 1963, Larry won a major event, the New Year's Buttercup meet, running a 409-ci Chevy motor in the Jeep. During the next two years, Larry won a number of sand drag events in Top Eliminator with the 409-ci Chevy motor in that Jeep at Bakersfield, San Jacinto, Pismo, Glamis, and Fallon, Nevada.

"We just liked Jeeps and liked racing," Larry said about his budding relationship with Hall. "We teamed up a few times and ran races and stuff like that."

That friendship took them from the Hemet Jeep Club to the first Mexican 1000, factory-supported drives, and a hand in shaping the sport from the very beginning.

Rod Hall

Rodney Alan Hall was born November 22, 1937, in Southern California. A lover of off-road excursions from a young age, Rod's first off-road vehicle was a motorcycle.

Later, at age 16, recognizing the advantages of toting along a sleeping bag and ice chest, he found a Jeep CJ-5 to take him into the wilderness. The Jeep was worn out previously, and Rod became a Jeep mechanic out of necessity to make it reliable.

By 1964, Rod was getting noticed after he won the club's signature event, the Afton Canyon Jeep Junket. Through the club, he had befriended others who proved that the teams from the Hemet Jeep Club were the teams to beat. Names such as Larry Minor, Jim Fricker,

Larry Minor. (Photo Courtesy Larry Minor)

Jim Loomis, and Carl Jackson all helped shape the sport in its infancy. All of those men eventually ended up in a Stroppe Holman-Moody Bronco because Bill Stroppe saw the quality of the Hemet drivers.

Out of high school, Rod worked at the Loomis Turkey Ranch and started dating the daughter of the owner, so you could say that Rod was dating "the farmer's daughter." It did not last long. However, he made friends with Jim Loomis and Larry Minor during his time at the Turkey Ranch.

Rod went on to own a gas station in Hemet while he expanded his resume as an off-road driver with the club. In time, his early adventures in the Baja wilderness turned into a career.

Rod Hall. (Photo Courtesy MotorTrend and Petersen Museum Archive)

Larry Minor and Rod Hall celebrate being the first vehicle to La Paz. They established a record for being the only four-wheel-drive vehicle to win an off-road race overall. They even beat the motorcycles. (Photo Courtesy MotorTrend and Petersen Museum Archive)

Arriving at the third checkpoint and in the lead of the race, Parnelli and Stroppe heard about the fatality and quietly abandoned their race and headed back north to see what they could do and help with the complicated arrangements of bringing home remains of people who died in Mexico.

Broncos took 1st, 6th, 7th, and 10th in the four-wheel-drive class and a record overall win that stands to this day.

The Lasting Legacy: Hall and Minor

With the results of the 1968 and 1969 Mexican 1000 showing the Bronco on top of a stacked field of Jeeps, Internationals, and every other make, it soon became the logical choice for teams looking to get into the sport to compete in the four-wheel-drive class. It was also not bad for Ford dealerships, as during those model years, roughly 37,500 Broncos were sold off showroom floors.

That translates to just over 1,500 sales per month. People believed that if it could slay the Mexican desert, it could probably handle whatever they were going to do to one.

When the Bronco program with Bill Stroppe ended in 1975, Minor went on to Stroppe's new program fielding the Ford Courier mini truck for a few years. Then, he went on to drag racing in 1978, building Top Fuel and Funny Cars for NHRA competition. The Top Fuel car was piloted by Gary Beck, who in 1983 was the first driver to break into 5.3 seconds with a 5.391-second quarter mile. Like in off road racing, Larry Minor stayed at the top of NHRA drag racing for many years with the sport's top drivers if he himself was not rocketing down the quarter mile.

You can take the man out of the desert, but you cannot take the desert out of the man. Larry returned several times to off-road racing, starting in 1982 with Parnelli Jones in a Chevrolet truck built by Walker Evans. Eventually, the truck ended up in the capable hands of Larry's hired gun, Steve Kelley.

After his Bronco days, Rod Hall and Bill Stroppe campaigned a Dodge 4x4 pickup for 27 years. In that period, Hall was the winningest driver in off-road racing history. (Photo Courtesy Marcus Clark)

At the end of his driving career, Larry Minor claimed residence in two halls of fame: the Drag Racing Hall of Fame in Gainesville, Florida, and the Off-Road Motorsports Hall of Fame in Jean, Nevada.

Rodney Hall went on to drive the Dodge 4x4 factory entry for Bill Stroppe for the next 20 years. His legendary racing career spanned more than 50 years in the desert. He left behind a long list of accomplishments. From an unprecedented winning streak of 37 straight races to winning 25 times in Baja's thousand-mile race to running every one of the first 50 of those 1,000-mile Baja races under three different sanctioning bodies.

He had more than 160 victories, 14 major championships, two wins in Australia, a second-place drive in the 1982 Marlboro Safari Rally in Africa, and finishes in the grueling Dakar Rally.

"I was never a fast guy, and I was never the first guy to the first checkpoint," Hall said in a video close to the end of his driving days. "But, I did learn that if you don't go any slower than you have to in the rough stuff, maybe you can just pull out a mile and a half faster than the other guys without beatin' up your car. Anybody can go fast in the fast area, but it's the slower areas, I think, where I learned how to win races."

Rod had remarkable relationships with manufacturers Ford, Dodge, and Hummer. BFGoodrich Tires stayed with Rod throughout most of his career, and he could be counted on to make appearances anywhere the company needed him around the globe. Hall was also an inductee into the Off-Road Motorsports Hall of Fame.

Someday soon, a space-age million-dollar four-wheel-drive chassis with a fiberglass truck body will probably take the overall win, besting the motorcycles. It will be revered as a great achievement, and it will be with the aid of GPS navigation systems, lightning-fast pit stops, radios relaying information to the drivers, nearly bulletproof computer-designed tires, and four times the wheel travel and horsepower. That's not to mention only two-thirds of the time behind the wheel to make the trip.

Into the 1970s

As the 1960s ended, the Bronco was firmly established itself in desert racing events and on the sales charts. More and more existing private teams moved into the Bronco or chose it as a starting platform.

The Stroppe team expanded technologically with the addition of the *Pony, Colt,* and eventually *Big Oly* itself. As good as the 1960s were to the Bronco, there was more history to made in the 1970s.

CHAPTER 3

THE 1970s
THE LEGEND GROWS

The 1960s had been good to the Bronco. Major wins dotted its resume from factory efforts and privateers alike. Lessons were learned along the way, and new innovations to safety and speed decreased times dramatically in races from just three years previous.

The 1970s provided challenges to the off-road racing community at large. The energy crisis, a move by the Mexican government to take over the Baja races, a new organizer, and radical changes to the 1,000-mile racecourse were just a few of those things.

Through it all, the Bronco did not rest on its laurels from the previous decade. New innovations to keep ahead of the competition from Jeep, International, and Toyota brought the Bronco to a whole new level. Long after the factory team stopped campaigning the Bronco, private teams kept winning for Ford. It would be 1989 before a factory-backed Bronco stormed the deserts again.

Meanwhile, back in Signal Hill, California, an experimental chassis arrived at the Stroppe shop and changed everything for Parnelli Jones. However, before that, another attempt to build a Parnelli-proof Bronco began in 1969.

This star-studded group of Stroppe drivers gathered before a race. From left to right are Larry Minor, Rod Hall, Walker Evans, Parnelli Jones, and Bill Rush. (Photo Courtesy Larry Minor)

Parnelli Jones and Bill Stroppe got an excellent starting position for the 1970 Mint 400 in the Colt *but still registered a "did not finish" (DNF). Success eluded them with the* Colt, *but good things were about to happen. (Photo Courtesy* MotorTrend *and Petersen Museum Archive)*

The *Colt*

In an effort to get Parnelli and Stroppe to the finish line, The *Colt* was devised to stand up to Parnelli's pace. The name *Colt* came about because a colt is lighter and faster than a bronco. Parnelli and Stroppe entered two events. After the tragic accident of the Smiths at the 1969 NORRA Mexican 1000, Parnelli and Stroppe willingly withdrew while leading to handle the aftermath. More information about this is in Chapter 6.

Then, they went out in the *Colt* again at the 1970 Mint 400 and with some help earned a sixth-place finish. The way several people remember it was Parnelli had a problem with the heat or was ill in some way. Larry Minor had parked his Bronco for a mechanical reason and was available to relief drive for Parnelli. Minor and Stroppe were able to get it to the end of the grueling race.

The *Colt* was then handed off to Larry Minor and Rod Hall for a few events. The first was the inaugural NORRA Baja 500 a few months after the Mint race.

"We were just out of San Felipe a ways and we were right on Parnelli's tail when we hit a rock," Minor said. "It blew the tire and folded the steel wheel around the caliper. We couldn't get the wheel off, so we slept in the desert. That was the last race Stroppe allowed steel wheels to be used."

Stroppe sold the *Colt* to Bill Rush. In 1972, Rush took class wins in both NORRA Baja events and the Barstow Fireworks 250. In late 1973, the Bronco was sold again to a team in Mexico. The Bronco continued to run competitively throughout the 1970s with new owner Alfonso Barbosa and his Coatzymoto racing team. The Bronco sat

The Colt *churns through bountiful Nevada sand against a rocky backdrop. It began life in 1969 as an innovative design. Technology moved fast, however, and it was obsolete for winning races overall very quickly. It briefly moved on to Larry Minor and Rod Hall for a few events before finding a home with Bill Rush through 1974. It was sold and found a new home in Mexico. (Photo Courtesy* MotorTrend *and Petersen Museum Archive)*

for many years until in 2019 Bronco enthusiast Andrew Norton found and purchased it.

The Inner Workings

Still, despite its failure to come through as hoped, the *Colt* was a radically upgraded Bronco where lessons learned went into the next two Broncos built for Parnelli. This Bronco was modified by sectioning the body two inches and channeled slightly. The floorboards and roof were lowered to give it a lower center of gravity. This also made the *Colt* friendly for shorter drivers. The effect of lowering the driver compartment caused the fenders to have to be lowered to match the body, so a bubbled hood was crafted out of fiberglass to keep it looking like a Bronco. The fender and door skins were also fiberglass. Everything else was stock sheet metal.

These modifications allowed the engine to be lowered and moved back to better balance the Bronco. The weight distribution of a stock Bronco makes it nose heavy, which makes the front end dive. The engine was a 302-ci 8-cylinder with a Ford high-rise intake and a Holley double-pumper carburetor. The engine was hooked to a 4-speed manual transmission and transfer case that were largely stock but were upgraded with the best components from the Ford parts bin.

The suspension was typical Stroppe with custom springs from F-Series chassis trucks, twin heavy-duty shocks per wheel, and many extra fabricated materials welded on the suspension and steering anchor points to handle the beating handed out by of the desert.

The *Pony*

In 1968, a gentleman recruited to Ford from General Motors named Semon E. "Bunkie" Knudsen had an idea to offer the Bronco in a two-wheel-drive package sold as a kit. It was a special project vehicle that did not get too far before the whole project was scrapped. The experimental chassis was offered to Bill Stroppe, who accepted it for an unknown reason.

Not long after the chassis arrived in California, Parnelli Jones was at the Stroppe team shop. In his book, *As A Matter of Fact, I Am Parnelli Jones*, he wrote, "I saw that thing sitting in his shop in Long Beach, and I said, 'Bill, that's our new racer. We don't need four-wheel drive and the extra weight and extra parts that go with it. Let's run that I-Beam Bronco.'

"Stroppe agreed. He added a roll cage and some good suspension pieces and worked on every part of that truck."

In sticking with the horse theme, the new chassis was named the *Pony* because it was shorter than any other racer in the shop.

For reasons lost to history, Rod Hall and Stroppe fabricator Chuck Looper entered the *Pony* in the 1970 Mint 400. One can only assume that either Jones or Stroppe wanted the *Pony* to be shaken down before the Baja 500. Several who were there agreed that the *Pony* finished and performed pretty well but did not win.

The *Pony* needed improvements after Rod Hall relayed what he learned about it during the Mint 400. The improvements were made just in time to make it to the 1970 NORRA Baja 500. It was so late, in fact, that Parnelli did not get a chance to pre-run the course.

Bill Stroppe poses in front of the Pony *circa 1972. (Photo Courtesy Larry Minor)*

Larry Minor spent more time in the Pony *than any other driver from 1970 to 1974. The* Pony *was a dependable off-road machine, and Minor was known as a finisher. (Photo Courtesy* MotorTrend *and Petersen Museum Archive)*

The Pony, under the heavy right foot of Larry Minor, was the star of the show at Mickey Thompson's first race at the Riverside International Raceway. (Photo Courtesy MotorTrend *and Petersen Museum Archive)*

In what turned out to be Larry Minor's last race in the Pony, *he was beaten for the win by a young upstart named Ivan Stewart with Bill Hrynko. (Photo Courtesy Trackside Photo)*

The Inner Workings

Stroppe and his crew built a beautiful machine with one sole purpose: go down the Baja Peninsula faster than anyone. To achieve this, Stroppe worked on the chassis that came to him with a stock Bronco frame and rear end and a truck Twin I-Beam front suspension. Stroppe worked his magic like he had on so many Broncos before by matching up heavier-duty truck coil springs with twin Gabriel shock absorbers and an Air Lift airbag setup. The *Pony* rode on high-floatation tires in the front and an aggressive off-road tread in the rear. Without the limitation of having to match tires all the way around (as was the case with four-wheel-drive), they could play with tire combinations that were not available to the four-wheel-drive units.

The 302-ci 8-cylinder small-block engine received a Ford High-Performance Pack, which included a high-rise intake, heads, a Holley 750-cfm double-pumper carburetor, and a special camshaft. The engine was coupled to a stock Ford C4 automatic transmission with gears being selected by a Mustang floor shifter. Without the need of a transfer case, the engine assembly was set back 10 to 12 inches into the chassis for better weight distribution. This was the first Stroppe Bronco racer to have power steering.

The body was lowered 3 inches right below the belt line. About 3 inches were chopped off the rear frame, and the body was shortened slightly. Fiberglass replacements were made for the hood, fenders, and door skins, and Stroppe custom made the aluminum inner fender panels. With these replacement body panels and the lack of four-wheel-drive parts, the *Pony* weighed a whopping 800 pounds lighter than the standard Stroppe racer.

Mint 400

March saw the third iteration of the Mint 400 again in Nevada. Jim Loomis and Bud Wright came up with a podium finish (second place) but were bested by Donnie Beyer and Don Richardson piloting a Jeep. Lighthearted rivalries between the two brands began to build as it was noted when a Bronco got stuck halfway up Graveyard Hill a Jeep fan yelled, "Get a Jeep and pull it up."

Later in the event, a Jeep encountered the same problem, and Bronco enthusiasts clamored, "Push it over the side and let it lay!"

The Bronco versus Jeep battle was entertaining for all.

The 1970 NORRA Baja 500: The *Pony* Debut

Just recently completed, the *Pony* was assigned the number 77 for the race, giving it a good starting spot given that there were over 230 entries. The meandering

Jim Loomis, a turkey farmer from Hemet, was one of Stroppe's early drivers. He and Larry Minor were related through marriage but had been friends for years. (Photo Courtesy MotorTrend and Petersen Museum Archive)

Duffy's Bronco *churns up some Nevada dust during the 1970 Mint 400. (Photo Courtesy James Duff Inc.)*

You can feel the frustration in this image. Steve Krieger and Jim Pfeifer attempt to dig out of the Mint 400 sand as a VW speeds by in what might be a better swath of desert. (Photo Courtesy MotorTrend and Petersen Museum Archive)

At the 1970 NORRA Baja 500, Parnelli's hunch that two-wheel-drive and a Twin I-Beam suspension would be the answer to building a winner was realized. With a big lead halfway through the race, Parnelli and Bill Stroppe take a pit stop for some fresh tires and fuel. (Photo Courtesy MotorTrend *and Petersen Museum Archive)*

The 1970 NORRA Mexican 1000

The 1970 peninsula run was largely forgettable for the Bronco arm of the Stroppe team, as the peninsula and Jeep won this round. One highlight for Stroppe's team was the emergence of Walker Evans in a two-wheel-drive F-Series pickup winning his class and coming home third overall. Ak Miller and Ray Brock took third in their class and fifth overall just 19 minutes behind Evans.

The other highlight was in the Production 4x4 class when Carl Jackson and Jim Fricker took second place almost two hours behind that pesky Jeep.

"I think that was the year they moved the North Star [laughs]," Carl Jackson said. "I was coming off the tidal flats between San Ignacio and La Purisima in the early morning hours, and somehow, I ended up going northeast. The worst part was I thought I knew the area like the back of my hand."

In the Production class, James Duff came home in fourth place another two hours back. Jim Loomis and Bud Wright were sixth, and the Quint's Bronco came in 11th after 34-1/2 hours. In the Modified 4x4 class, Don Barlow

course covering most of Baja Norte and stretching from the Pacific Ocean to the Gulf of California had something for everyone. There was fog in coastal areas and even some light rain reported, which was odd for June.

For the first time in an off-road race, Parnelli Jones put everything together that Bill Stroppe, his navigator, had been trying to teach him. He had a flawless run around the 500-mile course. The car, the driver, the pit stops, and everything came together, and the *Pony* finished in 11 hours and 55 minutes to take the overall win.

The winning Husqvarna motorcycle of Bill Silverthorn and Gene Fetty was 41 minutes behind. Jones had beat the previous year's best time set by Bud Ekins and Guy Jones in the *Baja Boot* on the exact same course by nearly five hours.

This win verified in Parnelli's mind that this was the setup he needed to dominate in off road racing—just like he had in stock cars, sprint cars, and at Indy. The die was cast, and he felt that all he needed was to improve upon the *Pony*. This is where the beginning ideas of *Big Oly* were conceived.

Bill Rush and Dan Shields had a long 1970 Mexican 1000. They overcame flat tires and an unspecified engine repair to take seventh place in the Modified 4x4 class. (Photo Courtesy MotorTrend *and Petersen Museum Archive)*

Don Barlow got his first chance at off-road racing at the 1970 NORRA Mexican 1000. Coco Corral had to do some talking to get him in the seat. Barlow envisioned a La Carrera-type race. He had a wild adventure, enjoyed himself, and came back for more for over a decade. (Photo Courtesy MotorTrend and Petersen Museum Archive)

One of the highlights for Team Stroppe in the 1970 Mexican 1000 was a second-place finish in Production 4x4 class. Carl Jackson and Jim Fricker trailed the winning Jeep by nearly 2 hours. (Photo Courtesy Carl Jackson)

brought the Coco Corral Bronco in fourth place. Stroppe drivers Bill Rush and Jim Griffin took sixth.

This was the first off-road event for Don Barlow in one of Coco Corral's Broncos. Barlow was a neighbor of the Corrals and a racer of jalopies and modified dirt cars. Coco asked Don if he would like to run the 1970 Mexican 1000. Barlow loved the old Pan American Road Races and was excited to try it and accepted the invitation. Later, he was at Corral's to see the car. When they walked inside, sitting there was a 1966 Ford Bronco. Barlow did not understand. Where was the car? After some explanation and convincing, he agreed to try off-road racing.

About 14 hours into the race Don recalled, "I hadn't had anything to eat since we started, and I was freezing because I did not have a jacket. In the distance, I saw the glow of a fire; a couple was pitting for another car. I pulled over and warmed myself by the fire, and they offered me something to eat. After about an hour, they asked me what broke on the Bronco. I told them nothing [broke but that] I was starving and cold. They said that only about seven or eight cars had been by and that I was doing pretty well. The guy lent me a jacket, [and] I put it on backward so it would warm me better and hopped back in."

Deciding to detour to the beach route to try and make some time, Don picked the wrong time—the tide was in. He slogged down the beach and headed back inland as the sun was coming up. Tired, cold, and wet, Don thought he was seeing things; it looked like water up ahead. By the time he saw it was a water crossing, he hit it, drowned the engine in the Bronco, and they were stuck. Soon after, a farmer came along and towed the Bronco out. Don started drying the engine out, and by the time the engine finally fired, another hour was lost.

Don Barlow and the Borrowed Bronco

Not every funny story comes from race day or pre-running the course. Sometimes it comes from building the racer, like in this case with Don Barlow and obtaining a fiberglass mold for the *Crazy Horse* body.

Barlow owned a Texaco gas station across the street from Coco Corral's Fillmore Ford dealership. The dealership was Barlow's sponsor, and Coco Corral was the man who got Barlow into off-road racing in the first place. In 1973, they were building a new Bronco to run a fiberglass body just like *Big Oly*.

One of the tougher jobs of making a fiberglass body is that a mold is needed to manufacture one, and if a mold is not commercially available, you must make your own. The problem was that the racer was already torn apart, and Barlow and mechanic Kenny Derwin did not know anyone with a body in good enough condition to get a clean mold. Barlow looked across the road to Coco's dealership, which was stocked to the gills with brand-new Broncos.

Don knew there was no way Coco would let him take a brand-new truck off the lot to make a mold. Following the old adage that "it is easier to ask forgiveness than permission," a Bronco was "borrowed" and brought

This fiberglass-bodied Bronco competes in the 1981 Parker 400. Fiberglass is easier to modify than metal. It also has the benefit of being lighter. (Photo Courtesy Trackside Photo)

over to the gas station for a fitting.

Luckily, all went well. There was no damage to the new Bronco, and *Crazy Horse* had a new body. No one interviewed for this book would say whether Coco ever found out about it.

Barlow stormed into the finish in La Paz with fourth place in his class. Don later found out he was only 40 minutes out of first place. A valuable lesson about Baja racing was learned early. Without just one of those mishaps, he might have won in his first attempt in a Baja race.

Big Oly's Debut as *Crazy Colt*

It should be noted that this event was the Mexican debut of the creation of Parnelli Jones and Dick Russell. It was not yet officially *Big Oly*; that came in 1971.

The *Crazy Colt* was still just that at its debut in Ensenada. It was draped in a Johnny Lightning paint job, the same company that sponsored Jones' winning Indy Car effort with Al Unser Senior. Running on propane for this event,

In its first race at the 1970 NORRA Mexican 1000, Parnelli Jones and Bill Stroppe were running away with the race by the third checkpoint near Punta Prieta in Crazy Colt. Soon after, it all went wrong with rear-end damage. That 350-mile test, as it turned out to be, showed Parnelli Jones that his creation was everything he hoped it would be. (Photo Courtesy MotorTrend and Petersen Museum Archive)

This is the **Crazy Colt** *when it was new and being tested before the 1970 NORRA Mexican 1000. Between this test and the race, the graphics were either completed or modified to match Parnelli's Indy Car team and the Johnny Lightning Special, which was driven to two Indianapolis 500 wins by Al Unser Sr.*

Parnelli started off very well. The *Crazy Colt* was running perfectly as designed. About 200 miles into the race, Parnelli pulled into his pit at Santa Ynez for fuel and service. Sitting there waiting for the crew to refuel and check over the Bronco, Parnelli saw what looked like Drino Miller's race car go by. What Parnelli did not know at the time was that it was Miller's pre-run car scouting the course ahead.

Parnelli took off like a man possessed and, admittedly, drove way over his head chasing what would turn out to be a phantom. Early in the race, Parnelli covered the opening 240 miles in a blistering 3 hours and 33 minutes, leading the field. An off-course excursion over some boulders broke the rear-end housing and an axle. Vic Wilson in a buggy passed the stricken Bronco.

He and Stroppe limped down the road for repairs, but the crew could not repair the broken axle shaft. They ran the next 400 miles in one-wheel-drive until the stress and strain broke the other axle 200 miles from La Paz. One of the Stroppe four-wheel-drive teams came by and was told to get to the end and send a crew back to make repairs. It took hours, but Jones and Stroppe limped into La Paz far down the order.

This is the view that many a competitor did not want to see in the rearview mirror: a determined Parnelli Jones chasing them down. You could not miss that "PJ" in the front grille. This is the 1971 Mint 400 with Al Unser riding along. (Photo Courtesy MotorTrend and Petersen Museum Archive)

Wilson brought the buggy into El Arco to hand the car over to Drino Miller. To add salt to their figurative open wounds, Drino Miller won the race and set a record in the process. In the end, it was a good shakedown for the new creation and offered great hope for the future.

1971

Ford, after seeing the racing program have trouble keeping the Dana 30 front ends alive, switched production to the stronger Dana 44 axle. Manufacturers who learn from their racing programs build better products.

The factory support for Bronco teams continued under Bill Stroppe's watchful eye, and after a promising debut at the Mexican 1000 in 1970, the *Crazy Colt* program continued for Parnelli Jones. Larry Minor inherited the *Pony*, and Rod Hall began splitting time between a Bronco and a Ford Maverick.

Bill Stroppe introduced the Baja Bronco production truck package with upgrades learned from thousands of miles of racing and pre-running.

Mint 400

March 21–23 were the dates for the now-prestigious Mint 400. An incredibly iconic pairing of Parnelli Jones and Al Unser, both former Indianapolis 500 winners (Unser the year before), were piloting the No. 45 Stroppe Bronco. Stalwart Bill Stroppe had Larry Minot in the No. 47 machine.

Parnelli Jones had a real love of racing in the desert, and he liked to share it whenever possible. The driver of his Indy Car, Al Unser Sr., was available for the Mint 400. He and his brother Bobby had run a Mint 400, or at least part of one, two years previous, so Parnelli offered Al a chance at revenge on the unforgiving Nevada desert. Stroppe slid over to ride with Larry Minor in the *Pony*.

In the first four laps that took

Parnelli and Al Unser charge through the Nevada desert in the Crazy Colt's *second outing. While it was not particularly successful in terms of a high finish, more information was learned for future races. (Photo Courtesy* Motor-Trend *and Petersen Museum Archive)*

place the first day of the Mint 400, Parnelli Jones and Al Unser covered the first few in fine form. Early in the third lap, the rear end failed on the Crazy Colt, ending their day and making them spectators for the next day's laps.

While Parnelli Jones took Indy 500 winning driver Al Unser Sr. for a ride, Bill Stroppe enjoyed the company of Larry Minor at the Mint 400 in the Pony. *Anyone who thinks that buggy just passed the* Pony *obviously does not know Larry Minor very well. (Photo Courtesy* MotorTrend *and Petersen Museum Archive)*

Bill Rush or Walker Evans try the inside line on a single-seat buggy during the 1971 Mint 400. (Photo Courtesy Motor-Trend and Petersen Museum Archive)

Wayne Minor, Larry Minor's brother, had a good run for a while in off-road racing. His growing business commitments kept him from driving but not before he notched a win at the 1971 NORRA Baja 500. (Photo Courtesy MotorTrend *and Petersen Museum Archive)*

NORRA Baja 500

The third annual loop race saw the usual suspects returning to Ensenada for another assault on Baja. NORRA was running like a well-oiled machine. Once again, it chose to run its established 500-mile loop for the third year in a row.

Wayne Minor (Larry's bother) and Gary Scarmella took the four-wheel-drive win in their Bronco, beating a field of Jeeps and fellow Bronco drivers.

Of all the great stories to come out of Baja racing, perhaps one of the most incredible was the story of a team that towed a trailer through the entire 500-mile race.

NORRA Mexican 1000

It was time to unleash *Big Oly* on the Baja Peninsula once again. Parnelli was confident. He put in the pre-run time and knew that Russell and Stroppe had Oly tuned and sorted out to the nth degree. This was his fourth attempt at the Mexican 1000, and he wanted it badly. Heck, it only took him two tries to win the biggest auto race in the world, the Indy 500. Team Stroppe arrived at the start in Ensenada ready to show what *Big Oly* could do.

Prior to the race, Parnelli sat in the San Nicholas Hotel with its owner and off-road racing supporter, Nico Saad. Nico knew that once the cars started and the officials were on the airplane headed to La Paz, there would be a betting pool for the overall winning time. Looking for some inside information, Saad asked what kind of time he thought he could turn in *Big Oly*. Parnelli said with confidence that he was sure he could make it in 15 hours flat.

Prior to the start of the 1971 NORRA Mexican 1000, Parnelli Jones parks Big Oly *in the impound lot after passing safety inspection. (Photo Courtesy* MotorTrend *and Petersen Museum Archive)*

Parnelli and Stroppe drew the No. 63 starting spot. They would have some passing to do before they got to clean air, but this was Baja, and most people knew what was behind them and kept an eye on their mirrors so

Parnelli and a crew member make their way through technical inspection prior to the start of the 1971 Mexican 1000. (Photo Courtesy MotorTrend *and Petersen Museum Archive)*

The Legend of the Sprite Trailer

Caravans International was a recreational trailer manufacturer out of Indiana that had a license to produce the Sprite, which was a 1,500-pound trailer that was designed and built in England. One of the executives was tasked with finding a way to show how tough the company's trailers were. He or she thought that it would be just the ticket if someone would tow a trailer behind them in a Baja race and finish within the official time limit of 30 hours.

Caravans International had a Southern California dealership owned by Wayne Lindsey, who was called and asked to head up the project. Lindsey knew that if anyone could pull this off, it was Bill Stroppe. It took one phone call for Stroppe to agree to do it, and he knew the driver in his lineup. This was a job for "Pretty Boy."

Wayne Lindsey drove to Fairway Ford, owned by Dick Landfield, and purchased a 1971 Baja Bronco. It was delivered to Stroppe's shop for preparation. Stroppe built a roll cage off of the existing rollbar, added different tires, and applied stickers. Some concern about the durability of the Class II trailer hitch was voiced by Lindsey, but Stroppe assured him that it was plenty tough for the job.

Carl Jackson and Jim Fricker make some time while the going was at least somewhat smooth. No one, not even NORRA, gave them a chance to make the 30-hour cutoff time. A lot can happen in 30 hours. (Photo Courtesy Carl Jackson)

Carl Jackson received a call to come visit the shop. Once there, Stroppe laid out the plan to hitch a Sprite to this Baja Bronco and finish the race. He paired Carl with Jim Fricker (one of his best ride-along mechanics), thinking that with "Pretty Boy's" driving and Fricker wrenching, they would get this crazy idea to the finish. To enhance the deal, Caravans International offered Carl a lot of money to just take the start, and if he finished within the official time limit, they would double it. Jackson did

Prior to the start of the 1970 NORRA Mexican 1000, most teams took a moment for a photo. Here, Carl Jackson (right) and Jim Fricker (left) pose with their Bronco before setting off for La Paz. (Photo Courtesy Carl Jackson)

Just before the start ramp, Carl Jackson talks with Wayne Lindsey of Sprite Trailers. (Photo Courtesy Carl Jackson)

With the wave of the green flag, Carl and Jim are off on a tour of Baja California towing what should not be towed over most of those roads. (Photo Courtesy Carl Jackson)

not remember the exact amount, but he remembered that it paid better than winning the race overall.

If you are wondering how Carl Jackson picked up the nickname, on the long pre-runs in Baja, personal grooming was pretty lax, but Jackson insisted on shaving every morning. The nickname stuck for years. Parnelli Jones and Walker Evans still call him "Pretty Boy" to this day.

What Do We Do with It?

NORRA did not really know what to do with the Bronco/Sprite entry. Certainly, it could not start where they would normally put a driver of Jackson's abilities, so they put them at the end of the 227-car field. NORRA officials did not give them a chance of finishing anyway.

One of the issues that concerned the team was the lack of alloy wheels available that would fit on the Sprite. Being a single-axle unit, it only had two tires on the road at any one time to take the abuse. Jackson and Fricker packed four spares in the trailer and placed more spares around the course at team pit locations.

Into the Wilds of Baja California

Not far off the start from Ensenada, Jackson and Fricker found that some areas were so rough that they were dragging the trailer over the inhospitable terrain. Attempting to access the low range in the transfer case, they found that low range would not engage. The linkage had been damaged when it was unloaded from the car hauler. So, four-wheel high range it was, but that had repercussions. The extra engine RPM, low speed, and the June heat in Baja meant that the Bronco's water temperature was at 220 degrees for most of the race.

Jim Fricker recalled the following in a 2006 interview at the Bronco 40th anniversary.

"Not far off the start, I looked back to check on the trailer, and it was bouncing all over the place," he said. "Right, then left. Well, I'll tell you, that was the last time I looked behind me for the rest of the race."

Then, the flat tires started, not so much from the tire itself being compromised but because those steel wheels would bend, allowing air to escape. In an effort to save spare tires, they pulled over and pounded the wheel back

The Legend of the Sprite Trailer CONTINUED

These are just two of the trailer wheels that fell victim to the terrain of Baja California. The tires are looking good— the wheels not so much. Poor Jim Fricker lost count of how many times they changed tires on that long day. (Photo Courtesy Carl Jackson)

to some semblance of round and re-aired the tire. That is, when they *could* pull over. Some flats were happening in canyons that were so narrow that there was no room to safely pull over to allow another vehicle to pass during a repair. Jackson had to drag that poor trailer along until the canyon widened out enough to safely pull over.

Finally, in San Felipe after a long night on the Puertecitos Road, the Stroppe pit crew repairs the trailer hitch. The repair was not necessary because it broke (it did not break—just as Bill Stroppe said it would not) but because it kept coming loose. It was nothing that a welder couldn't handle. Recently, the Baja Bronco used for this was found, and the trailer hitch was still welded in place. (Photo Courtesy Carl Jackson)

Even for the fastest racers in the best-prepared cars, the Puertecitos Road that headed north to San Felipe was a worrisome piece of road because it was the roughest, rockiest chunk of land in all of Baja Norte. For Jackson and Fricker, it was crucial to get through there and make it to San Felipe where the pit crew had extra spare tires. Sure enough, only halfway to San Felipe in the middle of the Cuestas, three nasty mountains to climb, they ran out of spare tires. It was slow going, and Jackson was wondering if he would be able to finish in the 30-hour time limit. They rattled and banged their way into San Felipe.

Once in San Felipe, Fricker told the pit crew that they had to retighten the hitch several times and even replace some lost bolts. Not wanting to have to worry about it anymore, the hitch was welded permanently to the frame. Now, it was just a question of navigating the final 150 miles back to Ensenada.

Loaded with spares again, Jackson just needed to stop by the fuel depot and fill the Bronco with gas. Back in those days, fuel was included in a NORRA entry fee, and volunteers manned the fueling areas. Arriving towing their trailer, none of the volunteers believed that Jackson and Fricker were actually entered in the race and refused to give them fuel. After some heated exchanges, the volunteers were convinced to fuel the Bronco.

They Said It Could Not be Done

Twenty-six hours and two minutes after leaving Ensenada, Jackson and Fricker returned triumphantly to do what no one thought possible. They finished four hours ahead of the time limit, were 19th in class, 105th overall, and beat 121 other entries back to Ensenada.

In a phone conversation with Carl Jackson in August 2020, he recalled that the trailer actually did very well and finished with minimal damage to the exterior. Inside the trailer, only a single curtain rod had fallen. One Caravan International official at the finish thought that the trailer looked too good and approached it with a large hammer to put some dents in it. Jackson intercepted the gentleman and convinced him that it would absolutely not look better with the added dents.

Caravan International wanted to enter the same Bronco and Sprite in the 1971 Mexican 1000. NORRA refused the entry, stating that it would not look good for the image of the world's toughest off-road race if a truck and trailer could finish it.

Wayne Lindsey drove the Bronco and Sprite combination back to headquarters in Nappanee, Indiana. The unit spent several years touring the 4x4 and RV show circuit with a poster that stated: "The travel trailer that beat Parnelli Jones in the Baja 500." It did not mention that Parnelli was not able to finish the race.

After starting 26 hours earlier, the Sprite trailer returned to Ensenada with four hours to spare. Jackson and Fricker did what no one excepted them to do, return with the Sprite intact. As a matter of fact, some people thought it looked too good. (Photo Courtesy Carl Jackson)

that they could move over voluntarily instead of having Parnelli "announce" his presence with the front bumper.

It sounds anticlimactic, but Parnelli and Stroppe had an exceptionally clean run down the peninsula and arrived in La Paz only 14 hours and 59 minutes after leaving Ensenada. It was just one minute off Parnelli's prediction, but it was close enough that Nico Saad won the betting pool.

Big Oly, with a little help from Parnelli Jones, did what it was designed to do: win the Mexican 1000 overall and beat the motorcycles. Malcolm Smith and Gunnar Nilsson on a Husqvarna were the first motorcycle entry to finish 1 hour and 52 minutes later.

Larry Minor and Jack Bayer managed fourth place overall and third in their class with the *Pony,* finishing 1 hour and 37 minutes behind *Big Oly*. However, the Stroppe team notched a two-wheel-drive pickup win. It was third overall with Walker Evans and Shelby Mongeon, and second in the two-wheel-drive pickup class with Ak Miller and Carl Jackson finishing seventh overall just to sweeten the effort. Maybe it took some of the sting out of not winning the four-wheel-drive class.

1972

United States President Richard Nixon started the year making headlines for visiting China. Later in the year, the word "Watergate" entered the American lexicon. The

Finally, Parnelli Jones and Bill Stroppe could call themselves winners of the biggest off-road race in the world. Ed Pearlman, the founder of NORRA, leans in to congratulate the winners. (Photo Courtesy MotorTrend *and Petersen Museum Archive)*

After the 1971 NORRA Mexican 1000, a very proud Parnelli Jones and his wife, Judy, seem to be taking a moment with Big Oly *in post-race impound. All the hard work and early disappointments paid off at the perfect time for Parnelli, Bill Stroppe, Ford, Olympia beer, and Firestone tires. (Photo Courtesy* MotorTrend *and Petersen Museum Archive)*

production Bronco, again learning from racing, was outfitted with large brakes front and rear. Meanwhile, back in Signal Hill, Stroppe was just as busy building racers as he was outfitting Baja Broncos.

Mint 400

The 1972 edition of the Mint 400 was in silty, dirty Tule Springs. For the 390 entries at this race, it was good news when it was announced that 1972 was the last year the race would be held there. As a farewell to the racers, the begrudging desert only allowed 32 percent of the field to finish.

The Mint 400 draught continued for the Bronco. This was in the Bronco's dry spell between 1969 and 1972, when no Bronco won its class at the Mint.

It did not stop a legion of bobtails from coming out and trying to knock Jeep off the top spot on the podium. This was the final year in Tule Springs, which was one of the roughest sections of Nevada.

Early favorite Parnelli Jones set a new record in the first lap, running approximately 50 miles in 1 hour and 7 minutes. On just the second lap of six, he broke an axle before a silt bed and buried *Big Oly*. Hours of digging netted no movement, and Jones had to call it.

The 4x4 class had 46 entries. Of those, only 9 made it to the finish. Among them was Rodger Ward, a two-time Indy 500 winner, who

Parnelli Jones and *Big Oly*

I feel confident in stating that if you took a vote among off-road racers past and present and asked what the single most iconic vehicle of all time is, the winner by a landslide would be the *Big Oly* Bronco.

As a case in point, at the 2019 Specialty Equipment Manufacturers Association (SEMA) Show in Las Vegas, Nevada, the Bronco was a featured vehicle of the show. Of all the iconic Broncos that lined the Ford displays and halls of the Las Vegas Convention Center, *Big Oly* had the biggest crowd around it every day.

Big Oly only ran for three and a half years, but for those four seasons, it influenced off-road racing technology for decades to come.

Parnelli Jones

Rufus Parnell "Parnelli" Jones was born on August 12, 1933, in Texarkana, Arkansas. The Jones family, looking for a prosperous life moved to Torrance, California. This is where Parnelli grew up and still lives near today.

Growing up, he did not take a liking to schoolwork and opted to leave public educational opportunities behind. Finding himself adept at working on and driving cars, he soon came up with a plan to start racing at 17 years old. While Jones was not a particularly notable name, Rufus was, and he needed to keep his parents from finding out he was racing while still a minor. His friend, Billy Calder, came up with "Parnellie" Jones and lettered the first jalopy he raced as such. Carrell Speedway in Gardena, California, was the first racing experience young Mister Jones had, and he liked it. The name stuck,

World-renowned photographer Boyd Jaynes arranged to get Big Oly *in his photo studio with unprecedented access to Dick Russell's handywork. One could argue that* Big Oly *is a piece of art as well as a functioning machine, and Jaynes's photo brings considerable credence to that argument. (Photo Courtesy Boyd Jaynes)*

Big Oly *on display at the 2019 Specialty Equipment Marketing Association (SEMA) Show in Las Vegas, Nevada, which is the biggest show of its type for aftermarket automotive products. In March 2021, news of Parnelli Jones selling his co-creation rocked the Bronco world to its core. No matter who the buyer is, it will always be Parnelli's truck in the eyes of off-roaders the world over.*

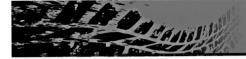

but the "e" fell off somewhere along the way.

As he learned the ways of driving a jalopy on dirt bull rings in Southern California, the wins started coming. His name grew popular, and soon he was courted to drive the West Coast NASCAR events. By 1958, he was terrorizing the stock car circuit. By 1959, he was on to sprint cars and again terrorizing the West Coast again in the winter and spring. By summer, he was driving IMCA events in the Midwest on drier and dustier tracks than he had ever seen. Once he figured out that you could see better if you were in the lead, winning became commonplace.

Parnelli was at home in the dirt as he tackled the toughest tracks all over the country alongside some of the toughest drivers, including A. J. Foyt, Mario Andretti, Johnny Rutherford, Jim Hurtubise, and many more. By 1961, Indianapolis car owners came calling, and by 1963, Parnelli could call himself an Indy 500 winner.

In the years that followed, he drove about everything from stock cars to sports cars and everything in between. At the end of his racing days, Parnelli found himself enshrined in no less than 20 different halls of fame and had his likeness on the BorgWarner Trophy.

He was a favorite driver of legendary car owners, including Agajanian, Vel Miletich, and Bill Stroppe. Now, I could go on and on about Parnelli's accolades outside of the desert, but you are here to read about Broncos and more importantly the *Big Oly* Bronco.

Big Oly Started as a Big Secret

A true racer never stops looking for a way to go faster. After running a four-wheel-drive Bronco in early events, Parnelli had a hunger to beat everyone, including the motorcycles. To do so, he knew he needed something two-wheel drive and completely custom built.

Before *Big Oly*, there was the *Pony* Bronco, which Stroppe built from a two-wheel-drive prototype that came from Detroit. Parnelli saw the chassis in Stroppe's shop and instantly thought it was the answer to his driving style. At his request, Stroppe built the chassis into a racer. It was a particularly good start taking the NORRA Baja 500 in 1970 overall, but in the end, Parnelli wanted more.

Stroppe heard the pitch from Parnelli about a more robust version of the *Pony* several times. Every time Stroppe turned it down. He enjoyed a good relationship with Ford and did not want to jeopardize that with an out-of-this-world take on the Bronco.

Parnelli Jones approached Dick Russell, one of Stroppe's best builders, and took him to lunch. With drawings on a napkin in hand, Russell started to build Parnelli's vision in his garage at his home. Such was the inauspicious beginning to what was initially called the *Crazy Colt*.

The Building of an Icon

Dick Russell was a fabricator of extraordinary ability and a big cog in the Team Stroppe machine. Russell had been building road race cars for the likes of A. J. Foyt, the Unsers, and Parnelli Jones. He was a highly regarded fabricator on Indy Cars too. Behind the wheel, Russell was a member of the 200-mph clubs at both El Mirage Dry Lake and Bonneville. In an obituary published in *Hot Rod* magazine in 2013, David Freiburger wrote, "Dick Russell was one of those unsung guys whose name you probably never heard before today but who very likely changed some part of your gearhead existence without you ever knowing about it. Godspeed, Tricky Dick."

Parnelli knew he wanted a racer built from the ground up with a space-age tube chassis made from TIG-welded 4130 chromoly. A highly modified Twin-I-Beam suspension was devised. Then, they figured that the engine needed to be set lower and back as far into the chassis as possible. From these early ideas, Dick Russell started laying out the *Crazy Colt* on his garage floor in the evenings and on weekends.

As the *Crazy Colt* was coming together in Russell's garage, the month of May was coming up, and Parnelli was in Indianapolis. Excited about his "secret" project, he started telling Mickey Thompson all about it (possibly bragging, as racers do). After the 500, Stroppe happened upon Thompson, who spilled the beans about the project. Stroppe was very unhappy upon learning what was going on behind his back.

The next time Stroppe and Parnelli got together, it devolved into a yelling match. Then, the cussing ensued. Eventually, cooler heads prevailed. Parnelli promised that it would have a fiberglass body that looked like a Bronco, which Stroppe figured he could sell Ford on. He told Russell to bring the chassis into the shop and finish it under his watchful eye.

Suspension

The suspension work began with taking pickup truck Twin-I-Beams and narrowing them down (how far was never noted). The stock-radius arms that helped locate the beams were replaced with trailing arms attached to the front of the chassis. Specially built coil springs were wound to allow the *Crazy Colt* to soak up the bumps. This design created more natural deflection when the suspension ran through its travel. In short, it made the *Crazy Colt* handle better over big bumps. Steering was controlled through a Ford Thunderbird steering box that had the preferred ratios for quick reaction from the driver. These adjustments gave the *Crazy Colt* almost a foot of wheel travel.

The rear suspension was a coil spring four-link system located with a transverse Panhard rod laterally centering the rear end. That system was good for 10 inches of wheel travel, which was more travel than anything else currently racing.

Engine and Drivetrain

The engine was going to have to be a strong unit with lots of torque. They settled on a small-block V-8 because they cooled better in the desert conditions. Stroppe and Jones used a Ford 351 Windsor small-block. They crowned the engine with a Cobra Jet high-rise single-plane manifold and a Holley 650-cfm double-pumper carburetor. Ed Iskenderian provided one of his legendary Isky camshafts, and some porting of the heads was done. The oil pan was baffled to keep the oil around the oil pump pickup no matter what gravity-defying driving was being done. Finally, custom headers and exhaust tubing expelled the spent gasses away from the driver and passenger. In the final configuration *Big Oly* produced 390 hp and had a top speed of 145 mph.

All of that power had to get to the final drive, and initially Stroppe had a Ford C4 automatic transmission matched up to the engine. However, after some early runs, everyone agreed that *Big Oly* needed the heavy-duty Ford C6 automatic transmission. Originally, Harrison coolers were used for the transmission and engine, but shortly after completion, those were switched out for Rapid Cool units on the transmission and engine oil. These coolers were mounted behind the passenger compartment in clean air flow.

A few feet back at the end of the driveshaft was a Ford 9-inch rear-end housing. It held a 4.11 gear ratio ring and pinion with a Detroit Locker differential. At each corner were Hurst/Airheart disc brake units because going that fast is not very beneficial in off-road racing unless you can stop for unexpected holes, broken cars, rocks, cattle, or cacti.

You have to be a pretty big deal to get Firestone to name a tire after you. (Photo Courtesy Boyd Jaynes)

*Parnelli opted to go with knock-off hubs on **Big Oly**. Until this point, knock-off hubs had been used many kinds of racing, but off-road was not one of them—not until **Big Oly**. After that, most large trucks ran them. In the desert, in the middle of a tire change, it is easier to keep track of one big spinner than five or six tiny lug nuts. (Photo Courtesy Boyd Jaynes)*

Wheels and Tires

All of this beautiful engineering stood on Firestone Tires. There were 9x15 tires in the front and 9.5x16 units in the rear mounted on alloy wheels. Parnelli had done a fair amount of damage to steel wheels over his short off-road career at this point, as had most every racer at some point, which made an alloy wheel the obvious choice. The wheels were held on by massive knock-off spinners instead of lug nuts.

*In this rear view of **Big Oly**, you can see the fuel filler setup on both sides of the truck. This allowed for quicker filling with NASCAR-style dump cans into the dual fuel tanks. (Photo Courtesy Boyd Jaynes)*

Fuel

There were two 22-gallon fuel cells supplying high-octane gasoline to the engine. One was mounted directly behind the passenger compartment, and the other was mounted low in the rear behind the rear axle. This helped with weight distribution. The higher-mounted cell fed the lower cell with the aid of gravity. From there, an electric fuel pump moved the fuel to the engine through braided stainless-steel lines. It is interesting to note that in its first two events, the *Crazy Colt* ran on propane instead of gasoline. Stroppe had experimented with propane often, but it became clear that *Big Oly* needed gasoline.

Wing

Let us not forget the most interesting bit of engineering that made *Big Oly* stand out: that wing. NORRA rules mandated a fixed solid roof on every vehicle at the time. Parnelli Jones, looking for every advantage, and Bill Stroppe, being a most innovative guy, decided to mount a big wing to help with the higher speeds seen in Baja.

However, why just mount a simple wing? Why not make it so the passenger could adjust the wing according to speed conditions? The wing could be adjusted up or down 40 degrees in 10-degree increments. The faster you went, the lower the wing position, and the higher the speed. But wait, there is more! Off-road races usually went into the night, and special lights like what the European rally cars were using were needed. Stroppe mounted lights in the wing that could flip up or down mechanically, again controlled by the passenger.

Cockpit

The compartment for the two occupants was all business. Two racing seats were mounted with a large console between the seats. This was the control panel for everything from the shifter to the gauges and control switches for electrical items. Mounted on the dash was the air filter assembly to cut down on ingesting fine dirt particles into the engine.

It was the $10,000-per-year sponsorship that was genesis of Big Oly's name. The Tumwater, Washington, brewery built a legion of fans due to some smart marketing. (Photo Courtesy Boyd Jaynes)

Stroppe liked information, so he had an array of gauges mounted in that center panel: transmission oil temperature, engine oil temperature, water temperature, fuel pressure, and amps. Electrical switches with safety covers numbered five: ignition, fuel pumps, and three for the off-road lights. Parnelli had a steering wheel and a tachometer, and that was it. It was all he needed.

You may think that was a lot of technology for the times, but wait, there is more. Remember, Dick Russell was smart. Using an idea that Colin Chapman devised on his Lotus race cars that Parnelli had driven previously, Russell built a two-piece channel that ducted air into the space where the windshield would normally be. What this did was create a curtain of air that kept dust from entering the passenger area.

After extensive hours of research, it has become clear that many of the races that Parnelli entered do not have an active archive for results. What we do know is recounted below. In some cases where race results are no longer available, I relay any memories gleaned during interviews and period press clippings.

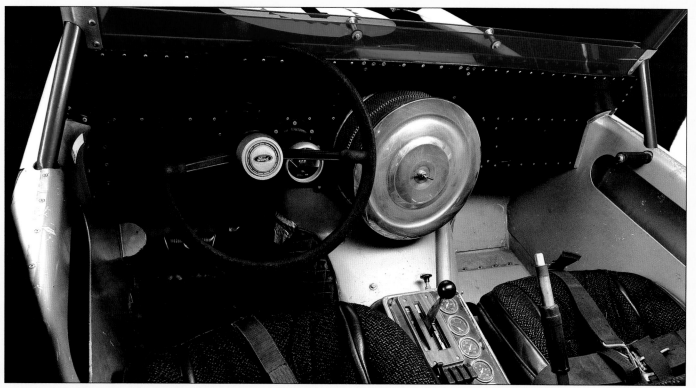

This is your office if your job description includes winning off-road races. The air filter in the dash kept a fresh supply of air flowing into the Holley 650-cfm double-pumper carburetor. Bill Stroppe assembled a collection of gauges that could not only tell him at a glance how the heart of Big Oly was feeling at that moment but also foresee problems. The lever next to the codriver seat controlled the angle of the wing. The shifter was out of a Mustang. (Photo Courtesy Boyd Jaynes)

Parnelli Jones and Bill Stroppe power their way down the Baja Peninsula and their first win in Big Oly. It was a long road to getting Parnelli in the proper state of mind to win off-road races, but the payoff was spectacular. (Photo Courtesy MotorTrend and Petersen Museum Archive)

Ben Bender and Mike Sherman were one of the many victims of the Nevada desert at the 1972 Mint 400. Here, they test the rugged Bronco with a small trip through a berm. (Photo Courtesy MotorTrend and Petersen Museum Archive)

teamed with Mel Larson in the same Bronco that took Larry Minor and Rod Hall to the 1969 Mexican 1000 overall spot. They met mechanical gremlins early and parked the Bronco.

Jeep took the top two spots in the 4x4 class as each Bronco encountered the trap-laden Nevada desert. Tule Springs was rough on every car, no matter how well-built it was.

NORRA Baja 500

Adventurous souls came great distances to challenge the competition at the 1972 Mint 400. John Freeman and Kenneth Pike from Michigan were only able to complete one lap in the Nevada desert, netting them a 33rd-place finish out of 46 entries in the class. More importantly, they probably had stories for a lifetime. (Photo Courtesy MotorTrend and Petersen Museum Archive)

Big Oly was a two-wheel-drive vehicle, and a broken axle came at a bad time just before a silt bed. Sometimes even with 650 hp, it was not enough to plow through unscathed with one-wheel-drive. (Photo Courtesy Trackside Photo)

This was another sad outing for Big Oly at the 1972 Mint 400. Parnelli ran alone in the car with Walker Evans in the place of Bill Stroppe. Parnelli took a wrong line in a silt bed and stuck Big Oly over the axles in the fine talcum powdery substance. (Photo Courtesy MotorTrend and Petersen Museum Archive)

This is Lou Puentes plowing through the loose stuff at the 1972 Mint 400. The Bronco contingent went into the event with a lot of confidence. Nevada had other ideas. (Photo Courtesy Trackside Photo)

It was rainy start to the annual loop around Baja Norte, and it finished with thick fog in the mountains surrounding Ensenada. However, Parnelli, Stroppe, and *Big Oly* had bigger problems than the weather.

Reports were that a truck purposefully parked across the road to disrupt the race as Jones approached. With no way around the parked truck, *Big Oly* used a winch to move the offending obstacle, which benefitted other racers more than it helped him. Without Parnelli and Stroppe's actions, racers could have been delayed for quite some time.

Further into the race, *Big Oly* threw a wheel and tire down a large gully that was parallel with the road. Parnelli and Stroppe spent 1½ hours looking for where the tire landed before they could make repairs and get going again.

Still, with all that going on, *Big Oly* stormed home in eighth place overall. Five months later, *Big Oly* and occupants were looking for redemption south of the border.

The NORRA Baja 500 was either feast or famine with Parnelli Jones. Here, in 1972, Big Oly tossed a wheel down a canyon. It took Stroppe 1½ hours to find the errant wheel. Still, they managed an eighth-place finish. (Photo Courtesy Trackside Photo)

A very silty Parnelli Jones takes another try behind the wheel to extricate Big Oly from a Nevada silt bed. Much time was lost digging with a shovel, trying to move, and burying Big Oly again before it was freed. The race did not end well for either Jones or Oly, but redemption would come at the Mint 400 soon enough. (Photo Courtesy Trackside Photo)

James Duff had better NORRA Baja 500s than his first attempt. Here, in 1972, with better-engineered parts under the Bronco, he is about to take the start. (Photo Courtesy James Duff Inc.)

NORRA Mexican 1000

Ed Pearlman was approached by Baja Governor Milton Castellanos to move the start line from Ensenada to the border city of Mexicali in an attempt to bring more money to the area. Wanting to help and to keep an excellent working relationship with the Mexican government, Pearlman agreed.

In the months leading up to the 1972 event, there was a hurricane that struck the peninsula that was followed by ribbons of torrential rain. The result was a series of washed-out roads from Ensenada southward past San Vincente. A reconnaissance mission on NORRA's part quickly showed that many roads were impassable or unnecessarily dangerous.

Moving the start to the city of Mexicali, a border town immediately south of El Centro, California, added 108 miles to the race and increased the race mileage to 912 miles. Therefore, the race record set by *Big Oly* the year before of 14 hours and 59 minutes was in no danger of being broken. Moving the start to the east side did not mean that there were no effects of the hurricane. Sandy washes were now a wet sandy bog akin to quicksand. Small washes to cross were now wide arroyos with 6-foot

This is a rare aerial photo from the 1972 NORRA Mexican 1000. Parnelli Jones and Bill Stroppe are on their way to their second consecutive Mexican 1000 win. (Photo Courtesy Justice Archive)

Carl Jackson and Jim Fricker

This is another early NORRA Baja 500 story, but this time, it centers on a pre-running incident. Baja demands preparation as well as ingenuity for when the terrain gets the upper hand. Carl Jackson and Jim Fricker were pre-running in a half-cab Bronco from the Stroppe team. Loaded down with supplies, tools, and extra gas, the pair finished the rough section over the Three Sisters and took a break in San Felipe to get gasoline and a cold drink.

Carl and Jim figured it would be a quick run working their way back to Ensenada. A ways out of San Felipe, the road winds like a slot car track up a dry wash, and you carry some good speed through this section.

Entertaining themselves with the fun road and making great time, the Bronco suddenly stopped dead in its tracks. Carl tried cranking the engine over, but it just spun. The experienced men knew that it was one of two things: spark or fuel delivery. Fricker jumped out and pulled the distributor cap, thinking it was dirty ignition points, which was a common desert occurrence back in the day. He had Jackson crank it over and found that it had excellent spark. That left only fuel delivery.

Fricker pulled a fuel line to the carburetor, and it was dry. The fuel pump seemed to be pushing air, so it was working. Another old trick to clear a clogged fuel line was to blow into the gas tank from the fuel filler.

The lanky Jim Fricker walked to the rear of the half cab and pulled the fuel cap, but before he could blow into the tank, he thought he saw daylight on the other side. Fricker looked under the truck.

Sitting in the drivers' seat waiting for Jim to work his magic, Carl heard from behind him, "The fuel tank is gone!"

Certainly, Carl did not think he heard that right. He hopped out and looked. Sure enough, there was a whole lot of nothing where a fuel tank should have been.

Fricker began walking back down the road looking for the tank. Now, Fricker is a tall guy. In the desert, you can see him coming and going from a long distance, but he disappeared down the road. A short time later, here was Fricker, holding a gas tank. The tank had landed upside down and emptied its contents onto the desert sand.

Carl Jackson dove into his tool and parts bag and dragged out a length of chain. It was one of those things that if you head down to Baja enough, you stare at it in your garage thinking that it could come in handy, but you do not know why. In this case, when the straps that held your fuel tank snapped, it made for a handy piece of equipment to hold it in place using the bolts from where the straps had been.

Thankful to be carrying extra gasoline, they dumped a can into the tank, checked to make sure there were no leaks, and soldiered on to Ensenada to finish their pre-run.

Carl Jackson and Jim Fricker are two of many great off-roaders to come from Hemet, California. You can be as great as anyone, but without a gas tank, you are not going very far. (Photo Courtesy Carl Jackson)

Big Oly *bottoms out the suspension on its way out of a wash. NORRA Mexican 1000 victory No. 2 was in the books at the end of 912 long and dusty miles. (Photo Courtesy* MotorTrend *and Petersen Museum Archive)*

drops. Dry creek crossings were now raging torrents that saw more than one light dune buggy set sail across the desert on the shoulders of a mighty creek.

Oly*'s Crown to Lose*

As defending champions, Parnelli Jones and Bill Stroppe were the target this year, and the competition came looking for a fight. Mickey Thompson had built a very trick Chevrolet pickup with the single purpose of

Racing legend Mickey Thompson purpose built the Big Red *Chevrolet pickup to beat* Big Oly*. Thompson boasted his 600-hp big-block engine could take* Big Red *to a top speed of 165 mph. While it was fast, it never beat* Big Oly *to the finish of any race. (Photo Courtesy Kurt Strecker)*

bringing the fight to *Big Oly*. Legend has it that Thompson called Stroppe to brag about the project and let him know he was going to blow *Big Oly* away. The 1973 model-year 3/4-ton pickup had a 600-hp big-block engine that Mickey bragged could do 165 mph.

Bobby Ferro was on a tear with his *Sandmaster* single seater, having won the 500 in June of that year and several other big races. Hundreds of horsepower less than *Big Oly* and *Big Red*, the *Sandmaster* was lighter, nimbler, and able to obtain a higher speed over the rougher terrain.

Ferro's challenge never materialized. Although he was only a few minutes behind *Big Oly* at the fourth checkpoint at Rancho Santa Ynez, Ferro's car was in rough shape. The skidplate was torn off on boulders, his brakes were cooked, and, more importantly, his shifter was broken. That spelled the end of the race for Bobby.

Parnelli was second off the start line. The first 85 miles were paved, and Mickey Thompson set a blistering average of 109 mph. Mickey was ahead on corrected time, but physically *Big Oly* was in the lead as he quickly dispatched the car in front of him.

At the second checkpoint, Thompson had bent a driveshaft, and his spare was down the peninsula in El Arco, which was the halfway point. Thompson radioed for a replacement to be flown up on a private plane. After replacing the driveshaft a few hours later, he continued for a short distance only to lose the transmission.

Parnelli roared into Checkpoint 4 at Rancho Santa Ynez as the first four-wheeled vehicle. As he stopped, he barked at his crew, "No front brakes!" The crew dove under *Big Oly*'s front end and found a small leak that was quickly plugged. Then, *Big Oly* roared out of the pit stop and into the desert.

At El Arco, the halfway point in the race, Jones and Stroppe made a very speedy pit stop and continued into the night, lights ablaze, showing the desolation of the Baja peninsula. At some point as Parnelli was pushing hard, Stroppe, in a bid to slow down Parnelli just a bit, said, "You know, there's all sorts of coyotes and snakes around here, so unless you want to sleep out here tonight next to a broken truck maybe you better slow down."

The last scheduled pit stop was Ciudad Constitución, which was about 130 miles from the finish in La Paz. *Big Oly* had a big lead, and the plan was to take on fuel only as the tires looked good for the final push. Unbeknownst to *Big Oly*'s occupants, there had been some kind of misstep in refueling the Bronco, and Parnelli and Stroppe roared on not knowing that they would be a little short on fuel. About 15 miles from the end of the race, with the lights of La Paz in sight from on top of a mesa, *Big Oly* sputtered to a complete stop. Stroppe determined quickly that they were out of fuel. Agonizing minutes passed on

There isn't a more iconic photo of Big Oly in Baja California than with it charging hard through the elephant cacti at the 1972 NORRA Mexican 1000. (Photo Courtesy MotorTrend and Petersen Museum Archive)

Bill Stroppe made a point of saving that very Tequila bottle that they used to transfer fuel from the passing Beetle. It sat in Stroppe's office for over a decade. Upon Bill's death, his family was instructed to pass it along to Parnelli Jones, which they did. (Photo Courtesy Parnelli Jones Collection)

Larry Minor and Jaimie Martinez took the Pony for a ride the length of the Baja Peninsula. They were 38 minutes behind Big Oly at the finish for a Stroppe team 1-2 finish. (Photo Courtesy Larry Minor)

that mesa when faint headlights appeared headed toward the stricken racer.

It felt like forever until a well-used Volkswagen Beetle approached them and stopped. Parnelli leaned in the window and asked if the two gentlemen had any extra fuel. Luckily, they had filled up the car not far back and had a full tank. The two occupants were also pretty tanked up, as Parnelli spied a half-drained bottle of tequila in the car. Jones produced a $20 bill and asked for enough fuel to make it to the finish. There was no gas can or container in either the VW or *Big Oly*, so Parnelli grabbed the tequila bottle and went to pour out the contents, but one of the men from stopped him and obliged by draining the bottle between him and his partner.

Stroppe ripped the windshield washer hoses out of *Big Oly* and started draining fuel from the VW into the tequila bottle. It was an agonizing and slow process as bottle after bottle transferred from the VW to *Big Oly*. Finally, Stroppe felt that they had transferred enough, thanked the men for their help, and roared off toward the lights of La Paz.

The fuel held out and *Big Oly* finished the race for its second overall win, this time in 16 hours and 47 minutes. It was the start of great finishes for Team Stroppe as it took second overall with the *Pony* of Larry Minor. Stroppe Broncos swept the first four positions in the four-wheel-drive class too. It was a perfect end to the 1972 season.

The little-known story is that Bill Stroppe had a one-two punch in the class with Larry Minor and Jaime Martinez entered in the *Pony* with sponsorship from Minolta cameras. The *Pony* was not as potent as *Big Oly*. However Stroppe knew that with Minor's driving ability and Martinez as a riding mechanic, if anything happened to *Big Oly*, Team Stroppe could possibly still get the victory. In this case, Minor brought the *Pony* home 38 minutes back in second place.

The Production 4x4 class was chock full of talent, and six Broncos made the finish, including the top four out of the top five positions in class. It was unfortunate that none of the players could relay what happened that day in the fight for the win, but after 900 miles, Bill Rush and Dan Shields brought the *Colt* into La Paz a scant 8 minutes ahead of Rod Hall and Jim Fricker. Dennis Harris and Bob Conrad finished in third place in just over 4 hours behind the leading pair.

Rod Hall and Jim Fricker brought the Bronco home 8 minutes shy of first place in the four-wheel-drive class. (Photo Courtesy MotorTrend and Petersen Museum Archive)

My First 1000: John Baker

In only his second-ever off-road race, John Baker ran an ultra-low-budget effort. He rented a trailer and borrowed a friend's Ford F-250 to tow his Bronco to the start in Mexicali. With no pit crew, he signed with F.A.I.R., which was Dick Landfield's independent pit crew service, and then sent some parts and tires down the course with them.

Paired with Steve Chikato, the two planned to race down to La Paz and then drive the race truck back up to Mexicali, where they left the truck and trailer. Luckily, the drive back to Mexicali was uneventful.

In a conversation with Baker, he recalled that first 1,000-mile race.

"We were wearing these overalls that were dipped in some kind of solution that was supposed to make them fireproof," he said. "Going through Villa Constitutión, I remember someone throwing a rock the size of a softball, and it passed through from right to left just in front of our faces!

"If you remember, there were no side nets required at that time. At one point just before La Purísima, we were lost and went into a small village in the wee hours of the morning, and it turned out to be a dead end. I remember that there was a guy and a bunch of kids that led us out of there and pointed us to the correct road.

"I remember coming across the finish line wondering why the people were lined across the road. I thought you sped through the finish line."

The effort netted Baker and Chikato a fourth-place finish in their class.

John Baker and Steve Chikato brave the Baja Peninsula in their first attempt at the race in 1972. The story of their first Mexican is not very different from many privateer teams. (Photo Courtesy MotorTrend and Petersen Museum Archive)

Crazy Horse

In 1973, Don Barlow received a phone call from Bill Stroppe, who asked if he wanted a new Bronco for only about $500. Stroppe knew that Don was wanting to build something a little wilder than the 1966 Bronco they had been running—but for $500 with only about 200 miles on it?

It turned out that the Bronco had been a rental or a service loan vehicle. A couple of guys had it, got drunk, and drove it right off the Long Beach Pier into the ocean. Well, when you are building a racer, you take everything apart anyway, so Don headed down to Long Beach from his Texaco service station that he owned and picked it up.

Don dismantled the Bronco and dried it out. Then, it went to Larry Derwin, who did most of the work on *Crazy Horse*. Barlow had him chop the Bronco and then add 10 inches of wheelbase to it. They took a cue from

Big Oly and added a fiberglass body to save weight and increased the track width. Derwin completed the job in just five weeks to have it ready for the 1974 season with sponsorship from Coco Corral's Fillmore Ford.

The engine was built by Kenny Detweiler, who installed a 351-ci Windsor engine that was putting out 400 hp at the rear wheels. The power was nice, but it was a lot for the front axles to handle, and Don found himself breaking them often. The solution was to disconnect the four-wheel-drive, which was legal as long as all the components were in place.

Everything was going nicely for the new rig named *Crazy Horse* until the 1974 short-course race at Riverside International Raceway, where the ocean plunge the Bronco took in 1973 reared its head. The salt water collected in an area of the frame, and it corroded that area and caused a break during the race weekend. Aside from that, there were no further effects of the salt water. The

The Crazy Horse Bronco was revolutionary for its time. Larry Derwin did the lion's share of the building along with driver Don Barlow. Getting Crazy Horse completed required some outside-the-box thinking and even a little treachery. It raced for many years under a few different owners. Crazy Horse is now retired to the auto show circuit and is owned by Bronco aficionado Ed Gudenkauf. (Photo Courtesy Don Barlow)

Back when Crazy Horse was still new, the crew checks it over just before the 1974 SNORE 250. (Photo Courtesy Ed Gudenkauf)

In 1978, Coco Corral and Don Barlow gave Ivan Stewart a chance to get out of single-seat unlimited cars and into a Bronco. Stewart did two events in Crazy Horse: a desert event and a short-course event. From this start, Corral built a full-size Ford pickup for Stewart. (Photo Courtesy Trackside Photo)

Crazy Horse cuts a striking stance at speed. This undated photo from the Pine Forest in Baja California shows how menacing it must have looked in competitors' rearview mirrors. (Photo Courtesy Don Barlow)

No one escapes the Mint 400 without some kind of damage. The Nevada desert claimed the front fender off Crazy Horse in the early 1980s. (Photo Courtesy Don Barlow)

Crazy Horse took its revenge by winning the Riverside race back to back in 1977 and 1978.

1973

Paul McCartney released his masterpiece album Band on the Run. American soldiers left Vietnam. Richard Petty won his fourth of seven Daytona 500s, and it was a year of change and transition in the world of off-road racing. NORRA was out; SCORE was in.

Mint 400

Tule Springs was gone, and the race moved south of Las Vegas into the little town of Jean, Nevada. There was not much in Jean except a popular little casino/bar called Pop's Oasis. Jean had been the start area for several smaller, local races, but this was the Mint 400, and a virtual city popped up in the middle of a desert.

The excitement of leaving the silt and rocks of Tule Springs behind was short-lived, as unseasonably cool weather moved in along with strong winds. Then rain started and at higher elevations, the snow began to fall. The unseasonable weather made for an entirely new challenge.

Big Oly was there, the perennial star of the Stroppe armada of Ford products that traveled from race to race like a carnival. *Big Oly* had just returned from an invitational race in Japan of off-road stars of which Parnelli Jones and his Bronco were the stars of the show. No one

By 1973, you had to be wondering if Parnelli Jones ever thought he would win a desert race in Nevada. Until this moment, he had truly little luck against Nevada. The 1973 Mint 400 changed all that. In what everyone who was there remembers as one of the coldest off-road races of all time, Parnelli and Bill bundled up and braved the rain, snow, and the mud to bring it home first place. (Photo Courtesy MotorTrend and Petersen Museum Archive)

Big Oly, *Parnelli, and Bill Stroppe storm through the desert, outrunning (as circumstance would have it) storms of rain, snow, and wind. It was the first and only overall win for Parnelli Jones in the Mint 400. This photo was taken early in the race, noting the lack of mud on* Big Oly. *The move south of Las Vegas was fortunate for several Bronco drivers, ending the drought of Mint 400 wins that dated back to 1968. (Photo Courtesy Trackside Photo)*

At the 1973 Mint 400, Larry Minor takes full advantage of the excellent approach angle of the Ford Bronco. Larry chased Parnelli Jones all over the Nevada desert for a second-place overall finish. (Photo Courtesy Trackside Photo)

The 1973 NORRA Baja 500 was the last event for the Colt before it was sold. Rush was looking to build something more state of the art. At the BSC Baja Mil, he debuted his Big Hoss Bronco. (Photo Courtesy Trackside Photo)

The 1973 Mint 400 was a cold, snowy, rainy affair. However, four-wheel-drive makes it better. Bill Rush took the Colt out for a romp but could not beat teammate Rod Hall for the win. (Photo Courtesy Trackside Photo)

told this to a young talented driver in a single-seater off-road buggy named Rick Mears, who won the race. Yes, that Rick Mears, the four-time Indy 500 winner.

The terrain around Jean was different than that north of Las Vegas. There were not as many rocks, faster roads, and less silt. It still was the Nevada desert, and it was plenty challenging and not be taken lightly. Combined were all of the ingredients that would help *Big Oly* shine as well as something that suited Parnelli's driving style.

Parnelli had been chasing a Mint 400 win for five years and had been denied every time. The Stroppe team, similarly, had not had any success at the Mint since the first. So, it was especially gratifying to the team and to the Ford Bronco and Parnelli Jones fans when *Big Oly* had no problems and took the overall win. A Bronco driven

by Rod Hall and Jim Fricker also notched a win in the four-wheel-drive class.

NORRA Baja 500

The 500-mile race in Baja was able to continue because at that time Mexico's government was able to guarantee the availability of fuels and a freeze on prices at its Pemex gas stations. That same promise could not be kept for the other Baja race.

Some races come to you, and others you must work hard for. *Big Oly* drew a high number, No. 307, which meant that there was much passing to do. While behind Ray Russell's Jeep and with limited visibility in the dust, Parnelli hit a dry wash wrong and rolled *Big Oly*. Luckily, spectators were there watching and helped get the Bronco back on its wheels.

Parnelli was flying now, trying to gain back some of the time he and Stroppe spent on the beautiful, winged roof. Several miles later, Parnelli made a clean pass on Russell at a rate of about 30 mph faster than Russell was going.

Before the first checkpoint, *Big Oly* was in trouble again as Parnelli missed a turn and slammed into an embankment. Arriving at Camalu, Bill Stroppe was visibly upset and threatened to get out of the Bronco. However, calmer heads prevailed, and Stroppe strapped back in. In hindsight, maybe that was not the best move, as Parnelli rolled *Big Oly* two more times.

Certainly, victory was lost, but the pair soldiered on into the night with only one working headlight. Word started getting to the Bronco that Bobby Ferro was out of the race, Mickey Thompson was slowed with a problem,

Gale Pike

In 1973, the Mint 400 was moved from north of Las Vegas to south of Las Vegas. The start/finish area was vast, and in an attempt to bring spectators, the organizers built a jump past the start line. The people were there to see Parnelli Jones and *Big Oly* fly off that big jump.

A few cars behind Parnelli was Gale Pike, the restaurant owner, in a Stroppe-prepped Bronco. He, like any fan, was watching to see what Parnelli would do. Behind Pike in the starting order was Don Barlow in the powerful *Crazy Horse* Bronco.

Big Oly launched off the start line with all 600 thundering horsepower turning the rear wheels and churning up pieces of the desert. Flying down to the jump, everyone was holding their breath. How far would he go? How high can that thing fly?

Suddenly, *Big Oly* nose dived under braking, pitched left over a berm going around the jump, went hard right around the back of the jump, and went left again to keep going down course.

Pike thought to himself, "That was a great idea. Why pound the Bronco a half mile into the race?"

As he staged up at the start line, Pike mashed the pedal and took off down the course. Approaching the jump, he started to slow to go around the jump just like Parnelli did.

Gale Pike flew the Bronco banner for a lot of years—and occasionally the Bronco itself.

What Pike did not know was that Don Barlow, starting 30 seconds behind him, had a much more powerful engine and did not brake to go around the jump. As Pike slammed on the brakes and eased around the jump, he looked up to see the *Crazy Horse*, which took the jump, flying over the top of his Bronco! Pike watched as Barlow's tires flew just over his roof, hit the dirt landing ramp, and sped off into the desert.

At a 2006 gathering of Bronco drivers, Pike said that it was still one of the greatest moments of his racing career. Don Barlow remembered it fondly as well.

This photo might imply that the 1973 NORRA Baja 500 was an unmitigated disaster for Parnelli Jones and Bill Stroppe. However, they won the event. Big Oly took a beating, getting rolled three times and at least one major shunt into an embankment. Note the low starting position (307th), which meant a lot of dust and traffic. This, and possibly a short-tempered driver contributed to what had to be one of Bill Stroppe's most bittersweet days in the right seat. (Photo Courtesy MotorTrend and Petersen Museum Archive)

A cold Olympia Beer probably never tasted as good as after a long day thrashing your racer and still arriving at the finish with the win. The look on Bill's face is perfect for the situation. (Photo Courtesy Trackside Photo)

Consider this a "before" picture of Big Oly *at the start of the 1973 NORRA Baja 500. It did not look anything like this at the end of the race, which was 12 hours and 18 minutes and about five crashes later. (Photo Courtesy Tom Madigan)*

and Malcolm Smith was reported to be broken down. *Big Oly* roared to the finish area looking like a complete mess. There was not one straight panel anywhere on the truck, and that beautiful wing was crushed down around the halo of the roll cage. A win, however, is still a win and history recorded this one as the last NORRA-sanctioned race in Baja California until 2010.

Big Oly took an epic win in a multiple-accident-laden 500-mile run across Baja for Parnelli and Stroppe!

There were high points of the weekend for the Stroppe team, as Rod Hall and Jim Fricker took the Stock

Even the late, great Rod Hall can have an off day. However, this was the 1973 NORRA Baja 500, and Parnelli Jones was flipping all over Baja Norte like a pancake. Maybe it was catching? One can only imagine the conversation in the Bronco between Rod and Jim Fricker. (Photo Courtesy Trackside Photo)

4x4 class. Bill Rush with Dan Shields took the Modified 4x4 class with his new Bronco, *Big Hoss*.

Walker Evans took the two-wheel drive class for pickups too, taking some of the string out of the weekend for Bill Stroppe.

One Bronco's Success

One Bronco driver who made the most of the shortened season was John Baker, a three-year veteran of the Bronco wars. Until 1974, he had three top-five finishes to his credit. Baker began the year with his first four-wheel-drive win at the California 400 in Barstow, California. This event went down in history for those who remember the race because it snowed in the Mojave Desert that day.

From there, Baker won in Barstow at the Firecracker 250, which was followed by another win at the WRA Casino 350 in Las Vegas, Nevada. When a driver learns his or her way to the winner's circle, it can be hard to keep them from it over and over. Such was the case for John Baker.

Mickey Thompson's Delco RV Spectacular

Mickey Thompson had a dream to bring a "chunk of Baja" to the masses but on a grander scale than anything previously done. His idea brought him to the world-famous Riverside International Raceway (RIR). RIR had a lot of excess land adjacent to the racetrack, which allowed Thompson lay out a 7-1/2-mile course.

Entries ran a one-hour heat race to decide class champions. Those who qualified ran a four-hour race to decide the grand champion of the event. In the heats for production-based four-wheel-drive trucks, Rod Hall and Jim Fricker took the win. In the Modified 4x4 class, privateers George Wallace and Rod Fish wheeled their roadster Bronco to the win.

Modified 4x4 winners George Wallace and Rod Fish outdueled the likes of Steve Mizel, Bill Rush, and a host of pesky Jeeps. (Photo Courtesy MotorTrend and Petersen Museum Archive)

George Wallace pulls off a pass on a pesky Jeep on his way to the first Class 4 Championship at the 1973 Riverside Races. (Photo Courtesy MotorTrend and Petersen Museum Archive)

Rodney Hall and Jim Fricker seem to be losing a shock absorber at the right front wheel on the second day of racing. Luckily, they recorded their class win the day before in the 1-hour race. (Photo Courtesy MotorTrend and Petersen Museum Archive)

Larry Minor ran in the buggy class with the *Pony*. At the start of the heat race, he jumped ahead to lead the first lap. In the second lap, the rough, obstacle-laden course took its toll on the *Pony*, and the suspension failed. The next day in the big race the *Pony* failed again.

Mickey versus Parnelli

On Friday during practice sessions, Parnelli rolled *Big Oly*, which necessitated repairs. Parnelli did not want to miss out on valuable practice, so he climbed in his Ford Econoline van that he used for pre-running desert races and went back out on course. Thompson was not happy with that decision and flagged Parnelli off the course.

Now here is where history gets a little muddy. Either Mickey was so upset that he disqualified Parnelli on the spot for being out there without a race car, or after getting flagged off the course, Parnelli went out again despite Mickey's warning to stay off the course unless in *Big Oly*. Whatever the actual events were, Parnelli was disqualified. Mickey refunded his entry fee and told him to leave immediately, which he did. The *Los Angeles Times* ran the story about *Big Oly* being disqualified, which cost Thompson at the spectator gate because some people were only attending to see Parnelli run.

Already rivals, this did not help make the two stubborn men become any closer to being friends. Although, there was always a mutual respect for each other's talents on the racecourse.

Baja Sports Committee 1000

With the change in organizers, there was uncertainty about the 1973 event. However, the Mexican 1000 by any other name was still the 1000, and teams came in good faith to support the Mexican government. After all, they had promised that proceeds from the event would go to helping the children of Baja. Any racer who spent any time in Baja knew that the children were in need.

The political atmosphere was tense however, as NORRA, in retaliation for losing Mexico, staged a 500-mile event in Parker, Arizona, known as the Dam 500. Bill Stroppe was under pressure to perform and give Ford a third 1,000-mile victory in Baja. He also had been loyal to Ed Pearlman and NORRA. Being a fair man, Stroppe sent three entries to Parker to support NORRA and the rest of the team went to Baja.

The split Stroppe team came with a large agenda on its plate. First was to make it three in a row for *Big Oly*. Then, it was to support Walker Evans in the two-wheel-drive pickup class and to continue racing the new Ford Courier mini truck. The main priority was *Big Oly*.

All the hopes and dreams and planning came to an early end as *Big Oly* coasted to the side of the road just 10 miles off the start line with a sheared pinion gear in the rear end. The damage was extensive enough to pack it in. It was a painful exit for Jones and Stroppe, who did not know at the time that this was the last 1,000-mile race for *Big Oly*.

1974

The 1974 oil crisis began in October 1973 when the members of the Organization of Petroleum Exporting Countries (OPEC) instituted an oil embargo. The embargo was targeted at nations perceived as supporting Israel during the Yom Kippur War.

The effect on off-road racing was the cancellation of the 1974 Parker 400, the Mint 400, and then the Baja 1000. As a result, only three major off-road races took place: the Baja 500, Mickey Thompson's Riverside short-course race, and an independent event designed to replace the canceled Mint 400.

Bonnie and Clyde 350

Walt Lott teamed with Peter Simon, who owned Pop's Oasis south of Las Vegas. Pop's Oasis was the home of the Bonnie and Clyde death car, and 1974 was the 50th anniversary of the death of the outlaw couple. Late April was selected for the race date, and to entice teams, a hearty $50,000 in prize money was posted. It attracted more than 200 entries looking to cash in.

Parnelli Jones brought *Big Oly* looking for the $5,000 for a class win and an extra $5,000 for the overall win. However, so did Mickey Thompson, Bobby Ferro, Malcolm Smith, and every other off-road hot shoe.

Parnelli Jones came out fast off the start and led the race early. The course was in the same area that he won his first Mint 400, so Jones had confidence. By the second and third laps, reports came back to the start/finish line that Jones was getting off the marked course, gaining an advantage. Jones was running solo it was reported. Whether it was bad navigating or a missed course marker, we will never know. At the end of Jones's third lap out of four, he was waved off the course and disqualified.

In the four-wheel-drive class, only two entries made the finish line. John Baker and Allan Sheldon took their Bronco to a commanding win over the pesky Jeep of Gene Hightower and Dale Frahm. Kurt Strecker had the Viva Broncos entry in the mix until his alternator failed late in the race. For the win, Baker took home $5,300, which adjusted for inflation is about $29,000.

Baja 500

The Baja 500 was the start of a new era in off-road racing. In 1973, the Baja government revoked permission for NORRA to be the sanctioning body for all races in Baja

John Baker was a fierce competitor. This photo is from the 1974 Baja 500. Baker was running up with the Stroppe Broncos before he suffered a mechanical failure. (Photo Courtesy MotorTrend and Petersen Museum Archive)

California. The Baja Sports Committee was formed to handle the 1973 Mexican 1000, which was a miserable experience for all concerned. Mickey Thompson was approached to take over sanctioning the races, and he did so under his Short Course Off-Road Enterprises (SCORE) that he formed to promote his Riverside closed-course races.

The energy crisis threatened the desert debut of SCORE. Talks were held between SCORE and the Mexican government. The Mexican government stepped up and guaranteed that there would be gasoline available to run the race without issues. It kept its word, and 279 entries showed up.

It was a bonanza day for the bulk of Team Stroppe, and at the same time a curtain was coming down on a golden era. Rod Hall and Jim Fricker won the Production 4x4 class, Bill Rush and Dan Shields won the Modified 4x4 class, and Walker Evans won the pickup class. However, the era of a factory-backed Bronco program was coming to an end, as Ford wanted to move on to other models.

Tragedy for Parnelli and Oly

In his book, *Boss: The Bill Stroppe Story*, Stroppe told Bill Madigan the events that led to the end of *Big Oly* as it was known.

Parnelli drew a late starting position for the race and had to do a lot of passing just like in 1973. *Big Oly* was passing on a continual basis, and Bill Stroppe had the best seat in the house watching Parnelli do what he did best. In the mountains outside Ojos Negros, they came up on some slower cars and entered a big dust cloud.

One Last Race for *Big Oly*

Author note: Photos in this section are from the Los Alamitos Horse Racing Track camera. They are from the second race. As such, the quality is limited, even with today's digital tricks. (Photos Courtesy Parnelli Jones Collection)

There was one last race for *Big Oly*. This story was relayed to the author by several people, but the version by Willie Stroppe (Bill's son) is probably the most reliable. He was there.

Sometime after the decision was made to retire *Big Oly*, Parnelli Jones was talking with fellow off-road racer Frank "Scoop" Vessels. Vessels, besides being a tenacious competitor in an Ford F-100 pickup, was a renowned breeder of American quarter horses. Vessel's stallion farm was known worldwide. His father was a founder of the Los Alamitos horse racing track. The discussion came around to racing—both horse and off-road. Vessels opined that his thoroughbred quarter horses could beat a race car. That was all Parnelli Jones needed to hear.

Big Oly was pulled out of its short retirement and brought to Los Alamitos, where it faced Vessels's best horse. *Big Oly* and its 600 hp was in its standard desert racing setup, and the horse was, well, a horse—they are hard to modify. The race started, and Parnelli and the horse were close going into the first corner, but by the time the backstretch was coming up, Vessels's horse pulled on *Big Oly*. The horse held off Parnelli down the back stretch and pulled away some more headed out of the final corner. The horse beat Parnelli Jones.

The crowd was a little stunned. Parnelli, being Parnelli, wanted another crack at racing the horse after he and mechanic Dick Russell did some modifications. So, the horse got to rest, and Dick Russell went to the service truck and pulled out some paddle tires, like you would use in sand dunes, as well as a bottle of nitrous oxide. Fill in your own imagination as to why there was a bottle of nitrous in the service van.

After the first race when the quarter horse won, Dick Russell worked a little magic for the second race. You can see that the horse still pulls on Big Oly off the start, but with the addition of some paddle tires and possibly some nitrous, things went Parnelli's way.

One Last Race for *Big Oly* CONTINUED

With the tires changed and nitrous plumbed, they lined up again. At the start, the horse and *Big Oly* were again neck and, uh, bumper. Coming out of the first turn, this time with a lead because of the tires, is probably when Parnelli hit the nitrous because he pulled away from the horse. It was no contest, as *Big Oly* took one more, albeit unofficial win before retiring *Big Oly* to the show and museum circuit.

Retirement and Legacy

Big Oly went back to the Signal Hill shop and was repaired and cleaned up for its new life on the show circuit appearing at events for Ford, Firestone, and wherever it was needed. When *Big Oly* is not sitting in Parnelli's private collection, these days it is loaned out to the Petersen Auto Museum in Los Angeles or in Las Vegas at the Specialty Equipment Manufacturers Association (SEMA) Show every October.

Looking back on the iconic vehicles that advanced the sport of off-road racing, the Myers Manx, the *Baja Boot*, and the Volkswagen Bug were all important. It was *Big Oly* that really influenced the sport for years after it stopped racing. What Dick Russell and Parnelli created was a blueprint for how to build a winner. Yet, aside from an attempt by Parnelli and Russell to recreate the *Big Oly* magic with a Chevrolet Blazer–bodied tube chassis, which saw little success, no one made it work like the Stroppe team.

In May 2021, Parnelli Jones put *Big Oly* up for auction, shocking the entire off-road industry. For weeks, speculation ran wild about who would buy it and for how much. When the day came, the winning bid for *Big Oly* was $1.87 million. The buyer's identity is a mystery at the time of this book's publication.

Today, the spirit of *Big Oly* lives on in trophy trucks that float over the desert at amazing speeds.

Frank Vessels is on the far left. In the middle from left to right is musician Doc Severinsen, the horse jockey, and Parnelli Jones. Bill Stroppe (wearing glasses) is fifth from the right.

Rufus "Parnelli" Jones (right) receives a trophy from musician Doc Severinsen. It was long road from Texarkana to fame at Indianapolis, Riverside, Ascot, and Baja. Not content with only racing wins, Jones won in the business world as well.

"We were running on a narrow trail with a sheer drop off on one side and a high bank on the other," Bill wrote in his book. "It was hard to see, but just out of the corner of my eye, I saw a guy lay a motorcycle down. At that same instant, *bang*! There was a tremendous blow, and the cockpit was full of fire.

"We were on fire! Parnelli slammed the brakes on and screamed, 'We hit a guy!' What had happened was two spectators, riding the wrong way on the course, had moved over for the cars in front of us but had gotten back on the course in the dust, and here we came. One guy was right in the middle of the track. We hit him so hard that his gas tank exploded and came right into our car. Parnelli jumped out, and just as he did, Stan Gilbert, another racer, came flying by and almost got Parnelli.

"It was a terrible mess. Parnelli was so distraught he could hardly control himself. He had never experienced anything like this in all his years of racing. I tried to tell him it was not his fault, but he took off down the embankment, threw down his helmet, and disappeared. I found him sitting on a rock, putting things together. When we came back to the scene, I went to get help in a movie helicopter that had landed to offer assistance."

Due to the laws of Mexico at the time, there was mandatory jail time if you were involved in an accident. The governor of Baja intervened due to the special circumstances and kept Parnelli and Stroppe out of jail. A subsequent investigation showed that Parnelli Jones was not at fault for the death of the motorcycle rider.

Riverside Off-Road World Championships

The second event for off-roaders at the famous Riverside Raceway was slightly modified from its original format. The course was shortened to a more manageable 3.2 miles, and the heats were shortened to 16 laps. The finals were shortened to one hour.

With *Big Oly* now retired, Parnelli Jones took up one of the single-seater race cars that was starting to get all the headlines. The *Pony* entered the two-seat class, and a smattering of Broncos mixed it up in the 4x4 classes.

In the 4x4 classes, the Bronco succumbed to the pesky Jeeps in both the Modified and Production classes. However, they were second place in both classes. Rod Hall and Jim Fricker ran Production for the runner-up spot, with Dennis Harris and Bud Wright taking third. Bill Rush took second in the Modified class. Larry Minor and Bill Stroppe teamed up in the *Pony* in the unlimited two-seater class and managed a podium spot with a fine third-place showing. Average speeds were tracked at the races. The Production 4x4 race had a higher average speed than the Modified class: 41.40 mph to 40.94 mph.

Presidential Notice

After the OPEC crisis ended, President Gerald R. Ford sent letters to only two event organizers thanking them for canceling their events for the good of the country. One was to the Mint Hotel and Casino for canceling the Mint 400. The other was to the organization that sanctions the Sebring 12-hour race.

The beauty of the Ford Bronco was that it did not need fancy, expensive parts to be a finisher. This Bronco is supported by the Viva Broncos conglomerate and a local auto parts store. They are running with the factory entries at a 1975 race in Arizona near the Colorado River. (Photo Courtesy MotorTrend and Petersen Museum Archive)

1975

With the OPEC shenanigans in the rearview mirror, racing returned to normal. However, things changed at Stroppe's shop. Parnelli Jones took Dick Russell and started his own team. Unrelated to that, Ford ended its official support for the Bronco program in off-road racing. Ford shifted its focus to promoting the Courier mini truck and the full-size two-wheel-drive truck.

Parker 400

Despite the factory abandonment of the Bronco, a hearty 11 of them showed up in Parker, Arizona. Parker, being the first event of the year, always brought big entry numbers.

In the end, it was a wild weekend with a very high attrition rate. It was not too surprising to see two Stroppe-built Broncos taking the class wins. In the *Stud* Bronco, Dennis Harris and Bud Wright took the Production class. Bill Rush and Dan Shields took the Modified class win.

After Jim Loomis stepped out of the driver's seat, his codriver, Bud Wright, joined with Dennis Harris, who would race off-road in a variety of different trucks for decades. Here, the pair is on its way to a big win at the 1975 Parker 400 in Production 4x4 class. (Photo Courtesy MotorTrend and Petersen Museum Archive)

The Baja Stove was aptly named because it ran on propane. Bill Stroppe was a believer in propane as a motor vehicle fuel. It never caught on with the American motoring public, however. Willie Stroppe put a lot of miles on the Baja Stove, as was done here at the 1975 Parker 400. (Photo Courtesy MotorTrend and Petersen Museum Archive)

Mint 400

As the Mint 400 rolled around, it featured the first race run out of the Las Vegas Speedrome. The course was used for the next dozen or so years and immediately became a favorite because it posed such a challenge. It featured 15 miles of volcanic rock that ate tires for lunch. Racers affectionately called it "the rock garden."

The Mint was interesting in that nine Broncos were entered in the event. Rod Hall and Jim Fricker had a

The year 1975 began on a sour note for John Baker. At the Parker 400, Baker took a jump too fast and landed the Bronco on its roof. (Photo Courtesy MotorTrend and Petersen Museum Archive)

Newly built and stretched for a smoother ride, Don Barlow takes off with Coco Corral out of the Las Vegas Speedrome at the 1975 Mint 400. The storied history of the Crazy Horse is interesting from its construction through its life as a racer. (Photo Courtesy MotorTrend and Petersen Museum Archive)

Dennis Harris wrinkled the front fender of his Bronco at the 1975 Mint 400. No one gets out of the Mint without some damage. (Photo Courtesy Trackside Photo)

John Baker

The Mint 400 can play havoc with man and machine alike. Its reputation as the toughest off-road race in America (at that time) was well deserved. The 1975 Mint 400 was the first to use the Las Vegas Speedrome (now Las Vegas International Raceway) as the start/finish area and run a 100-mile loop north of Las Vegas four times.

John Baker highlighted the toll it can take on your body and the element of human endurance one can find among the rocks, silt, and sand of the unforgiving Nevada desert.

"I remember the 1975 Mint 400 that my codriver, who was also my sponsor, and I were running," he said. "We were running fifth in class and trying to make up time by not stopping, but we really needed to make a personal pit stop. My codriver was able to relieve himself into a towel, but I unfortunately had to wait. When we got to the finish line, I remember that I had to really go bad, but it was like a lawn sprinkler that occasionally worked. Every so often, it worked unexpectedly. Unfortunately, this continued as I was walking through the lobby of the Mint Hotel."

Maybe file this under the "too much information" category, but it is interesting what men and women will endure to beat the desert.

Sadly, they never caught fourth place, either.

Stroppe-built Bronco that carried the Stroppe paint scheme but was labeled as *Hall's Ass*. It carried sponsorship from a Hemet, California, Ford dealership. Gale Pike was running his newly built Bronco, and the *Crazy Horse* was there as well. In the end, it was one of those pesky Jeeps that outlasted the field.

For the remainder of 1975, at each event, including the 500-mile race in Baja, the Riverside short-course race and some events in Barstow, there typically was 8 or 9 Broncos running. More often than not, the Blue Oval took a win.

*Even after the official Ford backing dried up, Bill Stroppe kept servicing his drivers until other opportunities came along. Here, at a 1975 short-course event, Rod Hall uses every little bit of traction to stay on a piece of the course called "Thompson's Ridge" that was named after Mickey Thompson, the event's founder. (Photo Courtesy Motor-*Trend *and Petersen Museum Archive)*

Baja 1000

For 1975, the Baja 1000 took on a new format to save teams from having to figure out the logistics and bear the expense of running the length of the peninsula and, just as importantly, the expense of getting the race team back home.

That year was an 801-mile loop format, starting and finishing in Ensenada. SCORE planned to return to the peninsula run about every four years.

In his first attempt at racing his Bronco in a Baja 1000, Gale Pike (teamed with Willie Stroppe) took the win in the stock four-wheel-drive class (Class 3). Except for a little dust and mud splatters, the Bronco looked as good as when it left Ensenada 25 hours and 24 minutes previously.

However, it was not all smooth sailing, as Willie Stroppe recently remembered. Pike and Jaime Martinez had taken the start and run the Bronco down to Rancho Santa Inez, the third checkpoint in the race. There,

Driving the last race Bronco ever built by Bill Stroppe, Gale Pike teamed with Willie Stroppe for a big win after 801 grueling miles in the Baja 1000. (Photo Courtesy Trackside Photo)

Steve Mizel hustles through the wilds of Baja California on his way to a big Class 4 win in the 1975 Baja 1000. (Photo Courtesy MotorTrend *and Petersen Museum Archive)*

Steve Mizel had a good few years with the heavily modified Bronco winning a few big events in Baja California in the late 1970s. Here, Steve tackles Riverside. (Photo Courtesy Trackside Photo)

Willie Stroppe took the wheel with Joel Silverstein riding shotgun. They got the Bronco down to the southern end of the course at Punta Prieta, where the course turned northeast toward the Gulf side.

Punta Prieta is infamous for deep silt beds. While churning through the silt, Willie caught sight of a motorcycle rider standing on a ridge watching the Bronco. Willie wondered where his motorcycle was when suddenly *bang!* He ran over this rider's motorcycle, which was buried in the silt bed. It did not cause any problems for the Bronco, but it was a wakeup call to keep an eye out for riders with no motorcycle nearby.

It was a long run for Stroppe around the bottom of the course and toward the gulf where the road gets rocky and unforgiving. He was looking forward to handing the Bronco over to Pike and Martinez at Puertecitos after a long night of driving. As they were rolling to a stop in the pit, Pike leaned in the driver's side and said, "Move over, Willie. Jaime is sick, and you need to ride with me the rest of the way." Willie's long night was going to become a long morning too.

In Class 4, for heavily modified four-wheel-drive trucks, the Bronco of Steve Mizel and Max Jamiesson covered the 801 miles in 22 hours and 58 minutes. Only 87 of the 239 registrants finished the race in the 38 allotted hours.

1976

The big news for the Ford Bronco is 1976 was the addition of factory front disc brakes and a vacuum assistant booster. Steering systems were also upgraded this model year with the steering box being upgraded from six turns lock to lock to just four turns. It was good news

for perspective buyers but great news for Bronco racers. To this day, the 1976 Bronco remains a favorite among collectors.

Riverside

The Ford Bronco had a good outing at Riverside in 1976. Don Barlow won the Class 4 race going away in the *Crazy Horse* Bronco. Barlow outran the potent Jeep of Ray Russell and Dennis Harris. Steve Mizel came home third in the same race, which gave Ford two podium finishes. In Class 3 for the production 4x4s, Kurt Strecker upheld the Bronco honor by placing third in the Viva Broncos entry.

Parker 400

The off-road racing season typically opened along the Colorado River in Parker, Arizona, for the Parker 400. Mickey Thompson's SCORE International organized the event and it pulled a big list of entries.

In the Production class, it was tight racing for more than 10 hours, as two Broncos and a Jeep battled for the win. John Baker and Paulo Solano drove a flawless race and still only took a narrow 1 minute, 20-second victory over the pesky Jeep of Sherman Balch. Just 9 seconds

In 1977, Crazy Horse *capped a good year with a win in Baja on a 500-mile course. (Photo Courtesy* MotorTrend *and Petersen Museum Archive)*

At the 1976 Parker 400, Gale Pike is happy to bring the last of the Stroppe-built Broncos home third in its class. (Photo Courtesy MotorTrend *and Petersen Museum Archive)*

behind Balch came Gale Pike and Willie Stroppe to pick up the final podium position.

In the Modified class, Steve Mizel nabbed second place 12 minutes after the winning Jeep.

WRA Casino 350

In early March 1976, Walt Lott put on a race in Laughlin, Nevada, called the Casino 350. He found sponsors to put up a $50,000 prize fund, which is almost $250,000 adjusted for inflation. Nothing brings out a stacked field of cars like a big prize fund.

At this event, Lott decided to make bigger prize pots by combining classes that were close in performance. Lott combined production four-wheel-drive cars, mini trucks, and the stock VW sedans into what was known as Class D. The modified 4x4s were lumped in with the two-wheel-drive full-size trucks.

John Baker in the yellow Bronco (No. 316) passes a slower competitor on his way to a dominating win at the 1976 Parker 400. The win at a major SCORE event helped launched Baker into a Chrysler factory ride. (Photo Courtesy MotorTrend *and Petersen Museum Archive)*

John Baker powers out of a corner at the 1976 WRA Casino 350. The event, run out of Laughlin, Nevada, was one of Baker's many victories in the mid-1970s. Baker chased down the leading Chevy Blazer for four laps as Bronco contenders fell by the wayside with mechanical issues. In the end, Baker came into the finish right on the Blazer's bumper, taking the win on elapsed time. He built an impressive resume that caught the attention of Dodge, where he was a factory driver well into the 1980s. (Photo Courtesy MotorTrend and Petersen Museum Archive)

March 6, 1976, dawned cloudy and cold with a wind—perfect conditions for an off-road race. It meant no dust for the 187 entries. The racecourse was a mix of sand washes, rocky trails through the Newberry Mountains, and fast-flowing desert roads. On paper, it seems like an even match in Class D. The rougher and twister parts favored the nimble Volkswagens, while the faster desert roads favored the horsepower advantage of the 4x4s.

Many of the Broncos that entered encountered troubles. Steve Mizel pulled over just before the second checkpoint with engine issues. Ken Rice remembered not liking being grouped with the big two-wheel-drive trucks,

"We were out-gunned," he said.

Racers being racers, Rice and Sealund tried to run with the group

Kurt Strecker is the founder of the Viva Broncos out of Santee, California. He slogged his way through the 1976 Baja 1000, which was a watery, muddy event thanks to Hurricane Liza. (Photo Courtesy MotorTrend *and Petersen Museum Archive)*

but fell out early with a broken track bar that was fashioned out of 4130 chrome-moly tubing. Early in the fifth lap, Rod Hall and Jim Fricker pulled over and were out of the race as well.

This left John Baker and Paulo Solano in their Bronco to battle for the win with a Chevrolet Blazer driven by Lonnie Woods. Baker used four consistent laps to catch Woods, and because off-road races are won on elapsed time, Baker knew he had the win when he and the Blazer came across the finish line nose to tail. Baker remembered that the racecourse was so rough that he felt like he was still bouncing two weeks after the event.

Baja 1000

Kurt Strecker, the founder of Viva Broncos, took a third place at the 1976 Baja 1000. It was a very wet and muddy affair to the point where the start was delayed 24 hours to let the torrential rains of Hurricane Liza pass.

"I remember every rock," Strecker said. "But, at every pit, there were people cheering us on, and that kept us going. It was a spike in a race of endless ruts and roads."

1977

In Detroit, Ford Motor Company decided that 1977 was the final year of the short Bronco body. After 1977, the move was made to the "big" Bronco, which ironically did not see much success in off-road racing until 1989. Rod Hall and Jim Fricker were lured over to Chrys-

ler starting in 1977, leaving the Bronco faithful short one very successful ally.

Parker 400

A new era began at this race. Rod Hall and Jim Fricker moved over to Dodge and promptly won the production 4x4 class, which was a habit they would not often break for the remainder of the 1970s, 1980s, and most of the 1990s. All was not bad for the Bronco, though. Steve Mizel won the Modified 4x4 class handily by nearly an hour over a pair of pesky Jeeps.

Baja Internacional (500)

By this time, Jeep was forming a better support system than users of their vehicles had since the inception of off-road racing as we know it. Add to that the sudden support that International Harvester was starting to throw into desert racing programs, and you have the recipe for less incentive than ever to run a Bronco.

Fortunately for the Blue Oval crowd, there are die-hards and those who felt that the Bronco was still the answer to winning races. Steve Mizel flew the Ford flag proudly at this event and took a commanding win in Class 4.

Riverside Off-Road World Championships

Don Barlow did not stop there. Hot off his Baja win, he came right back and outran two of the fastest Jeeps around for another big win but this time on a big stage.

There are spectators in Baja, but they are largely outnumbered by the scorpions and rattlesnakes.

Baja 1000

For 1977, the big race was a short loop totaling 660 miles (1,062 kilometers). Of course, "short" is relative in Baja. It does not mean easy in any way. Of the 346 entries, only 123 saw the finish.

In the 1977 Baja Internacional (NORRA would not allow the use of "Baja 500," so the event was renamed), the sole highlight for the Bronco faithful was a big win by Don Barlow in the Crazy Horse. (Photo Courtesy Don Barlow)

Don Barlow flies the Crazy Horse to a 1977 Riverside Off-Road World Championship win. (Photo Courtesy Don Barlow)

Ford walked away with two podium finishes, one each in Class 3 and Class 4. Gale Pike put in a 22-hour drive for third in Class 3 after some downtime for a suspension problem. In Class 4, the Colt, now owned by Alfonso Barbosa (but still prepped at Stroppe's shop) had a number of problems reportedly ranging from suspension to engine issues but took third place in class.

1978

The year 1978 saw a precipitous decline like never before in the ranks of Broncos running in major off-road races. The numbers may have been down, but the competitive nature of those driving was as keen in the 1960s and 1970s.

Mexicali 300

Sometimes the unexpected happens, like it did to Sal Fish in 1978. The Parker 400 was supposed to be run on March 18, but due to insurance issues, the nearly 400 race teams found themselves in Mexicali, Baja California. It all happened with about a week's notice.

Fish always laid out a backup plan just in case something like the insurance crisis of 1978 made his first choice unavailable. In short, SCORE was unable to procure liability insurance necessitating the move. A 300-mile alternative course was enacted, and everyone just moved 174 miles to the southwest.

What nearly made the whole thing go more off the rails than it already had was the torrential rains moving into the area. The evening before the race, Sal Fish spent the night traversing the racecourse to make sure that it was passable. Come the published start time, Fish was still out checking roads, and the race was moved two hours later to allow Fish to complete his recon.

The Class 4 race was a close one, as 27 minutes covered the top three finishers in class. While two pesky Jeeps got ahead, it was Ken and Greg Rice who took the final podium spot for the Blue Oval.

Mint 400

An unusually wet winter made the racecourse north of Las Vegas even more rutted and rocky than usual, which made for an even more supreme challenge to man and machine than normal. Even though no Bronco recorded a win, Broncos took second in the Stock and Modified classes.

Gale Pike and Jamie Martinez powered the Stroppe-built Bronco to a strong second in class 3. Steve Mizel and Max Jamiesson took their stretched Bronco to a solid second in Class 4.

SCORE Baja Internacional

The desert is supposed to be a hot place, but for this event, the weather surpassed hot by a lot. In some places on the east side of the racecourse, temperatures were recorded at 125°F. This made the act of simply finishing this race an extreme accomplishment.

Steve Mizel and Pancho Weaver broke the seal on 1978 Bronco wins at this event taking Class 4 in 11 hours and 52 minutes.

SCORE Baja 1000

After another shutout at the Riverside races where only one Bronco raced and did not finish, it was time to head south of the border again. SCORE laid out a loop race totaling 580 miles, or just short of 1,000 km. Sounds easy, right?

The first half of the race was dry, but going into the last 250 miles, a storm soaked the peninsula and made the course muddy. Heading into the checkpoint before San Felipe, Ken Rice remembered being about a half mile behind Steve Mizel and seeing him take a different road. Mizel missed the checkpoint, and despite beating Rice to the finish was disqualified for the infraction, which handed the Class 4 win to Ken and Greg Rice.

1979

At the close of the decade, there was not a lot for the Bronco contingent to crow about. There were entries at Parker, the Mint, the Baja Internacional, Riverside, and Barstow, but there was a trophy draught.

Chuck Johnson remembered his trip to California from Illinois for the Riverside race.

"I had great practice runs and qualified third for the race," he said. "The truck felt great. Then, just a few seconds into the race, I had an accident."

That sort of sums up 1979 for a lot of Bronco racers. In saving the best for last, however, there is the following story from the Baja 1000.

Baja 1000

After loop races the last four years, it was back to a peninsula run to close out the 1970s. There were 260 entries that came out for a chance to relive the grand adventure that is a peninsula run. Standing between racers and an official finish was 975 miles and a 44-hour time limit. It required an average speed of about 22 mph.

Ken and Greg Rice made the run in 31 hours and 41 minutes, which was a 30.8-mph average. Everything was

Chuck Johnson is a Midwest off-road racer who made the annual trek west to run with the desert trucks at the Riverside International Raceway. It was a long way to tow to end up like this on the first lap, but that, as they say, is racing. (Photo Courtesy MotorTrend and Petersen Museum Archive)

going according to plan as the Bronco made its way down to the halfway point at San Ignacio and a scheduled pit for gas and tires. Suddenly, the electric system stopped charging. The sun was going to be going down very soon, and they would need every bit of light they could to get through the next section where the racecourse turned towards the beach. This was a place where you did not want to be late or worse yet stuck when the tide came in.

This is the Bronco that transported Ken Rice and Hal Sealund to the winner's podium at the 1978 Baja race. Then, it repeated a Modified class win in 1979. Now retired, the racer still draws crowds at car shows. (Photo Courtesy Ed Gudenkauf)

Upon reaching their pit, there were no spare parts. This was a fuel and tire stop only. The chase truck was well over an hour away. After running up and down the pit road asking for a Delco single wire alternator, there was none to be found. All they could do was sit and wait.

When the chase truck arrived, the alternator and voltage regulator were scavenged off of it and installed on the Bronco. The chase crew had to wait for daylight to buy new parts in San Ignacio and make its way down to La Paz. Off they went after never seeing any trucks in their class, and by all radio accounts, they seemed to be the only Class 4 still running. Ken made his way down to the beach before the tide. Several stuck cars and trucks were pulled out by the Bronco along the way.

At Ciudad Constitución, about 200 miles from La Paz, the Bronco broke a power steering fitting. With no way to repair it, Ken soldiered on, steering the Bronco by brute strength. Every place they could, they dumped oil into the power steering pump—not in hopes of making it work but to keep the internals lubed up enough that the water pump and alternator belts would keep working. Shortly after sunrise, the Bronco roared into La Paz as the winner and sole survivor in its class.

Heading into the 1980s, things did not get much better for the Bronco contingent until 1989, but the Bronco flag few proudly at many events, and as always, they would be the crowd favorites.

Rod Hall and Jim Fricker are two boys from Hemet who have done well. If you never had the pleasure of meeting the pair, this photo encapsulates their personalities. What they did for the Ford Bronco program, both separately and together, raised the quality of the team. They went on and did the same for Dodge and then Hummer over nearly three more decades. (Photo Courtesy Trackside Photo)

CHAPTER 4

BIG CHANGES TO
THE STOCK BRONCO

The 1980s was the decade that no one saw coming. Big hair, big fashion, breakdancing, new wave, and punk rock dominated the scene. Things were changing in the deserts of the American Southwest and in Baja as well. Technology was about to start running amok on every single component of an off-road racing machine. In the first five years of the 1980s, suspension travel on trucks went from 6 to 8 inches to more than a foot.

The body change in 1978 to the Ford Bronco brought some advantages and some disadvantages. No longer was Detroit designing the Bronco for strictly off-road performance. Ford basically chopped down a Ford F-100 4x4 frame. It added 12 inches of wheelbase to a smoother-riding 104 inches. However, Ford extended the body and lost what was that excellent departure angle that early Bronco owners enjoyed.

Flying high on the first lap of the 1984 Mint 400, it is hard not to show off for the giant crowd at the Interstate 15 underpass early in the race. Sponsored by his restaurant and gas station in Baker, California, the Pike family built a business empire from its well-known pit stop on the road between Los Angeles and Las Vegas. Gal Pike at the writing of this book is 90 years old and going strong.

In 1978 and 1979, Ford stuck with the solid-axle front end for the Bronco, which limited suspension performance compared to 1980, when Ford introduced the Ford/Dana twin traction beam independent front suspension system.

The curb weight of the Bronco went from 3,585 pounds in its original configuration to a bulky 4,663 pounds in 1978. In 1980, the independent suspension dropped the curb weight to 4,374 pounds, which was still a long way from the original configuration. This made getting the new Bronco to be competitive a daunting and expensive task compared to its ancestor.

The Ford Bronco was, above all, an affordable way to go racing. For the cost of the vehicle and a few thousand dollars in performance and safety equipment, you could be out there bashing over the same roads as the factory drivers. For most of the privateers back in the earliest days, it was more about the adventure than trying to beat Larry Minor or Parnelli Jones. (Photo Courtesy Trackside Photo)

The Rule Book KOs the Bronco

For the first time in 14 years, the Bronco was no longer the dominant force in the deserts of the American Southwest. SCORE rules separated the 4x4 classes by modifications instead of wheelbase. This meant sending the stretched Broncos into Class 4, while Broncos that still met stock wheelbase specifications went into Class 3, which was for production-based 4x4s. This put 92- and 104-inch wheelbase Broncos up against Jeep Honchos and Dodge Pickups with 120 inches. That is a world of difference on a rough road.

Still, a good driver in a well-prepared first-generation Bronco still had a chance going into any race for a podium finish. However, to overcome the Dodge and Jeep advantages of wheelbase, factory support, and the driving talents of Rod Hall (now driving for Dodge), Roger Mears, and Don Adams made a victory difficult.

1980

The new decade arrived, and the new season of racing held great promise for everyone. It was the 1980s, and technology was on the forefront of everyone's mind. *Saturday Night Live* was still funny, at least for another season, and off-road racing was getting national exposure in all forms of media.

Mexicali 250

Ken Rice and Hal Sealund began 1980 with a win in Class 4 at the Mexicali 250 in late March. Preparation is everything in off-road racing; one of the keys is a good pre-run of the racecourse. At this event, Ken Rice finally

The 1980s began well for Ken Rice and Hal Sealund, as the pair took the Modified 4x4 victory at the 1980 Mexicali 250. (Photo Courtesy Trackside Photo)

made his two-wheel-drive Ford truck reliable enough to take a look at the course.

Ken and Hal started 4th out of 13 entries and quickly dispatched the three trucks in front of them. They never saw another vehicle in their class the rest of the day. At the finish, Rice and Sealund took the win by a hearty 30 minutes and 3 seconds over Don Adams's Jeep.

Baja 500

One of the few highlights for the Bronco contingent at Baja was the third-place finish in Class 4 by Ken and Greg Rice. The race started with a wild moment while still within sight of Ensenada when Ken was running along a paved road and suddenly launched into the air. His efforts to control the bouncing Bronco helped avoid a spectator disaster.

However, the wild bouncing save did manage to break Ken's seat back, which made for an uncomfortable

Sometimes it is not even what happens in the car that highlights the strange world of motorsport. Shortly after purchasing the *Crazy Horse* Bronco, Don Barlow, Dwayne Steel, and Mark Vest were at the 1980 event in Parker, Arizona. The event is comprised of a 110-mile lap in California, then a 2-hour break to get the race car to the Arizona side, where you continue with two laps of 90 miles.

While running the California lap, Barlow smacked the front end and bent one of the radius arms. Barlow muscled it back to the California finish. Vest headed straight to the Ford dealer in town, Parker Motors, to get a new arm. The problem was that they were out.

Heading into the parking lot thinking that he might check a wrecking yard, Vest spied a Bronco on the street. The owner worked in the dealership. Vest tracked him down and offered him money for the part. Right there on the street, the owner let Vest jack up his truck and dismantle the front suspension. The part was installed in the *Crazy Horse* in time, and despite a throttle linkage issue, they went on to a top-five finish in the event.

The **Crazy Horse** *was flying high at a closed-course event at Riverside International Raceway. Built for the desert, it did not take much modifying to lighten it for wheel-to-wheel action. (Photo Courtesy The Vest Family)*

Mark Vest flies off a cattleguard during a Baja California race. To have some fun with spectators, note the eyes on the hood scoop (Photo Courtesy The Vest Family)

time trying to sit up and drive. Arriving at his first pit stop, the broken seat was tack welded as well as it could have been, and Ken was off again. The seat still moved more than he liked, but it was better.

Just past the halfway point in the race, in the heat of the late afternoon, the Bronco trudged through a notorious sand wash, and about an hour was lost to cooling the overheated engine. Yet, with the stops for repairs, the K Bar S Bronco was still able to claim the last podium spot.

1981

The Bronco contingent did not get a good start to 1981, as no one was able to win any of the first few events, including the Parker 400, Mexicali 250, and California 400. Gale Pike parked his Bronco and took up Rod Hall's first Dodge truck for much of 1981 and 1982, lessening the number of bobtails. There would be some

Ken and Greg Rice endured a broken driver's seat and overheating issues but plugged along to make a strong third-place finish. (Photo Courtesy Trackside Photo)

Mark Dulaney ran a Bronco for several years in the early 1980s. The rules debacle worked against him and others who ran the bobtails, but in true racer style, it did not stop him from trying. Here, he gives his suspension a workout at the 1981 Parker 400. (Photo Courtesy Trackside Photo)

In their swan song to off-road racing, the Rice brothers (Ken and Greg) went out in style with a well-earned victory at the 1981 Mint 400. (Photo Courtesy Trackside Photo)

redemption on the horizon as racers made their annual pilgrimage to Las Vegas.

Mint 400

Ken and Greg Rice had been racing the K Bar S Bronco for a while now with some notable successes. At the end of 1980, their main sponsors pulled out, and as 1981 started, they found themselves self-funded. A new engine had been installed (the 351-ci Cleveland engine was swapped for a Windsor), so they decided to see if they could make the Mint 400 pay off for them. With no testing on the new engine and very limited pre-running done, they found themselves on the start line with Ken driving the first two laps of four.

This Mint 400 was a record-breaking event as 512 entries flooded the Nevada desert in search of racing glory. Of those, only five were Broncos, and most of them were in the Modified class. As a matter of fact, the entry was so large that some of the fast single-seater cars came around for Lap 2 before some of the 4x4 classes had even started.

Ken drove two perfect laps and brought the Bronco back into the pit area with a lead and a few pesky Jeeps uncomfortably close. The course was littered with four broken Broncos as Ken handed the sole remaining Bronco off to his brother Greg, and away he went into the fading afternoon sun. As he pounded his way through the third lap, the crew relayed that he was getting caught.

So, doing what any good racer would do, he went faster. The extra stress caused his motor mounts to break.

Now, Greg was trying to stay ahead of the Jeeps and trying to keep the engine in the cradle until he reached a pit area. Ken had got in with his chase crew and met Greg. Together they took ratchet straps and chains and tied the motor in place as well as they could. Greg soldiered on, not losing his lead.

In the final lap, the Jeeps encountered issues, leaving Greg to motor around the rest of the way unmolested but listening to his engine strain against the chains that were holding it in. The victory was sweet as the Rice brothers decided it was a fitting way to go out while on top.

Baja 1000

Off-road racing is tough, but the Baja 1000 is the toughest. Case in point was Steve Mizel's 1981 Baja 1000. I point this out because he was the only Bronco entered.

Steve Mizel had a miserable experience at the 1981 Baja 1000. Broken water hoses, getting stuck, distributor issues, and getting lost were a few of the issues to just name a few. They all cannot be happy endings. (Photo Courtesy MotorTrend and Petersen Museum Archive)

How strange does that sound? It was the event that built the Bronco legend. The 1980s were a strange time, indeed.

Mizel took off from Ensenada with the best of intentions of finishing well. Baja had different ideas. Early in the race, Mizel had two water hoses break and lost time with repairs. Not long after that, while chasing down another vehicle, he took a rock in the windshield, which had to be pushed out. In the dreaded silt beds of Punta Prieta, his distributor packed with silt stalled the engine. While making repairs to the now-stuck Bronco, another vehicle plowed into the back of the Bronco. Much time was lost there, but they did get out, unlike many other cars and bikes. Later, while headed for Santa Catarina in a sand wash, locals pointed them in the wrong direction, which cost another 30 minutes. Reportedly, Mizel arrived at a checkpoint beyond the official closing time and had to abandon his attempt to finish.

1982

After years of complaints from Ford, Jeep, and International drivers, the sanctioning bodies finally separated the four-wheel-drive classes by wheelbase. This brought the Bronco back to a level playing field for a win in Class 3, the Dodge and Jeep honchos populated Class 4, and modified 4x4s went into Class 14 in most sanctioning bodies. SCORE went with this configuration until 1984, when they rewrote the Class 3 rules excluding V-8 engines. The High Desert Racing Association (HDRA) stayed with the wheelbase rules.

Still, the Broncos did not really start to come back out until later in the season. Gale Pike even returned to the Bronco ranks late in the season from his stint in a Dodge pickup. Sadly, there was nothing much to celebrate for the Bronco. The 1982 season belonged to Jeep and International. However, the rules change would pay dividends in the coming years.

Mark Vest continued to run through the rule changes. The former Crazy Horse *Bronco was modified extensively enough that it was competitive against the pickup trucks. Here, at the 1982 Parker 400, he thrashes through the Arizona side on the first lap. He made another lap but ended as a DNF.*

1983

Organizers had hoped that the 1982 rule change would bring out a lot of garaged Bronco racers, and eventually it would, but it was slow in happening.

Riverside Off-Road World Championships

The Riverside races always brought out the cream of the crop from the Midwest where short-course racing is king. One of those was Chuck Johnson, who drove an orange Bronco. This was not his first attempt, as he had about three years of experience on the Riverside track, which paid off.

Mark Vest and Dwayne Steele compete at the 1982 Mint 400.

Chuck Johnson is shown en route to his best Riverside finish in his Bronco: second place at the 1983 Riverside Off-Road World Championships in Class 3. (Photo Courtesy Milan Mazanec)

Riverside races used the "Oklahoma Land Rush" start. Vehicles lined up in a straight line like a drag race. At the drop of a flag, racers flew down a constantly narrowing road until they hit the first turn. In this year's Class 3 race, it became clear that the race was between the factory-backed Jeep of Don Adams, a buffalo rancher from Colorado, and Chuck Johnson, a privateer from Illinois.

Adams got the jump (or possibly the horsepower advantage) on Johnson, and the two ran within easy reach of each other. The chase was thrilling to watch lap after lap, and toward the end, if you were there (and I was), it was Adams's race. Chuck Johnson tried everything (to his credit), and he did come away with his best Riverside finish to date.

Frontier 500

For the 1983 edition, 10 short-wheelbase 4x4s showed up to race. They called it a race, but it was more of a survival exercise. Every single one ran into major repair issues at one point or another. Don Adams's Jeep, which was winning everything in sight thus far in the 1980s, had a transmission failure right off the start and was way behind early.

Steve Mizel jumped out into the lead and ran strong all the way until Virginia City, where his Bronco ran out of fuel. It took a long time for his crew to find him, and his lead was gone. Still, there was a chance, and Mizel took off. Adams was in his sights, but Gale Pike and Jaime Martinez were closing in from behind. What looked to be a runway event was now looking like a close finish after 485 grueling miles. Adams completed the run in 15 hours and 49 minutes in his pesky Jeep. Mizel stormed across the line after 16 hours and 2 minutes, and Pike came roaring in just 15 minutes later.

At the 1983 Frontier 500, it was looking like a runaway for Steve Mizel until his Bronco ran out of fuel near Virginia City. The crew had a hard time getting fuel to him, and he lost over an hour and the lead. He pushed hard after getting going again to salvage a second-place finish. (Photo Courtesy Trackside Photo)

Ken and Penny Snyder came from Northern California to try their luck in the 1983 Frontier 500. They and many others saw their race end in the nasty silt beds between Pahrump and Beatty. (Photo Courtesy MotorTrend and Petersen Museum Archive)

Baja 1000

The 1983 SCORE Baja 1000 had a different format than in years past. This event was two laps totaling 815 miles. There was also an overnight halt in San Felipe. Many old-time Baja racers did not like the idea of stopping in the middle, but the siren call of Baja still brought them all down.

Michael Wilson was brought on by Hal Sealund to take over the K Bar S Bronco. The pair saw Don Adams out early with a broken front end when he hit a boulder. They soldiered on, battling their own issues to nab a second place in the race.

Barstow Classic

There is something about seeing a second generation come along in any sport. Off-road racing is no exception. Gale Pike handed his venerable Bronco over to his son Matt and Steve Hummel. In their first race, they managed

Michael Wilson and Hal Sealund kept a steady pace around the 815-mile loop to bring bobtail fans a well-fought second-place finish in the 1983 Baja 1000. (Photo Courtesy Trackside Photo)

In 1983, at the SCORE Barstow Classic, Matt Pike and Steve Hummel took the family Bronco out for a spin as their first race. They took second place for their efforts.

to navigate four laps though the Mojave Desert to nab the second place in Class 3.

Frontier 250

Short-course expert Chuck Johnson, fresh off a second-place finish at Riverside a few months prior, wanted to try a desert race. Eight Class 3 trucks arrived in Las Vegas to try their luck at four laps around the Nevada desert. Johnson ran his truck in basically a short-course setup but with a spare tire, tools, a codriver, and some parts loaded on board. No one thought he had much of a chance.

While it was another Jeep win, as it had been for a while, Johnson had a very clean run and brought his Bronco home for second place a half hour ahead of some desert veterans. Mike Wilson brought the K Bar S Bronco home fifth as well. This ended the 1983 season on a high note for the Bronco troops.

1984

In yet another major rules shakeup, SCORE decided that the smaller SUV 4x4s deserved a place to run and be competitive, so they changed Class 3 by limiting engine displacement to 2.85 liters and no more than six cylinders. Thus, it loaded anything with a V-8 engine into Class 4, and reintroduced the wheelbase paradox for Bronco, International, and CJ racers. However, the HDRA did not change its rules, leaving the class split by wheelbase alone.

Parker 400

Even with the rules change, the lure of Parker, Arizona, is hard to resist, and 13 big-engine 4x4s came to race in the Modified class. Mark Vest and Dwayne Steele

Mark Vest and Dwayne Steel had some quick repairs to do after a disastrous California loop. They recovered nicely, cranked out two good Arizona laps, and wound up in third place. (Photo Courtesy Trackside Photo)

had some rear-end problems with the *Crazy Horse* Bronco on the California loop. During the 90-minute downtime before the Arizona loops, they repaired the issue. Vest and Steele made two solid laps on the Arizona side and outlasted 10 competitors to bring home a nice third-place finish to start their season.

Mint 400

The Mint 400 brought out the short-wheelbase racers, as 19 started the race. This edition of the classic race was particularly nasty on the class, as only 3 completed the required four laps.

In 1984, Mark Vest tackles the Nevada desert at the Mint 400. The Mint races always had the biggest entry numbers for Broncos. This time, the desert won, as Vest and 15 other 4x4s failed to complete the race. (Photo Courtesy Trackside Photo)

At the 1984 Mint 400, Gale Pike battled for 400 miles only to come up 34 minutes short at the finish line for second place. (Photo Courtesy MotorTrend and Petersen Museum Archive)

Gale Pike and Steve Hummel took the old Bronco out again and proved that the Bronco was still a viable platform. They took a very strong second place (trailing by only 34 minutes at the finish) and set an identical last lap time as the winner.

Barstow Fireworks 250

The 14th annual event for off-road racers was the Fourth of July bash thrown by HDRA in Barstow. It was a hot event, so the start of the race was traditionally at 4 p.m. Fewer laps in the hot sun made for a safer race overall.

Ken Nance and Dennis Alhemire turned some consistent lap times and managed to bring home a fine second place finish in their class over a stack of Jeeps.

Frontier 250

While its big brother, the Frontier 500, was a lengthy point-to-point race, the 250 was a conventional-lap race south of Las Vegas around the Jean Dry Lake. The first part of a lap was a rocky affair strewn with washouts across the road. The second part of the lap was fast and flowing and labeled by many as some of the best roads in Nevada.

Gale Pike trod out the old Bronco again and showed that Bill Stroppe built a heck of a machine as he ran a patient race and nabbed a strong third place at the end of the four laps.

1985

At the midpoint of the decade, Broncos were seeing a little bit of resurgence in the desert. Largely, it was because SCORE realized that Class 3 was not attracting the entries it hoped for. With that, SCORE returned the class to a short-wheelbase format, and the entries came back.

Parker 400

Eight short-wheelbase rigs came to Parker to celebrate the return of V-8 engines to the class. Parker was run in February, and even in Arizona, it could be a cool day in the desert.

The superior design of the Ford Bronco allowed it to take a lot of abuse, whether it was asked to push a snowplow, traverse a sandy beach, or, in this case, race the 1985 Mint 400. (Photo Courtesy Kurt Scherbaum/The Lensman Photography)

Second place was well earned by Kenny Nance in his Go For It Off Road Center Bronco at the 1984 Parker 400. (Photo Courtesy Trackside Photo)

Even though they did not make it to the finish of the 1985 Frontier 500, Mark Hutchins and Gary Stewart outlasted all but one competitor to Checkpoint 4, where they were forced to stop racing by a checkpoint closing time. It was still good enough for second place in Class 3. (Photo Courtesy Ed Gudenkauf)

However, this particular year was very cold at the outset, and it was not long before the snow started falling. Pit crews were building snowmen as racers fought carburetor icing and their windshields or goggles fogging for the entire day.

Kenny Nance ran clean and strong for just over 10 hours to take the second spot, just 20 minutes ahead of Matt Pike, who took third.

Great Mojave 250

In 1984, in a herculean effort, SCORE was prevented from staging the Baja Internacional as planned. SCORE President Sal Fish worked with the U.S. Bureau of Land Management (BLM), got a course near Lucerne Valley, California, and dubbed it the "Baja in Barstow." Lucerne Valley enjoyed the attention and the bank deposits after a weekend of thousands of visitors to their town. SCORE returned in 1985 with the Great Mojave 250.

The desert in the Lucerne Valley was challenging, as six of the Class 3 trucks were about to find out. One Jeep had the battery die before he even moved a foot. Another Jeep, a strong contender, twisted the driveline and then needed the radiator and power steering to be replaced. Challenger after challenger fell victim to this particularly inhospitable piece of the Mojave. That is, all but one: the Bronco of Kenny Nance and Dennis Alhemire.

Frontier 500

The annual adventure from Las Vegas to Reno was curtailed into a loop race because the roads could not be found to run the usual Vegas to Reno format. The race was still was gaining a reputation as being shorter than the Baja 1000 but harder to finish. That point was easily made for the five short-wheelbase 4x4s that started the race. That year, the winter rains and the dry summer made

In a lightly attended 1983 Baja 1000, Philip Dean and Bob Lehrer fought for 31 hours through Baja's toughest terrain and netted a second place for their efforts. (Photo Courtesy Trackside Photo)

the course even rougher than usual. This resulted in not one truck from the class reaching the finish within the time limit.

In off-road racing, you could win a race as long as you went the farthest. Jim Yacksyzn and Mark Hutchins were in Hal Sealund's K Bar S Bronco and managed to coax the Bronco to about halfway before calling it. They knew they could not make the cut off time to the next checkpoint. It was good enough for second place, though.

Baja 1000

The 1985 edition of the Baja 1000 was an 822-mile loop that was an exercise in endurance and perseverance. Only three trucks showed up for the grand affair through the desert, forest, mountain, and silt beds. Philip Dean and Bob Lehrer took on a pair of pesky Jeeps and split the competition with a second-place finish after 31 hours battling the Baja and averaging 26 mph.

1986

The year 1986 saw a resurgence of sorts in Class 3, as more people were looking to run big iron through the desert. Unfortunately, the ranks of Bronco entries remained stagnant and were all but missing from the finish lines the first half of the season. Later, they showed up and even earned a big win.

Barstow Fireworks 250

The annual Fourth of July weekend bash around the Mojave (even with a late start time of 4 p.m.) was a hot race. Mark Hutchins and Gary Stewart kept their Bronco cool and avoided troubles that a rough Barstow course can hand out to the unsuspecting. With 12 trucks starting, it was going to be the smarter drivers that got to the podium.

Hutchins and Stewart were sitting fourth after the first of four laps and then second by the halfway point

The K Bar S Bronco powers through the rough Barstow terrain on a hot summer afternoon in 1986. Mark Hutchins and Gary Stewart powered the K Bar S Bronco to a third-place finish.

The K Bar S Bronco led early in the 1986 Frontier 500. (Photo Courtesy MotorTrend *and Petersen Museum Archive)*

Matt Pike and Burt McCready fought hard and were able to come away with the Class 3 win at the 1986 Frontier 500. (Photo Courtesy MotorTrend *and Petersen Museum Archive)*

with wily desert veteran Don Adams closing. In the closing laps, the Bronco could not hold off Adams and slid into a third-place finish.

Frontier 500

Again, this year the organizers could not make the run north to Reno or even the modified race they ran the year before. So, they created a course south of Las Vegas and put together a 111-mile lap that had to be traversed four times. There were 10 Class 3 entries that came to try their luck, and it was a stacked field.

Three of the Jeeps were out on the first lap, which thinned the herd a bit. Mark Hutchins and Gary Stewart had the K Bar S Bronco out front early followed by a Jeep and then Matt Pike in the family Bronco. By the end of the second lap, only 4 of the 10 starters were still running. Matt Pike had a clean run and moved up into the lead, a Jeep was second, and Hutchins had a long lap but was still third.

Pike stayed out front and brought home the win by more than 25 minutes. The Jeep was next, limping across the finish with steam escaping the radiator. Hutchins and Stewart disappeared on the last lap and never made the finish.

Budweiser 250

December in Barstow, California, can mean a lot of things, but rarely is one of them rain. It favored the four-wheel-drives, though, and a few were there in several classes. In the Modified class, it was a wire-to-wire win for Steve Mizel in his stretched creation. Steve outran 5 other trucks and won by 1 hour and 15 minutes.

Matt Pike brought the family Bronco back out, but he had a myriad of problems, and it was all he could do to salvage a fourth-place finish just 40 seconds out of third place. Still, having two Broncos at the event and both finishing was good for Ford fans.

Mark Hutchins and Gary Stewart held on for third place at the 1986 Frontier 500. Still, it had to be good to see another Bronco win the class. (Photo Courtesy MotorTrend *and Petersen Museum Archive)*

Steve Mizel outran five other entries in the Modified 4x4 class at the 1986 Bud 250 in Barstow, California. (Photo Courtesy Trackside Photo)

1987

Mark Hutchins and Gary Stewart were upholding the pride of Bronco fans everywhere with two second-place finishes in a row at the Gold Coast 300 and the Great Mojave 250. They followed that with third place at the Mint 400 against eight other trucks. It was a good start to a year where they could not campaign every event, so they skipped the Baja Internacional and waited for Barstow in July when they took a disappointing fourth place. They called off their 1987 campaign after that event.

Steve Mizel had made some appearances at a few races during the season but had no finishes.

At the Baja 1000, Rick Sieman debuted his *Big Oly* Bronco II. After a long day and night and part of another day of racing and repairs, he made the finish and nabbed a nifty third-place finish in Class 3.

1988

Toward the middle of the 1987 season, Matt and Gale Pike moved away from the Bronco and were now running a trick Dodge Ramcharger. Everyone thought that it was the end for the 1973 Bronco that started life in Bill Stroppe's shop. However, they were incorrect. Another Pike caught the off-road racing bug, as Christian Pike, Matt's younger brother, inherited the family Bronco.

Rick Siemen was the editor for Off-Road *magazine. He took his idea to build a tribute racer to* Big Oly *and ran the build as a series of articles. The 1987 Baja 1000 was his debut, and despite the teething problems, he managed a third-place finish in his class. (Photo Courtesy Trackside Photo)*

In their first race, Christian Pike outlasted his dad and big brother, Matt, to take a win in his first race, the 1987 SCORE Great Mojave 250. (Photo Courtesy Trackside Photo)

Gold Coast 300

Eight trucks started the Gold Coast race: a bevy of Jeeps, a few Ramchargers, and two Broncos (*Big Oly II* and the Pike Bronco with a brand-new driver). Jeeps led early after one lap but started falling by the side of the road one after another with repairs or terminal issues.

Setting a consistent pace, Christian Pike and John Lemieux paced themselves across the Nevada desert. Big brother Matt was leading for a time, but he too fell by the wayside. Suddenly, the younger Pike had the lead going into the last lap. He brought it home with a quick time and took a win in his first start as a driver.

Big Oly II would have been credited with third place but was disqualified for excessively rough driving after reports came in from three separate vehicles.

Nevada 500

Racing as a family had its rewards, but winning together as a family was even better. Of the nine trucks entered in Class 3, two had the last name Pike. Matt was in the Dodge Ramcharger and brother Christian was in the Bronco. One other Bronco was entered, that of Rick Sieman.

The route started and finished in Pahrump at an oval track speedway. The loop race did a giant tour of western Nevada, winding up to Tonopah and looping back to Beatty before retracing the route back to Pahrump. It was 485 miles.

The Jeeps jumped out to the lead through Beatty before a large hill spelled trouble for the leading Jeeps. Matt Pike took advantage and stormed into the lead on his way to Tonopah before turning south for the long run back. Rick Sieman held third place until near Tonopah, where his race ended with an engine fire. This launched Christian Pike into second place, a place he held all the way back roughly three hours behind Matt.

1989

What happened in 1989 was Enduro Racing with David Ashley and the late Dick Landfield. There is a lot more to the story further on in this book. However, the synopsis was that the new Bronco these men built laid the foundation of the Ford Roughriders program. That program fundamentally changed the way that off-road racing sponsorships work. Ashley won the majority of races in 1989, and at the Baja 1000, he averaged better than 50 mph in a peninsula run.

Into the 1990s

The 1980s saw off-road racing mature and technology soar in many classes. Yet, the stalwart short-wheelbase 4x4s remained largely the same with minor benefits from shock absorber technology and off-road lighting. The sneak peek of the future came with Enduro Racing, and in the coming decade, they rewrote the book on how to race in Class 3.

David Ashley closed out the 1980s by winning Class 3 in the Baja 1000 in a big way. Enduro Racing took a Bronco that ran as a largely stock unit in 1988 and revamped it into a class killer. (Photo Courtesy MotorTrend and Petersen Museum Archive)

The Bronco II

The Bronco II was designed in concert with the Ford Ranger pickup using many of the same parts on a shorter platform than the Ranger. The downsized version of the Bronco was remarkably close in dimensions to the original Bronco. Over its 7-year production run, 700,000 units were sold, but it was not universally embraced by the old-school Bronco community.

A few of the downsized Broncos made their way onto racecourses when Class 6 was reclassified from strictly a sedan class to a downsized SUV class. This effort was made to accommodate teams that wanted to run the new Bronco II, Chevrolet S-10 Blazer, Jeep Cherokee, and later, the Ford Explorer. All of those vehicles could not be built to be competitive in the short-wheelbase 4x4 class.

Their day in the desert was short in comparison to other more legendary Broncos, but they picked up a few wins in Class 6. Most teams abandoned the Bronco II platform by 1993 and went where there was more opportunity for sponsors with the Ranger.

One of the more successful Bronco IIs that raced was the Herzog Racing entry. In 1990, with Danny Ash-

craft behind the wheel, it won the 1990 1,000-kilometer (665 miles) Baja race. It was probably the most notable win for the baby Bronco in its short competition life.

Herzog and Wagenblast fly past one of the many cattleguards in Mexico as they set the pace in their class early on. The platform on the Bronco II was tough enough like its big brothers, but the popularity was not there. The introduction of the Ford Explorer put an end to the competitive life of the Bronco II. (Photo Courtesy Trackside Photo)

Only a couple of Ford Bronco II trucks ran in organized off-road races. The most successful of those was the Herzog Racing entry. It did very well in the SUV class. (Photo Courtesy Trackside Photo)

CHAPTER 5

PRIVATEERS CONTINUE THE LEGACY
BRONCO

B y the end of the 1974 racing season, Bill Stroppe was informed that the Bronco program was coming to an end. Stroppe began to look for homes for some of his racers. Some of his creations had already found new homes, and the occasional enthusiast hired him to build a Bronco. Stroppe was far from out of the off-road racing business, as Ford still had him running full-size trucks and the Courier mini truck.

What Ford had built would prove to be a durable racer for decades to come and in some cases into the new millennium. It took a hearty breed to run a Bronco, and the people highlighted in this chapter were some of the diehard enthusiasts that kept the Bronco tradition going.

Victor Abruzzese

Victor Abruzzese is most likely the first Bronco privateer. An avid

Two of the most successful privateers in a Bronco are the Moss brothers from Sacramento, California. Hastily built in 2000 for an extra-long peninsula run in Mexico, the brothers spent 68 hours completing the race. Since then, the black Bronco has been improved and perfected to record many wins in Mexico and the United States. (Photo Courtesy Trackside Photo)

Ever since the first organized races, the friendly spirit of off-road racing has been preserved over the years by the privateer teams. Here, at a 1977 race in Mexico, the Fulton family Bronco flies off a cattle guard running down the Baja peninsula. Teams like this often band together and work closely with one another through a pit crew for hire, such as Mag 7 or F.A.I.R. (Photo Courtesy Trackside Photo)

weekend explorer, like most of those first Mexican 1000 entrants, the 49-year-old naval shipyard electrician could not resist the adventure of that first Mexican 1000. The driver of a Renault sports car, he knew he needed something else to ensure seeing the end of the race. With no delusions of trying to win the race, he bought a new 1968-model Bronco. He and codriver Irv Hanks added a roll bar and some Gates Commando tires and called it ready.

At the end of that first Mexican 1000, NORRA promised a great banquet. This captured Abruzzese's imagination and fostered the idea of being properly dressed for

the occasion even if he arrived in La Paz late. Tuxedos became the official attire along with helmets and gloves for the intrepid pair. The new Bronco was dubbed the *Banquet Bronco*, a name that stuck.

Abruzzese made a majority of the races over the next 10 years. He never finished better than sixth place in class in his racing career, but fewer people had more fun. The *Banquet Bronco* went from a basically stock unit to a proper racer over the years, as Vic performed the work himself.

Blessed with a tremendous sense of humor, the Bronco appeared at races with a massive ship searchlight mounted to the roll cage or an air cleaner mounted on a 4-foot pipe with hoses running to his helmet for the dusty races. You could always count something different.

By 1977, the Bronco was tired, and Vic retired from racing. Several years later, Abruzzese was killed in a tragic accident while walking across the street. The Bronco went to Texas, where it ran some short course races then was neglected for decades. Recently, it came back to California, where a collector is refurbishing it for use in the NORRA races.

Don Barlow

Don Barlow came up racing jalopies on the Southern California dirt tracks based out of the Texaco service station that he owned and operated. As he competed at tracks all over the Los Angeles area, he had the good fortune to see Parnelli Jones race for the first time as a 17-year-old kid. Little did Don know that years later he and Jones would meet again competing in the wilds of Baja.

Victor Abruzzese was there from the very first Mexican 1000 in 1967 through 1977. Resplendent in their tuxedos, Vic and his variety of codrivers were the best-dressed team in Baja California. They were even once mistaken as toll-booth coin-takers during the 1967 Mexican 1000. It may never have been a frontrunner, but the Banquet Bronco was always a fan favorite. Here, Vic and his codriver await the start of the 1970 SNORE 250 outside of Las Vegas, Nevada. (Photo Courtesy Trackside Photo)

By the 1970 Mint 400, Vic was trying hard to reduce the dust fatigue factor associated with many off-road races. His helmet skirts holding in filtered air taken from above the roof line was the precursor to what eventually became the Parker Pumper system. (Photo Courtesy MotorTrend and Petersen Museum Archive)

Brought up on the dirt tracks of Southern California, Don Barlow spent much of his early life racing one kind of car or another. An invitation to Baja from longtime friend Coco Corral was the start of his tenure in off-road racing. Seen here at an early Mickey Thompson short-course event at the Riverside Raceway, the iconic **Crazy Horse** *is driven by the former Jalopy racer. (Photo Courtesy Don Barlow)*

Prior to the 1970 NORRA Mexican 1000, Don's friend Coco Corral asked if he would like to race in Mexico. Don had always admired the La Carrera racers in their big iron running the roads in Mexico, so he agreed. Coco had him meet at his garage to go over the vehicle. When Don entered the garage, he was looking for the race car, but all he saw was a Bronco. Coco pointed at it and said, "That's it!"

It took a little convincing, but Don signed on to drive even though it was not what he thought it would be. A true racer rarely says no to any opportunity.

Don took fourth in that first race and was hooked on off-road racing. Partnered with Coco Corral and his Fillmore Ford dealership, Don often took Coco's wife, Charlotte, whom he had known since childhood, with him. The two made a good pair and soon appointed each other the nicknames "Baja Gorilla" and the "Cactus Queen."

Don went on to build and drive the *Crazy Horse* Bronco and win two 500-mile races in Baja. Don retired from off-road racing in 1980 after 10 years of bouncing all over the American Southwest and the Baja Peninsula.

Gale Pike

If you have been on Interstate 15 through the Mojave Desert between Barstow and Las Vegas, you have probably stopped in Baker, California. It is a popular place to stop for gas and food. Standing in the middle of it was Gale Pike's restaurant and gas station.

Gale got his start in off-road racing when he bought a used Saab 96 race car. The start of Gale's racing career was marred with all kinds of problems with the car. It took Gale 12 hours just to get to Camalu. Realizing he needed a better rig, he was intrigued by the new Ford Courier mini trucks, so he approached Bill Stroppe to build him one.

Gale was familiar with Bill already. Back in the 1950s when Stroppe tested his Lincolns before the La Carrera Pan America races, he tested them in Death Valley, California. He and Gale became friends from those frequent visits and when the Stroppe team headed for Las Vegas for off-road races.

Gale plunked down his money and let Stroppe do his magic as he entered the 1974 1,000-mile race in Baja.

The lonely roads in the middle of the desert were a change for Barlow from the crowded and short oval dirt tracks on which he cut his racing teeth. When the desert gets into your blood, there is something refreshing about the new challenge of you against nature instead of 30 other drivers piling into Turn 1. Don embraced the desert, immediately running up front in his first race in a while. (Photo Courtesy Don Barlow)

Gale Pike has been a fixture in off-road racing since 1974, when a miscommunication between Pike and Bill Stroppe saw Pike get a brand-new Bronco instead of the Courier mini truck that he thought he ordered. Fortunately for Pike, the Bronco was the right way to go and it graced desert trails for more than 20 years. This was the last race Bronco built by the Stroppe team.

Somewhere along the way, instead of building the Courier, Stroppe had built him a Bronco. Not any Bronco, either, but the last one completed in the Stroppe team shops. Pike liked it a lot and took it without complaint. That Bronco ran for nearly 20 years winning many big races along the way.

John Baker

In 1970, John Baker was a college student in Minnesota working his way through school by running a landscape business on the side with an 4x4 Marmon Herrington dump truck. That same year, John also bought a brand-new Ford Bronco for $3,300. He had planned to fit it with a snowplow to earn money plowing driveways and private roads when winter came.

Before that first winter hit, John moved to Southern California, purchased a Hallmark store, and joined the Stump Jumpers Four Wheel Drive Club. Not long after joining the club, a fellow member named John Barr started talking Baker into entering the Bronco in the

1972 NORRA Mexican 1000. After some thought, Baker decided that it was just the kind of adventure he was looking for.

The Bronco went to Sandy Cone for a roll cage and fabrication work on the suspension to add extra shock absorbers. The Bronco was named the *Bronco Buster*, and Baker finished fitting two spare tires and larger fuel capacity. To strengthen the axles, he had the front Dana 44 and the 9-inch Ford rear end strapped. Safety equipment was added (as per the rules), and as a test before Baja, he took it to Las Vegas for the 1972 Southern Nevada Off Road Enthusiasts (SNORE) 250. That first race was a DNF (did not finish), John remembered.

"I remember hitting a large rock so hard that it exploded the wheel," he said. "I had several flats and couldn't complete the race because I ran out of tires."

With lessons learned the hard way, on he went to the Mexican 1000 with a little experience under his belt and a long trip ahead of him to the finish in La Paz.

After the race, John was sitting near the beach in La Paz watching the celebrities of the sport, like Parnelli

John Baker began his off-road racing career in the Bronco he purchased with the idea of plowing driveways during the long Minnesota winters. Fortune took Baker to Southern California before he fitted the snowplow. There, he transitioned to recreational off-roading and then racing at the urging of a friend. From this all-too-common beginning, Baker parlayed his hard work into a notable racing career. Here, at the 1973 500-mile race in Baja, John churns through a washed-out section of road. (Photo Courtesy Trackside Photo)

Jones, standing around talking together and he thought to himself, "I want to be a factory sponsored driver." In 1973, John garnered some second- and third-place finishes. Then, in 1974, he broke through with two wins.

John Baker raced that Bronco for another four years. It became obvious that the sponsorships were going to the full-size two-wheel-drive pickups. John had been using a used F-150 pickup to pre-run events in, so he raced that for two events. In doing so, he won the 1976 California 400 and took second at another event.

While it was the end of John's time in the Bronco, he went on to build on what he learned in that bucking Bronco and nabbed a sponsorship starting in 1977 with Chrysler to run its full-size two-wheel-drive team. Two years and a handful of wins later, Chrysler approached John to start a mini truck program for the Dodge D-50. Walker Evans took over the full-size truck program, while John set Class 7 on fire for the next six years. But, it all started with a brand-new $3,300 Bronco in Minnesota.

Lee Epstein

Lee Epstein purchased a wonderful piece of history in 1975 when Bill Stroppe sold him the *Pony*. It was the same Bronco that carried Parnelli Jones to his first off-road racing victory and was the inspiration for *Big Oly*. The *Pony* had built a legendary string of finishes and wins with Larry Minor at the wheel between 1970 and 1974. Now, with Stroppe thinning the herd of Broncos (pun intended), it needed a new home.

Epstein paid Stroppe to prep the *Pony* at his shop and funded some upgrades to the old girl. Out came the 302-ci engine and in went a 351-ci Windsor, upgrading its nickname from *Pony* to *Super Pony*.

The *Pony* ran about two more years with Epstein at the wheel before the car was destroyed in Mexico and reportedly scrapped.

Lee Epstein bought the Pony *from Bill Stroppe in 1975. He used it for several years and upgraded the engine along the way. He had some solid finishes in his short time behind the wheel of it. (Photo Courtesy* MotorTrend *and Petersen Museum Archive)*

Cal Wells

Yes, *that* Cal Wells, the mastermind behind Precision Preparation (PPI) and Toyota's success in short-course and desert racing for 16 years. A young Wells was hooked on off-road racing at age 14, when his father took him down to Baja to help pit for the Stroppe team.

Cal Wells bought his first Bronco at age 15 when a flood-damaged unit out of North Dakota became available for a deal. Wells rebuilt the Bronco in his parents' garage and prepped it for the 1973 NORRA Baja 500. The first race ended with a broken engine, but Cal was hooked.

Going into the 400-mile race in Parker, Arizona, in 1974, the Bronco crashed and exposed some deficiencies in the roll cage. Luckily, no one was hurt, but the Bronco went to the Stroppe shop for a new cage and aluminum dash.

At age 18, Wells was riding with a friend in a Datsun 620 pickup when there was a big accident. Wells received injuries that were serious and took some time to heal. In a difficult decision, Cal retired from off-road driving and sold the Bronco in 1975. He still wanted to be involved any way he could. His skills as a mechanic and attention to detail saw him transition to a mechanic and car builder for Joe MacPherson at his Chevrolet dealership, then for the legendary Drino Miller, and finally for renowned engine builders FAT Performance.

In 1979, Wells decided it was time to make it on his own. This was a humble beginning for PPI. One of his first customers was Jeff MacPherson for whom he built a Baja Bug and then a Funco Class 1 car. By 1983, he had a deal with Toyota to prepare two trucks for the Mickey Thompson Off Road Championship Grand Prix, which was quickly followed by a desert program.

After 28 years, Wells closed PPI after Toyota shuttered the off-road program. He moved on to the world of NASCAR when Michael Waltrip Racing approached him with an executive position. At the end of that, Wells established LNGA Consulting, where he continues to advise several NASCAR teams.

Mark Vest

Mark Vest and his friend Dwayne Steel were looking to get into off-road racing and put together a deal with Don Barlow to purchase the *Crazy Horse* Bronco. Part of that deal was that Don wanted to drive for 1980. That way, Vest and Steel could learn from one of the best.

Family-run teams, such as the Wells, were the backbone of off-road racing. Factory interest alone could never support an organizer like NORRA completely. Not many other forms of racing could see such a level playing field simply because the unknown was such a big factor in these early races. On any given day, you could have your clean run and beat a hot shoe, such as Larry Minor or Carl Jackson, who was not having the best day. (Photo Courtesy Trackside Photo)

It all began with a flood-damaged Bronco bought by a young Cal Wells with dreams of off-road racing with his family. From there, Wells accrued knowledge and contacts while working in the off-road industry until he opened Precision Preparation Inc. In this image from the 1973 500-mile race in Baja, Wells seems to be looking back at a two-wheel-drive pickup that he either just passed or was about to pass him. (Photo Courtesy Trackside Photo)

At the 1983 season-opening race in Parker, Arizona, the annual 400-mile race is a big favorite with off-road racers. The event featured a 110-mile opening lap on the California side of the Colorado River. Then, after a 2-hour break, there were 2 90-mile laps. (Photo Courtesy Kevin Vest)

Normally, a modified Bronco carried a number starting with a four. For many years, the Mint 400 went with a non-traditional numbering system. All these years later, there is no mistaking which photos came from the rough-and-rocky patch of Nevada north of Las Vegas. (Photo Courtesy Don Barlow)

Crazy Horse was in rough shape when they took possession. The 351 Windsor engine had a connecting rod hanging out of the side of the engine block. It also needed a transmission. A new engine was built, and a transmission was procured from B&M. Then, the already-stretched Bronco from its initial build was stretched another 10 inches looking for a smoother ride.

Barlow drove the Bronco for much of 1980, while Vest and Steel traded off codriving and doing pit crew. By 1981, Barlow was eager to spend time with family, so Mark and Dwayne took over from 1981 through 1983, when Steel needed more time with family. Mark Vest carried on through 1986 before he threw in the towel as well and sent *Crazy Horse* on to a new home.

Moss Brothers Racing

Don and Ken Moss have one of the most impressive runs of wins in a single class since Rod Hall. In a time where seeing a Bronco on an entry list was a curiosity rather than normal, the Moss brothers brought one back to the winner's circle many times.

Don Moss was raised in Bishop, California, a small town on Highway 395 at the base of Mammoth Mountain. Not known for being a motorsports mecca of any kind, there was the demolition derby event at the county fair every year. That is where the racing bug bit hard. From there, it was racing with Cal Poly San Luis Obispo and then circle track racing in Roseville, California.

His time at Cal Poly taught Don one thing, he could not afford to be an off-road racer. It did not quell his desire to be one, so he kept an eye open for opportunities. Along came the new millennium and with it a brave

Don and Ken Moss are not shy about getting their Bronco airborne. (Photo Courtesy Moss Brothers Racing)

The 1979 Ford Bronco had all the right components that Don was looking for to make a competitive off-road racer. From the 351-ci Windsor engine to the tough C6 automatic transmission and the proven combination of a 9-inch Ford rear differential and a Dana 44 up front, it had the right bones. Over the years, slight modifications and strengthening of parts within the existing rules made the Bronco one of the most successful ever. (Photo Courtesy Moss Brothers Racing)

It takes a lot of help to run a program like the Moss brothers do. The side of their Bronco is plastered with multiple companies that lend support. Some are contingency programs that are based on performance, and others are straight support in the form of money, parts, or labor. (Photo Courtesy Moss Brothers Racing)

announcement from SCORE that the 1,000-mile race in Baja that to commemorate the new millennium, that year's event would be a 2,000-kilometer race (1,242.7 miles). Don knew he had to be a part of it.

The Bronco

Don and his brother, Ken, and his father-in-law, Tom Baker, began with a 1979 Ford Bronco chassis. The 351 Windsor engine was outfitted with a Holley 750-cfm double-pumper carburetor feeding the engine through an aluminum intake manifold. A Mallory distributor with a Pertronix ignition system fed spark to the plugs.

The power from the engine flowed through a C6 automatic transmission and was divided by a New Process 205 gear-driven transfer case. The rear axle was a built up 9-inch with Cone axles, while the front was a Dana 44 with custom trussing. The final-drive ratio was a set of 4.88 gears. Steering commands came from a UMP power steering box.

King shocks soaked up the bumps front and rear with extra travel available due to West Coast Broncos' lengthened tubular radius arms. The rear used a Deaver leaf spring pack.

The Baja Experts

Since that first race, the Moss brothers and their band of volunteers continue to dominate in their Bronco to this very day. As of the publication of this book, the team has amassed 15 wins in the 1,000-mile (or more) Baja race, 9 wins in the 500-mile Baja race, and 7 wins in the

Suspension is the most important functioning system on any off-road racer. A big engine is not going to help if the terrain does not allow all that power to get to the ground. As you can see in this photo, the Moss brothers are using all of their available suspension travel at a 2009 race in Laughlin, Nevada. (Photo Courtesy Trackside Photo)

The 2000s belonged to the Bronco once more with the domination of the Moss brothers and the resurgence of NORRA. (Photo Courtesy Trackside Photo)

All the horsepower and suspension are not much good unless you have tires that can grab at any terrain. Every tire company imaginable has come and gone from the off-road racing scene, but several have stayed and helped build the sport. The Moss brothers count on BFGoodrich for their pit support and technological advancements. (Photo Courtesy Moss Brothers Racing)

250-mile race on the east side of Baja. Add to that more than 20 wins in races in California and Nevada.

While the Moss brothers trail Rod Hall in number of class wins in the Baja 1000 (Rod had 25), they have one more than the legend, Larry Roeseler, who has won on two and four wheels. That puts them in with some rather good company.

The brothers had to reluctantly miss the 2020 Baja race due to two issues. The first was a nasty rollover accident at the VORRA 250 that necessitated a frame and body change. The second was related to the pandemic, but given the treacherous nature of the 900-mile loop, maybe that was the right one to miss.

Kurt Strecker

The founding member of the Viva Broncos began his off-road journey after safely returning from Vietnam in 1968. With a dream of graduating law school, Kurt applied himself to the college grind. He had a wife, Ginger, who was a nurse, and a 10-speed bicycle for transportation.

His hatred for that bicycle and his new boss at Ginger's hospital in El Cajon, California, who had a Bronco inspired Kurt to save up for a 1966 Bronco. His boss got him into the Los Badadores 4WD Club, and Kurt was now driving hard in club events anywhere and everywhere. Looking hard for a new color to paint the Bronco he came across a color called "Hot Ginger." Perfect.

Kurt and Ginger were avid surfers with fiberglass boards, and the ability to fashion fiberglass turned into Kurt making himself some fender flares. As happens in clubs, one guy comes up with something, and everyone else wants one. Suddenly, Kurt's life took on a new direction, and just like that, the off-road lifestyle saved the world from one more lawyer.

Soon, Bill Stroppe came calling. He was impressed with the quality of Kurt and Ginger's work and asked if he could distribute them. It was time to get serious about running a business. Viva Broncos delivered the flares to Bill Stroppe's shop in Signal Hill, California, and there laid out before Kurt was the world of off-road racing. Soon after, Stroppe came calling again for hoods for his Broncos from Viva Broncos.

As happens to many a young man hooked by the off-road bug, Baja came calling. Turning *Hot Ginger* into a racer allowed him to use it as a test bed for new parts. Kurt also already had Baja experience from numerous surfing trips to Baja's wave-rich Pacific side. Better than

Kurt Strecker is your above-average renaissance man turned off-road racer. He is a Vietnam War veteran, law school dropout, maestro with fiberglass, and one heck of a surfer. He is also the founder of Viva Broncos. (Photo Courtesy Kurt Strecker)

Hot Ginger *storms down one of the lonely desert tracks in Baja California in 1976 Baja 1000. Kurt Strecker had the passion to race, but that passion often led to broken parts. (Photo Courtesy Track-side Photo)*

The 1976 Baja 1000 was a very wet affair. Areas that never were known for having flash-flood-carved washes now had them. Kurt and his Viva Broncos team never shied away from a challenge like this or any other. (Photo Courtesy Trackside Photo)

that, he could go really fast, which appealed to him and his friends. The Viva Broncos Racing Team debuted at the 1969 NORRA Mexican 1000. *Hot Ginger* continued to run until 1976 before life temporarily took Kurt away from racing. He returned later to revive the Viva Broncos brand.

Rick Sieman

As editor of *Off-Road* magazine, Rick Sieman knew all about the off-road racing scene and its history. He determined that he could build a race truck and use it as a feature in the magazine that in turn would generate sponsors to help defray the cost, and he could go racing. What would he build? It would have to be something that got attention, and what vehicle gets more attention than anything out there? *Big Oly*.

Big Oly II

Through his connection with Dennis Garman and his fabrication company, Rick decided that a late-model Bronco might get more attention than trying to build an exact replica of *Big Oly*. In that case, he called it *Big Oly II* and ran it in Class 3. The build was chronicled thoroughly and reported in many issues of *Off-Road* magazine between 1987 and 1988. Garman Fabrication finished with the build in time for the 1988 Baja 1000.

Garman started with a 1987–1991-style body and frame. Mike Evans built a 351 Windsor with great power and torque to propel the 4,640-pound Bronco along. The suspension was comprised of modified twin traction beams and coilover shocks in front that provided 15 inches of wheel travel. The front could have gotten more travel, but the front axles were the limiting factor. In the rear, Garman started with a trick swing-arm setup based on motorcycle suspensions. In theory, it seemed like an innovative setup that gave Sieman 18 inches of wheel travel in the rear. However, the swing arm was not dependable, so they went to a four-link system that cured the problem.

Early Retirement

Big Oly II was a big favorite with the crowds that lined courses at every race it ran from 1988–1990. The truck garnered attention from the sponsors, such as Valvoline, and the rest of the press. What it did not garner was many finishes or wins. Its best finishes were a few that were third place in class. After two years, Sieman retired the Bronco.

Steve Mizel

If Frankenstein's monster were a truck, it would belong to Steve Mizel.

In this 1988 photo from the big Baja race, **Off-Road** magazine editor Rick Sieman flies Big Oly II off of a cattleguard. The wheel travel that the Bronco was flexing can be seen. If not for an innovative rear suspension that needed some more research and development time, the Bronco may have recorded more finishes than it did. Still, it was a fan favorite. (Photo Courtesy Trackside Photo)

At the 1989 Barstow Fireworks 250, Sieman comes off one of the many off cambered jumps that dot the landscape east of Interstate 15. By this time, the rear suspension was corrected from the experimental swing axle to a more dependable four-link system. Still, the truck compiled more DNF results than finishes. (Photo Courtesy Trackside Photo)

Mizel started off-road racing at the 1969 NORRA Baja 500 in a Toyota Landcruiser. It did not take long for Steve to move on to the Ford Bronco, as he was looking for a faster ride. In 1975, he took his only win in the 1,000-mile Baja race, and in 1978, he won the 500-mile Baja race. Other wins followed, as his Bronco creations with chief mechanic Billy Rohrbacher roared across the deserts as well as on rally stages and up the famous Pike's Peak International Hill Climb.

Occasional second driver David Bryan remembered Mizel as both a character and a complex man. An accomplished businessman, Mizel branched out into oil exploration, owning a cable television company in Denver, Colorado, and as a financial manager based in New York City. Through it all, he stayed involved in off-road racing for many years.

Steve ran a few different Broncos, both two- and four-wheel drive over the years. Looking for every advantage, his creations kept getting longer and wider with more suspension innovations. On the final Bronco that they ran, Billy Rohrbacher devised a front suspension that utilized no springs at all, just nitrogen-charged shock absorbers. These creations were always fast, but troubles with his four-wheel independent design kept meeting with problems keeping the CV joints alive. I remember a conversation with Jeep driver Don Adams in the mid-1980s who said, "If he ever figures that suspension out, we'll all be chasing him."

Kirk Kovel

Brothers Kirk and Kim Kovel from Colorado Springs got their start in off-road exploration in 1968 when they procured an old Jeep. Being young men with gumption and little cash, they struck a friendship with the owner of Don's Jeep and traded work on vehicles for Jeep parts from his junkyard.

Later, through Don's Jeep they met Jerry Coulton and were introduced to racing, which was something Kirk was excited to do. Kim had a 1961 International Scout that Kirk purchased and turned into a racer. He got started at Rocky Mountain Off Road Racing Association events at Indian Springs Raceway near Canyon City, Colorado.

By 1981, Kirk was transferred to Seattle, Washington, and he took the International with plans to run in local Jeep events and some in Canada. On the way to Seattle, Kirk had an accident and rolled

You could count on Steve Mizel to lose the front-end fiberglass early in a race. The lack of a hood or fenders gave spectators a good view of the revolutionary front suspension and near-mid-engine design. When it worked, the Mizel Bronco was spectacular to watch.

At the 1985 Mint 400, Mizel comes out of the Las Vegas Speedrome for his second lap, looking more like an Unlimited class car.

The Mizel Bronco is set up for a short-course race at the Glen Helen Raceway in Southern California in 1985. A desert-built racer usually did double duty as a short-course racer at the few spectator events that were popular. Drivers could race wheel to wheel by taking out the spare parts and tires and unloading the codriver. Some even went as far as to install a smaller fuel cell.

Steve Mizel powers his "funny" Bronco ahead of the pesky Randall family Jeep Honcho. The short-course race was organized as part of the High Desert Racing Association championship for 1985. Mizel went on to win his class at the event.

Kirk Kovel thought about handling like you would with a sports car but in an off-road situation. A solid front axle design leaves few adjustments, but there are items that can make a difference. Kovel utilized spring choice, bump-steer adjustments, and stabilizing links to his advantage. (Photo Courtesy Kovel Family Collection)

Kirk Kovel was a fiercely smart competitor who began with a low-budget racing team that was built around family and friends. Through perseverance and a tenacity that got him wins, he had a well-funded team built around family and friends. (Photo Courtesy Kovel Family Collection)

Kirk Kovel pops up out of the desert at the 1994 Nevada 400 where he notched his first big win. Kovel went on to more wins, more sponsors, and many more years in the desert that he loved. (Photo Courtesy Kurt Scherbaum/ The Lensman Photography)

Nevada means silt, which is a super fine talcum powder-like substance that likes to trap unsuspecting racers. Kirk's Bronco was built for unfriendly terrain such as this and was often blasting through deep silty ruts. (Photo Courtesy Kovel Family Collection)

his Ford pickup and the trailer that had the Scout on it. Eventually everything was righted and at home in Washington.

At the end of his time in Washington before heading back to Colorado, Kirk decided he wanted to do desert racing and knew the International was not up to snuff. He purchased a Bronco that was already built for racing and hauled that back home, where he made extensive modifications so he could be competitive in the major desert events of the day.

Planning for his first event, the time schedule did not mesh with his work schedule, so Kirk asked a friend to drive the truck and trailer for him, and he would fly in with his brother Kim. Along the way, the friend managed to roll the trailer with the Bronco on it. That made for two rolled racers while on the trailer, but fortunately it was also the last. The unfortunate accident did however cost Kovel his first race.

As Kirk built a reputation as a quality off-road driver, sponsors made their way to him, including BFGoodrich Tires and Ford. The race team was exclusively made up of friends and family and competed in five or six events a year. In 1994, the team broke through and won the Nissan (formerly Mint) 400 in Class 3.

Getting ready for battle, Kirk straps into the Bronco. He's a long way from those early days of stripping parts at Don's Jeep in Colorado with Kim. Kirk culled his passion and abilities to make his mark in off-road racing. (Photo Courtesy Kovel Family Collection)

Kirk Kovel was a staunch Bronco supporter and a fierce competitor. (Photo Courtesy Mike Ingalsbee)

Trying to get to the church on time, Kovel launches the Bronco. (Photo Courtesy Kovel Family Collection)

This photo almost wound up on the side of a carton of milk. What do you do when your driver goes missing in the middle of the desert? (Photo Courtesy Kovel Family Collection)

His victories were all the more impressive considering that Kirk took the passenger's seat out of the Bronco. He was worried about hurting someone else. This is not altogether uncommon in off-road racing.

Kirk Kovel tragically lost his life when he was involved in a car accident in Miami, Florida, in 2015.

Chuck Johnson

Not all the privateers got their Bronco start in the American Southwest or Baja. As a young man in Rockford, Illinois, Chuck got his first Bronco in 1973. He started with club-style obstacle events in the upper Midwest. Chuck's first visit to Crandon, Wisconsin, when he flat-towed his Bronco to the event, netted a second-place finish to Geoff Dorr, who was the hot shoe of the day.

By 1975, Chuck had built the Bronco into a full-time racer and battled Dorr for race wins and championships. In 1977, he obtained Bronco body molds and made the decision to move out of the stock 4x4 class into Class 4 for modified 4x4s. Johnson kept the stock frame but built everything else off of the tube structure. In the same year, Chuck became a full-fledged electrician.

In 1983, Chuck Johnson slides by the spectators at a Firebird Raceway event organized by the High Desert Racing Association. His early forays out West laid the groundwork for his later successes with Ford in both desert and short-course events. (Photo Courtesy Trackside Photo)

In 1979, Chuck ventured west to try racing at the Riverside Raceway in Class 4 with his Bronco. In a spirited drive, Chuck took third in qualifying. Going to the tire trailer to get tires mounted for the upcoming race, he brought the tires and his inner tubes. The technician told Chuck that he did not need the tubes. Accepting that the technician was correct, he allowed the installation of the tires without tubes. What escaped the tire technician's attention was that Chuck was not running an aluminum rim with a deep bead.

In 1983, Chuck Johnson competes at Riverside Raceway. The Riverside events, originally founded by Mickey Thompson, drew huge crowds all weekend for almost two decades and pleased the sponsors and large crowds. Chuck claimed a well-earned second-place finish in his race. Later that year, he ran this same Bronco in the Frontier 250 outside of Las Vegas.

Going into the first corner after the Oklahoma Land Rush style start, Chuck laid the Bronco hard into the corner and the tire slipped off the bead, which sent the Bronco into the retaining wall and over on its side. It was a short race for Chuck that year, but he would be back.

In 1982, he took third place, and in 1983, he took second place. To end 1983, he traveled west again to run the HDRA Frontier 250 in Jean, Nevada, on an accelerated schedule that allowed for no pre-running, and he did not have a chase crew. In a solid drive, he finished second behind the hottest short-wheelbase 4x4 driver of the day, Don Adams. Anyone who was around back then can tell you that was an accomplishment.

At the end of 1983, Chuck Johnson sold his Bronco and went into the mini truck class in another Ford product, a Ranger. He had a lot of success in the Ranger, including being part of the Ford Roughriders team.

Ken Rice and Hal Sealund

Ken Rice met Hal Sealund while he was still in high school working on a Jeep restoration, as he and Hal used the same auto parts supplier. Sealund was keeping his Jeep CJ-5 in shape. This was in 1965 (before the Bronco was introduced). They became friends and started doing some off-road trips together.

Rice and Sealund made a good team and had some success in the biggest races, such as the Mint 400 and a long Baja race. By 1981, Rice had other priorities and moved on from the sport but not before going out with a big win. (Photo Courtesy Trackside Photo)

The original K Bar S Bronco raced by Ken Rice now has a home with Ed Gudenkauf, who ran some events with it but now has retired the Bronco to the show circuit. The history that this Bronco carries with it over 30 years of racing makes it one of the most venerable racers that ever tackled the desert. (Photo Courtesy Ed Gudenkauf)

By 1972, Ken started helping around an off-road shop and doing some pit crew duty for their team. Sealund had his Bronco there getting some work done, reuniting the two men. After a mishap with Sealund's Bronco, the project was stopped until Ken and Hal decided to work together to get the Bronco to the 1975 Mint 400 with local engine builder Paul Fischer driving and Ken riding shotgun. The 351-ci Windsor engine disqualified them from entering the stock 4x4 class, so they went into the modified 4x4, Class 4.

This was the first year the Mint started on the paved road course at the Las Vegas Speedrome. Fischer and Ken went into the first turn with an excess of velocity, and the Bronco went up on two wheels. Fischer caught it in time and brought back down on the four Firestone Parnelli 1000 tires.

Those Firestone tires were the best to have in those days. Although, they had an inner liner feature that was the cause of their first-lap exit from the race. The inner liner had leaked, which had over-inflated the tires and made the ride completely unbearable over the vicious Nevada terrain. The team at the time could not figure out the issue and parked the Bronco.

Next was the 500-mile race in Baja in June. Fischer dropped out of the team for personal reasons, so Ken was now the driver after learning at the Mint fiasco that he was not built for the right seat. Ken started the race and got down the Pacific side until he rolled the Bronco but was able to continue. About 100 miles later, the Bronco lost a steering sector shaft and came to an unceremonious stop. Ken flagged down a mini truck that was racing by and got a ride in the bed to the pit area at Santo Tomas. By the time the pit crew worked its way back to the disabled Bronco and fixed the broken shaft, it was too late to continue.

Finally, a Finish

Third time is the charm they thought as they went on to the 1,000-mile race in Baja. With more experience under his belt, Ken drove smartly through the 801-mile loop and the Bronco took third place in Class 4.

After the race, SCORE made a major rule change regarding roll-cage tubing sizes. After some unfortunate accidents, the head technical inspectors changed the rule to tube size by vehicle weight. This meant that the entire cage had to be redone, causing the team to miss the first event in 1976.

Finally, a Win

Things came together in 1978, as Ken and Hal won the Baja 1000 (which was actually only 580 miles). The start was in Mexicali that year, and a big rainstorm prior to the start made things difficult in the mountain passes that separated Mexicali from the finish line in Ensenada. It was good to have four-wheel drive at this event, as out of 219 starters, only 56 finished.

After the first win, the team decided it was time to rework the former Hearst Bronco, as some sponsors started coming on board after their inaugural win. The Bronco got stretched 12 inches at the front, which was different than Don Barlow's *Crazy Horse* at 10 inches. However, more importantly, while Barlow stretched out the rear, Ken stretched the front on his, which allowed the engine to be mounted further back from the front axle. The finicky C4 automatic transmission was replaced with a beefy C6, and the old 351 Windsor engine was freshened up. Other changes to the axles improved reliability, as some of the 1979 events saw the Bronco not finish because of axle issues.

The Long Road to La Paz

When the 1,000-mile event rolled around for 1979, it was a return to the original format of starting in Ensenada and finishing in La Paz. The 987-mile course had 244 starters, and 121 finished. For Ken and his brother Greg, who was driving the first half of the race, confidence was high for a good finish with all the new improvements.

Ken took a magazine writer with him on his leg of the race, which was at El Arco, the traditional halfway point in the race. Greg delivered the Bronco in good shape, and drivers were changed while the crew serviced the Bronco for the last half of the race.

Ken got underway with his rookie codriver as they made their way out of the pit area and southward on the two track road. About 50 miles into his drive, Ken noticed that his codriver was sick with his head hung over against the window nets in an attempt to eject the contents of his stomach out of the Bronco. At each stop, Ken offered to let his codriver out of the Bronco, but while he was weak in constitution, he was determined to make it. To his credit, he stayed in the whole way.

It was not a clean run, though. At San Ignacio, the alternator packed it in, and Ken knew that the loop over to the Pacific Ocean and back was too long to manage it solely on battery power. Ken waited three agonizing hours for the chase crew to catch up with another alternator. Underway again and surprisingly still in it for the win, Ken thundered down the peninsula.

With 300 miles to go, the steering wheel input suddenly told Ken that the power steering had a problem. With a quick look under the hood, he could see that an aluminum fitting failed. With no good option that he knew of at the time, Ken got the workout of a lifetime muscling the Bronco for hours to the finish. Perseverance paid off, as the Rice brothers took the win in Class 4.

It turned out the power steering fitting that broke was the same as a Holley carburetor inlet fitting that Ken kept as a spare in the Bronco.

The Last Race

When the Mint 400 rolled around for 1981, racing was taking a toll on the Rice brothers, so they decided to hang it up after the race. They picked a historic event to end, as over 500 cars started the event, which is a number that has not been equaled.

Earlier in the year, they made an engine swap from the reliable old Windsor engine to a Cleveland. This offered some extra power but required some serious fabrication, as the Cleveland engine shares little in common with the Windsor as far as engine mounting goes.

Things went along well for three of the four 100-mile laps, as Greg had a 45-minute lead headed out of the Speedrome and into the desert. Not far into the lap, the engine mounts started breaking one by one. Quick work in the field secured the engine, and they babied the Bronco to make the finish and collect another win in their farewell to the sport.

They Carried the Torch Well

The privateers highlighted here are just a sample of the great men and women who carried the Ford and the Bronco banners long after the factory support dried up in 1974. It was further proof, as if any was needed, that Ford built a superior product right from the factory floor that could and did beat the Baja.

This unknown racer is running the 1970 Mint 400. The Colorado state flag is being used for his or her sand flag, and the Bronco looks to be stock from the dash, aside from the aftermarket tachometer. (Photo Courtesy MotorTrend and Petersen Museum Archive)

Uncle Bob's Bouncing Bronco *was Bob Lewis's name for his racer. Lewis had Southern California dealership Galpin Ford help build the Bronco. Lewis was the first off-road racer to use and get sponsored by KC Hilites. Uncle Bob is seen here tackling the hills during the cold and snowy 1973 Mint 400. (Photo Courtesy MotorTrend and Petersen Museum Archive)*

This father-and-son team competed with the Quint Family Bronco. Many families use racing to help keep everyone close. From looking at this photo from the 1973 NORRA Baja 500, the Bronco was prepared well, including painting the hood flat black to reduce glare. (Photo Courtesy MotorTrend and Petersen Museum Archive)

Rod Fish drove the United Truck Driving School Bronco, while George Wallace rides shotgun. Wallace co-owned the school. The pair show up in many photos from the early-to-mid 1970s. Fish was known to defect and drive some pesky Jeeps from time to time. (Photo Courtesy MotorTrend and Petersen Museum Archive)

Gary Gabelich was once the fastest man on earth driving the Blue Flame land speed jet car at speeds of 630 mph. He also had speed records on water as well as for NASA. After a 1972 crash of an experimental four-wheel-drive Funny Car, Gabelich had to slow down a bit. Mike Edwards provided an outlet for Gabelich to get his racing fix from time to time. (Photo Courtesy MotorTrend and Petersen Museum Archive)

Slick Gardner was a jack-of-all-trades racer of some note. He spent time in sports cars, stock cars, and off-road racing. His son Racin Gardner was an Indy 500 driver. Back in those days, many racing drivers switched disciplines regularly, such as Parnelli Jones. (Photo Courtesy MotorTrend and Petersen Museum Archive)

The sport owes all the small private teams a debt of gratitude. They were the backbone of the sport. They competed against big-money factory teams and hoped it would be their day, and more than occasionally, it was. (Photo Courtesy Mark Atherton)

The Quint Family Bronco competes at the big Baja race. The Quints had a reputation as pure sportsmen who were always willing to help anyone in need. That is not a bad legacy to have associated with your time in off-road racing. (Photo Courtesy MotorTrend and Petersen Museum Archive)

CHAPTER 6

THE 1990s: THE FORD
ROUGHRIDERS

In what would be the truck market-ing coup of the 1990s and a shift away from the traditional way of marketing off-road racing, here came the Ford Roughriders. Since the start of organized off-road racing, it was hard to get big-time sponsorship. If a team could get $50,000 for a sea-son, that was considered big money in the 1970s and 1980s.

Largely, manufacturers had a dim view of off-road racing. It was hard to spectate, hard to film, and took place away from major popu-lation centers. However, there has always been manufacturer support of one kind or another in off-road racing. After all, even in its infancy, it was Honda that financed that first peninsula run record in 1962.

Ford, which had been there from the beginning with the Bronco, had floated in and out of the sport with manufacturer support. Since off-road racing was never as big of a draw as

One of the most prolific Broncos began life as a stock truck for media types to drive. Then, Dick Landfield of Enduro Racing built it up as a stepping stone to something bigger he had in mind. The Ford Roughriders truly started with this Bronco. (Photo Courtesy MotorTrend and Petersen Museum Archive)

The 1969 NORRA Baja 500 was Dick Landfield's first race. (Landfield is leaning out of passenger's side.) Irv Hanks took him on a wild adventure that lasted several days. Despite the adventure, the racing bug bit Landfield hard, and he started to use his Ford dealership to promote the sport. If he sold a few more cars and trucks, it was all the better. (Photo Courtesy MotorTrend and Petersen Museum Archive)

NASCAR or NHRA drag racing, it fell victim to the corporate axe on and off over the years.

One man had a passion for the sport and the connection to Ford's upper echelon of executives, and he had a unique idea.

Dick Landfield

Enter Dick Landfield. Dick first competed in off-road racing at the 1968 NORRA Baja 500 in a Ford Bronco with Irv Hanks. Like most people, after his first encounter with racing, he loved it even though things did not go as planned. His adventure during that first race would have stopped lesser individuals from coming back. The following year, he formed Enduro Racing and ran it out of his Southern California Ford dealership, Fairway Ford.

Dick was an off-road racing innovator from the start. He founded a group called FAIR (First Association of Independent Racers). This allowed racers to group together and combine people and supplies at pit stops throughout the racecourse. This saved small teams time and money, and still does today.

In 1972, he got Ford to finance the costs of starting a mini truck class with NORRA.

By 1990, Landfield had formed a marketing idea to make the manufacturers of trucks and tires and various other parts needed in off-road racing come together. He

Dick Landfield has had a varied career behind the wheel of Fords of all types. Here, he competes in a Ford Courier in 1973. (Photo Courtesy MotorTrend and Petersen Museum Archive)

envisioned being the one to get the ball rolling and then hand off the actual running of program to someone with the executive acumen to see the project through. As you can tell, Dick Landfield is an idea man, which has served him well in both business and racing.

Frank DeAngelo

After brainstorming with Dick Landfield, Lee Morse, who was second in command with Ford Special Vehicle Operations (SVO), made a call to Frank DeAngelo and offered to hand the entire Roughrider program over to him to manage. DeAngelo remembered the process.

"Ford SVO and Ford truck marketing got the idea of a big team effort from Dick Landfield," he said. "Ford SVO, run by Lee Morse, then bid the idea out to three motorsports marketing companies asking for budgets. The head of the program would, aside from the marketing of the teams, be in charge of coordinating sponsors, ensuring technological sharing among the teams, and coordinating the schedule for each race. My company won the bid not based on budget but creativity and program elements."

DeAngelo was no stranger to off-road racing, he had been heading the BFGoodrich Tires off-road racing effort and pit support for many years. In 1989, he struck out on his own with DeAngelo & Associates, a marketing company. Morse offered to turn marketing, budgeting, and associate sponsor acquisition over to him as well as deciding on the line up of teams. DeAngelo proposed that all four desert truck classes be represented at first: the two mini truck classes, the four-wheel-drive class for the Bronco, and the two-wheel-drive full-size truck class. There were also short-course programs involved.

For the next four years, DeAngelo traveled every week from his home in Ohio to Detroit for mandatory meetings at Ford Motorsport. He devised an innovative marketing strategy as well as a sharing of technology between the teams on everything mechanical and extensive tire testing with BFGoodrich.

After the close of the Roughrider program, Frank could still be found at most off-road races representing his company for 10 years until he closed that and went to work with Jackson Motorsports to continue representing BFGoodrich in off-road racing.

At the 2020 Baja race, Frank DeAngelo was honored by being chosen as the Grand Marshall of the event. An honor long overdue.

David Ashley

David Ashley came to the Enduro Racing program with an impressive resume of wins on two wheels in the

Frank DeAngelo is the man who oversaw the Ford Rough Riders program. He was a longtime supporter of off-road racing through positions with BFGoodrich and eventually with his own company. (Photo Courtesy Trackside Photo)

David Ashley drove, managed the team, and fine-tuned the Bronco's unique suspension. (Photo Courtesy Trackside Photo)

United States, Baja California, and in Europe. Ashley was still in high school at the age of 18 riding for Yamaha when he won the Six Day Trails of Austria. Ashley gave Yamaha the first Japanese factory win in a European Six Day event.

A winner from the start, he won his first event in the Novice Class at the Adelanto Grand Prix at age 13. By 1976, he was involved with developing the mono-shock suspension system. According to Ashley, at that time, teams were not really developing suspension at the shock and spring level. He learned through testing the importance of a proper setup, which was a skill that served him well on two and four wheels.

Before leaving two wheels for four, David racked up an impressive list of wins. David had known Dick Landfield since he was 13 years old, so it was no surprise that

Nearly a legend on two wheels while racing for Yamaha at the age of 18, David Ashley captured the first-ever Six Day Enduro title for Yamaha. Ashley cemented that legend status on two wheels with wins in the biggest Baja races among his trophy collection. He transitioned into four-wheel competition, racing a mini truck for Enduro Racing before moving over to head the Bronco program. Here, he pilots the Bronco to a win at the 1989 Mint 400. (Photo Courtesy Trackside Photo)

At the 1989 1,000-mile race, Ashley pilots the Bronco over one of Baja's many cattleguards that launch racers off the ground. Note the 10 Bosch off-road lights mounted on the front of the Bronco. From inside the cab, the drivers can run the lights in various configurations depending on the amount of dust in the air. In heavy dust, the lights highest up are turned off because they reflect off the hanging dust. (Photo Courtesy Trackside Photo)

Dan Smith was classified as a "did not finish" (DNF) at the 1991 Gold Coast 250, and looking at this photo, it is not hard to imagine why. (Photo Courtesy Trackside Photo)

he wound up working with him on a short-course and desert program for a Ford Ranger. According to Ashley, it was Ford that requested him to be involved with the setup and driving duties for the Bronco in 1989. This was 2 years prior to the initiation of the Roughrider program and the addition of Dan Smith.

When Ashley hung up his helmet, he finished with 154 victories on two and four wheels. He is a member of the Off-Road Motorsports Hall of Fame Class of 2014. He is also a member of the 2013 Class of the Riverside Sports Hall of Fame in Riverside, California, joining other motorsport luminaries, such as Malcolm Smith, Dan Gurney, Walker Evans, Les Richter, and Rex Mays.

David Ashley passed away on May 4, 2020, from complications of COVID-19.

Dan Smith

Dan Smith was another convert from a successful two-wheel career to the Enduro Racing team. How successful? Dan Smith won 59 AMA District 37 desert races, the 1983 1,000-mile Baja race, and the 1984 500-mile Baja race. He was a Whiskey Pete's World Champion (winning the inaugural event) and won the Barstow to Vegas motorcycle race. His career on two wheels was largely with Husqvarna, but he finished with Kawasaki.

A badly broken leg while practicing for a motorcycle race was the catalyst for Dan to start thinking about four wheels instead of two. A test drive in Ivan Stewart's factory Toyota truck convinced him that he could make the transition.

Dick Landfield knew that expert motorcycle racers transitioned into cars and trucks well, so he added Smith in 1991 with Ashley. The rest, as they say, is history.

The Enduro Racing Bronco

Included among the Roughrider teams was a Class 3 (short-wheelbase four-wheel-drive vehicle) Ford Bronco. In 1988, this Bronco was built by Enduro Racing for two women to attempt to finish that year's Baja 1000. It was largely a stock truck at that time with safety equipment and basic upgrades to shocks and tires. The team was nearing the finish when it was involved in an accident with a parked civilian vehicle. It damaged the truck enough to keep the team from finishing the race.

Arguably one of the greatest Broncos ever built began life as a near-stock racer for an all-woman media team. Ginny Commander and Parker Gentry wrote about the experience. The Bronco almost made it all the way around the course, but close to the finish line, they collided with a dump truck and heavily damaged the Bronco. Dick Landfield rebuilt the Bronco as a Class 3 killer, put David Ashley in the driver's seat, and ruled the desert for the next six years. (Photo Courtesy Trackside Photo)

Dick Landfield purchased that Bronco from Ford and went about building a proper Class 3 killer with the help of Dave Ashley.

The Engine

One of the upgrades that was allowed in the Class 3 rules at that time was a 430-ci aluminum block sprint car engine. David Ashley fondly remembered the power

The Enduro Bronco began life mostly stock for its initial race. Then, after the rebuild, it was fitted with a 430-ci sprint-car engine that had impressive power and torque. A rules change saw that engine become illegal in Class 3, so Enduro turned to NASCAR technology and Jack Roush Racing for a new powerplant. This photo is from the 1993 1,000-mile Baja race, where Dan Smith piloted the Bronco to a class victory. (Photo Courtesy Trackside Photo)

The Enduro Racing Bronco set a new standard for short-wheelbase four-wheel-drive suspensions. Led by David Ashley and his knowledge of suspension setup, the Bronco took obstacles at speed unlike any previous 4x4. Special components helped provide the necessary wheel travel and stay within the rules. Here, at the 1993 Nevada 400, Dan Smith launches out of a dry wash in route to yet another Roughrider victory. (Photo Courtesy Trackside Photo)

that was available on demand. The team enjoyed that engine until the rules were changed in 1990 to abolish aluminum-block engines in the class.

Starting in 1991, Enduro Racing went with a tall-deck NASCAR engine equipped with an iron block, as per the rules. The powerplant was good for in excess of 600 hp, and because it was a design proven in hundreds of thousands of miles in NASCAR, it was reliable.

Suspension

Ashley worked his magic on the suspension, designing it for optimum spring and shock performance and maximum wheel travel. Going back to his days racing on two wheels, he knew the value of getting just the right shock/spring combination. The front boasted highly modified twin traction beams with coilover shocks good for over 16 inches of wheel travel. The rear suspension featured a four-link rear end and quarter elliptic leaf springs. More coilover shock assemblies put travel at 20 inches.

Drivetrain

Power went from the engine through a E4OD automatic transmission and modified transfer case. A 9-inch rear end put down the power to the ground through

Dan Smith flies to a win at the 1993 Nevada (formerly Mint) 400. (Photo Courtesy Kurt Scherbaum/The Lensman Photography)

BFGoodrich tires. The front wheels churned their power through a modified unit based on a Dana 60 with modified axles, which according to Dave Ashley, were the hardest parts on the truck to keep alive.

Helping Build Better Broncos

Ford was using the Enduro Racing Bronco as a test bed for stock body and suspension parts, such as door hinges and suspension bushings, to run under race conditions and see how long it took for the stock parts to break down. Landfield said that according to his discussions with Ford engineers, they could learn more about a parts durability in one 1,000-mile race better than in 50,000 miles of real-world testing.

1989 and 1990: Before the Roughriders

The Enduro Racing Bronco debuted at the 1989 Parker 400 resplendent in a red, white, and blue paint job. The fiberglass cap was still covering the rear compartment, but that was gone for the Mint 400 a few months later. Parker did not go as smooth as the team wanted, dropping one to a full-sized Jeep.

Onward to the Mint 400, where in consideration to the desert tortoise population, the race was designated as a no pre-run event. Some teams used aircraft to check the course, which was legal but hardly provides the information you glean from feeling the road. Despite some tremendous competition, Dave Ashley brought the Bronco home for its first win. It was the first of many.

The season went on with more wins than disappointments as the Bronco continued to get refined. Before long, it was time for another 1,000-mile drive around Baja. The 1989 race was a peninsula run to La Paz total-

In 1989, the Baja 1000 was a peninsula run to La Paz. Ashley and Mike Bakholden, who built the Bronco, set the course on fire, blistering the Class 3 field. (Photo Courtesy Trackside Photo)

ing 1,058 miles. The peninsula runs really bring out the old iron.

Dave Ashley teamed up with Mike Bakholden. They were one of a trio of Broncos entered up against a tough field of Jeeps and Chevrolets. It took the Bronco 21 hours and 4 minutes to traverse the peninsula for an average speed of just over 50 mph. In comparison, the Bronco did the race faster than all three factory-backed mini trucks, which included Roger Mears in his high-tech Nissan, the John Swift Class 7 4x4 Ford Ranger, and Chuck Johnson's Class 7S Ford Ranger.

The year ended with Dave Ashley gathering up the Class 3 season title as well as the overall Heavy Metal Championship.

1990

The new year came with little change to the Enduro Racing Bronco team. The year 1989 had gone pretty well, and the competition was still playing catch up. As the season wore on, the boss, Dick Landfield, put the wheels in motion to establish the Roughriders. He needed all the Ford teams to put in a great year to solidify the deal.

The annual trip to Parker, Arizona, worked out to Enduro's advantage, as Dave notched another win to start the year out as well as was possible. The momentum continued into the Nissan (formerly Mint) 400 with another dominating win. For the second year in a row, the Bronco stumbled at the 500-mile run in Baja, but it was of little consequence, as the next month at the Barstow Fireworks 250, they were on top again by winning Class 3.

At the end of the year, the team was staring at Baja, a 1,000-kilometer-loop version of the race. However, the course was laid in a sadistic way by having teams crawl over the legendary summit early and then loop through Borrego twice, which is a particularly unforgiving chunk of Baja. The summit is a small mountain range that racers have to traverse that separates the west and east coasts of Baja Norte. It is rough. It is a single lane with big drop-offs on one side of the road. Just one stuck or broken-down vehicle can bottle up dozens of racers until a way past them becomes available.

At the end of pre-running the Baja race, Dave Ashley knew one thing, it was going to be a rough one and a lot of vehicles were going to be breaking down. The strategy was going to be running at their own pace and maybe counting on a little luck, which is something Baja does not hand out very often. Also at stake, besides the Class 3 race, was the possibility of another Heavy Metal Championship if Robby Gordon had trouble with his Ford pickup that ran in the two-wheel-drive class.

As luck would have it, there was a bottleneck on the summit that saw many racers stuck behind a

David Ashley is on his way to a big win at the 1990 1,000-kilometer Baja 1000 race that sealed his Heavy Metal and Class 3 championships for the year. A late starting slot and the misfortune of others on the rough crossing of the "summit" played into David's hands just as he anticipated. From there, it was smart driving that brought the Bronco an astounding fourth-place overall finish among all vehicles on four wheels. (Photo Courtesy Trackside Photo)

The year 1992 was difficult for Dan Smith and his Bronco. Seen here at the 1992 Baja Internacional, he overcame front suspension damage to claim a second place. (Photo Courtesy Trackside Photo)

broken-down truck. Buggies and trucks were lined up dozens deep, waiting for quite some time until the bottleneck cleared. Some did not navigate around the truck very well and got stuck on the cliff side of the road. What worked out for Ashley and the other Class 3 vehicles was that their class left the starting line toward the end of the group, as starting order is determined by average speeds, and short-wheelbase vehicles rarely go fast enough to break into the top of the running order. As Ashley arrived, the bottleneck was nearly sorted out. He passed the obstructing pickup, and it cost him little time.

While Ashley knew the attrition would be hefty, he could not have anticipated the carnage throughout the rest of the field. Among the wounded was Robby Gordon, who broke a sector shaft early and lost hours. By the halfway point in Borrego, the Enduro Bronco had a full hour lead over second place. It was hammer down all the way to Ensenada as reports came in from around the course that the Bronco was in the top five overall. It had been unheard of since the time when the Broncos ruled Baja 20 years earlier.

At the finish line in Ensenada, the Bronco earned a fourth-place overall finish, the year-end class championship, and a second Heavy Metal championship in a row.

An off-road racer must be able to handle all conditions–more than the usual hot, dusty, and rocky kind. It is not uncommon to have a water crossing or challenging weather conditions from rain, snow, fog, mud, or strong winds that you can get a vehicle airborne and move it of its intended path. This water crossing was encountered in June 1993 at a Baja race. Dan Smith went on to win that race. (Photo Courtesy Trackside Photo)

The Ford Roughriders Years

At last, Dick Landfield's vision was a reality. In late January 1991, there were eight different classes of Ford Trucks between the desert and short-course racing formats. All of the trucks were painted identically with crews all clothed identically. They were introduced to the press just two weeks before the first race in a media event with all the trucks, drivers, and team owners.

Things were vastly different for the Enduro squad going into 1991 with Dave Ashley being moved into a brand-new Class 4 pickup truck, which left the seat open in the Bronco. In walked Dan Smith. He soon learned that life at the back of the pack was a lot dustier than at the front on two wheels.

1991

In his debut at Parker, the drivers changed but the result was the same, as Dan Smith paired with veteran Ford wheelman John Swift won on his first try. So far, Dick Landfield's promises to Ford that a Roughrider would win at least one class per race was holding true.

The Nevada desert shut the Bronco out of victory lane at the second event of the year as well as the third in San Felipe. It was back on top in Baja in the 500-mile race but then no victory again on the Fourth of July weekend in Barstow or the Nevada 500. Off-road racing can be a real rollercoaster ride, except it is your finishing position that can rise and fall at the whim of the desert. Nevada shut out the Bronco for the season, as it was a no-win weekend for them, even as the other Roughrider teams notched five class wins for the event, which was their best yet.

The final event of the year in Baja was another bust for the Enduro Bronco, as it was beaten by one of those pesky Jeeps. It was not all bad, though, as at the end-of-the-year banquet, Dan Smith earned the Rookie of the Year award. The year 1992 looked promising.

1992–1993

Things were largely unchanged for the Bronco contingent going into the new season. Smith still held the driver's seat, and the team was counting on his experience gained in 1991 to make 1992 more successful.

The big race in Baja that year was a peninsula run to La Paz that totaled 1,032 miles. Dan Smith did the run in 21 hours, 11 minutes, and 8 seconds. The only reported issue was that the starter failed on the Bronco along the way. Luckily, there was a stock Bronco parked in the area, and its starter was generously donated.

While it was a great win for Smith and Ford, the Jeep of Mike Leslie had a better year overall and took the class championship.

The year 1993 was much better for the Bronco with Smith sweeping the Baja races and taking the championship for the Roughriders.

All Things Must Pass

At the end of 1993, Enduro Racing decided to fold the Bronco program and move Dan Smith over to a new Class 8 truck paired with Dave Ashley. The two made a lethal pair and continued their success in not only the two-wheel-drive Class 8 truck but also in a trophy truck, where they continued those winning ways.

The corporate world can be cruel to racing fans. At the end of the 1994 season, Ford declined to renew the Roughrider contract. Dick Landfield's dream was at an end for himself, but the practice of bundling sponsors into a larger package continues to this day in every form of racing.

The End of the Enduro Bronco

It was not in the cards for Enduro Racing to keep the Bronco. Enduro had its hands full, handling its other truck programs and looking at campaigning a trophy truck. Landfield put the Bronco up for sale. It was quickly snatched up by a team in Baja California that ran it in many local events as well as some major races. The last it was seen was around 2000. The Bronco was in disrepair with crash damage and mechanical neglect. Since then, it has not been seen for many years.

The 1992 Baja 1000 win was a big one for Dan Smith and Enduro Racing. They overcame a few issues and won the race handily. (Photo Courtesy Trackside Photo)

After two races with disappointing results, Smith and Enduro Racing were back on top at the 1991 Baja 500 (the name was changed back from Internacional to 500). (Photo Courtesy Trackside Photo)

CHAPTER 7

THE 2000s
NORRA IS BACK

The year 2000 brought with it two separate 2000-themed races. The first was from the Best in the Desert series called the Nevada 2000. It featured one Bronco on the entry list from the Sunderland family, which did finish.

Then, the organizers of the Baja races also jumped on the 2000 bandwagon and pieced together a meandering masterpiece across the Baja peninsula. It was not quite 2,000 miles, but it was more than 2,000 kilometers.

The Baja 1679

Recognizing the new millennium, organizers decided that the usual 1,000-mile race should be a 2,000—but in kilometers (actually 2,702 kilometers, which was 1,679 miles of racing). It meant crisscrossing the peninsula six times to pick up the needed extra mileage.

Don and Ken Moss compete with one of the most iconic Broncos in the new millennium. Their wins and championships dotted the first 19 years of the 2000s. (Photo Courtesy Mike Ingalsbee)

The 2000s saw the resurgence of NORRA, and with it, the resurgence of the Ford Bronco. In NORRA rally-style Mexican 1000s, no Bronco has been more successful than that of Boyd Jaynes. He converted a dune runner Bronco into the most successful vintage racer to date. (Photo Courtesy Boyd Jaynes)

A total of 262 teams started the race in Ensenada for the marathon run down to Cabo San Lucas, which is the farthest southern point in Baja. The time limit that was necessary to be considered an official finisher was 72 hours. Just imagine: three days of racing and always being on the clock. The pre-race guess was that the overall winners would take about 32 hours to cover the distance.

The Class 3 racers figured they were in for about a 48- to 50-hour race, and they were not far off the mark. Of the 9 entries in the class, 5 finished. The winners were in a Kia Sportage after 49 hours and 17 minutes. The only Bronco to finish was a whole story. This is where it all started for the Moss Brothers Racing Team.

68 Hours

Some argue that starting your off-road racing career with a full peninsula run is a foolhardy idea. Starting with a full peninsula run that was more than 650 miles longer than usual is akin to learning to swim by jumping into the Pacific Ocean from the flight deck of an aircraft carrier. It is not that it cannot be done; there are just eas-ier ways to get your feet, umm, dusty.

Once in Ensenada for the start, the fledgling team agreed that it was there to finish. There were no delusions of grandeur of winning. The team would run its own race against the clock. The competition was all veterans with vehicles that were sorted out. That was not the case with our heroes.

The team picked up the Bronco in Chico, California, and drove it home early in 2000. The brothers worked on it right up until the start of the race. There wasn't even a chance to paint it, so it started with black paint and a white hood.

By mile 50, the brothers realized that the spring rates they chose were way too soft, so for the next 1,629 miles, they were bashing the bump stops. Later in the race at a BFGoodrich pit, they pumped air into the shocks, and that helped a little.

By mile 125, the stock rebuild on the C6 transmission, which started slipping early, was now not moving the truck anymore. The team fitted an aftermarket deep pan on the transmission, and it came with a conversion to a very fine Chrysler-type inlet filter. Don Moss realized the filter was plugging with debris from the failing internal parts, so they pulled the pan, cleaned the filter, and were able to continue.

By mile 300, the transmission was really getting bad even though they had pulled the deep pan and installed the stock pan with a coarse-screened Ford filter. The transmission ended up welding itself together internally, so it was basically a direct drive with a torque converter. There were no other gears and, more importantly, no reverse. There was a junkyard spare, but that was a last resort because no one wished to do an in-the-field change of the transmission.

At about mile 1,200, the pinion shaft in the rear axle twisted off. They had the stock spare axle, but it had the stock 3.50 gears in it while the front axle had 4.56 gears. They went ahead and swapped it and then used four-wheel-drive sparingly because the two axles would fight each other violently. If they needed a lower gear, they used low range.

After the rear axle change, they did not bother to hook up the rear drum brakes on the stock axle. Ken drove it for one section with only front brakes. Don drove it a section and then decided to stop and hook up the rear brakes after scaring themselves nearly to death too many times.

By about mile 1,400 near La Paz, the main rear leaf spring broke just behind the axle. Luckily, at a nearby BFGoodrich pit, they were able to locate scrap metal and weld a box around the broken leaf that held the rest of the way.

Not long after the welding was done, just south of La Paz, they took a sharp turn that they did not turn hard enough for. In the process of turning around among the cacti in the dark, the Bronco got up against a tree, and with no reverse, they could not back up. They ended up chopping the tree by hand enough that they could drive over it.

Another issue that dogged the team all race long was the tire choice. Don wanted to use 35-inch tires, but only 33-inch tires were available. This made for several unsuccessful attempts to get across some of Baja's silt beds. In the end, they finished after 67 hours, 44 minutes, and 50 seconds.

Summing it up, Don said, "It was ironic that two of the strongest drivetrain parts that we had chosen this specific vehicle for were what failed. It turned out that both needed just a little more refinement to survive in the racing world."

NORRA Rises from the Ashes

In 1972, NORRA put on its Mexican 1000 race not knowing it would be its last in Mexico. In 1973, the Mex-

By NORRAs second event, entries were coming in big numbers. From this humble relaunch, NORRA was off and running only to become a political casualty just five years later. (Photo Courtesy Larry Minor)

Brad Lovell started in rock-crawling competition and built a resume of six championships. From there, he went on to short-course racing and then Ultra 4 races. Desert racing followed with his vintage Bronco. Now, Lovell is a factory driver for the Ford Ultra 4 racing effort. (Photo Courtesy Trackside Photo)

ican government informed Ed Pearlman that he was no longer welcome to organize events in Mexico. The government formed the Baja Sports Committee (BSC) to put on the races. NORRA continued with its Parker, Arizona, Dam 500 for another year until Ed Pearlman pulled the plug.

The BSC was an absolute failure financially, and the Mexican government realized it was not going to be the cash cow that they thought it had been for Pearlman. In stepped Mickey Thompson at the urging of several Ensenada businesspeople with a whole new off-road racing sanctioning body to take over the two Baja events. While it was a big score for Mickey Thompson, it caused NORRA to lay dormant for three decades.

Mike Pearlman relaunched NORRA in much the same way as his father. Instead of an all-out race, Mike made his NORRA a rally-style event. That format is more friendly to vintage machines. (Photo Courtesy NORRA Photo Archives)

Mike Pearlman

Ed Pearlman has a son named Mike, who looked to carry on the NORRA name but in a completely different fashion than the 1967–1973 NORRA. Mike crafted a NORRA website and posted some of his old photos from the early events, hoping to sell a few and make a few bucks. As old racers do when they gather, even on the internet, racing kept coming up. Mike had not planned on putting on a full-scale race, but they wore him down.

In the 30 years since NORRA shut down, off-road racing became a profoundly serious business with an equally serious price tag for all but a few car classes. Mike remembered the fun those early events were and wanted to bring back that fun aspect as well as those cars from that early era. He just had to plan a way to make the rigors of off-road racing a little easier on the aged equipment.

The event ran in a rally format from Ensenada to Cabo over three days of stage and transit sections. Eventually, the format was lengthened to five days. This served a multitude of purposes. First, it kept the field of diverse off-road racers bunched together within a compact area.

Mike Pearlman was not looking for all the million-dollar teams to come to his event, although some did just for the fun of it. Mike knew there were hundreds of old off-road race cars and trucks, and it was time get these cars and trucks out into the desert again. It was also nice to get some of the people out there again who had been gone from the sport for way too long. Thus, it was not difficult to get Parnelli Jones to be the first grand marshal of the event and to compete, albeit in a Chevrolet Blazer.

It was a boon for the Bronco crowd, as bobtails now had a place to race and be competitive.

2010

At NORRA's the first reincarnation, five vintage Broncos came out to seize the desert once more. Three were the original squarebody Bronco, and two were 1980s vintage. It had been a long time since five Broncos had graced an entry list.

The inaugural event started in Mexicali, which was not the planned starting location. It was planned to start in Ensenada. Mother Nature unleashed a hurricane on the Baja Peninsula just before the planned September 2009 start, which delayed the event. The damage from the hurricane did a real number on the West Coast roads, so the NORRA team moved the start across the peninsula to Mexicali. It was an interesting move tinged with déjà vu because the last NORRA Mexican 1000 in 1972 started in Mexicali.

Chuck Atkinson came from Kerrville, Texas, to compete in the 2009 Mint 400. The team was credited with fourth place in Class 3. (Photo Courtesy Mike Ingalsbee)

NORRA was back, and it was not shy about advertising it. It was big news for not only old Bronco owners but also hundreds of vintage off-road racer owners. (Photo Courtesy NORRA Archives)

The Red Rocket took the inaugural win for the Mexican 1000 in rally format. Chris Wilson set a blistering pace in the class. (Photo Courtesy Chris Wilson)

The Kriegers took the first-place trophy in the first category, Vintage Open Truck. (Photo Courtesy Trackside Photo)

On Easter Sunday, just before the start date for the rally, a major earthquake rattled the Mexicali area, threatening to delay the event again. The hearty nature of the city of Mexicali and the equally hearty nature of off-road racers avoided damaged areas and were able to start the rally on time.

When the event finally was underway, 80 entries took the start in 12 different classes. Cars drove at legal speeds to the start of the first stage at the top of Laguna Salada, a dry lake bed that was well known to off-road racers from any era.

Because the different classes were categorized by year, the newer Bronco and the older Broncos ran in different classes. Chris Wilson topped the older Bronco squad with his 1968 racer in just under 17 hours of driving over

three days. That beat the newer Bronco winner, Chad Krieger III, by 2-1/2 hours. Chad Niernberg, who was also in a 1968 racer, took 20 hours to complete the stages and brought home second place.

It was a promising start for NORRA as an organizing body once again. For the Bronco, however, the word reached the Bronco community, and its members started to envision themselves bombing down the peninsula like their heroes. It didn't happen overnight, but as was said in *Field of Dreams*, "If you build it, they will come."

The 2011 NORRA Race

The next year, the entry list stayed static at 82 overall entries. However, bigger names were coming out to

The Moss Brothers and a Turkey

In 2010, at the full run down the Baja peninsula, the old adage that "you cannot make this stuff up" comes into play. When you are making your way 1,000 miles through the most untamed areas of Baja, the road is at times the least of your worries.

A bird in the hand is worth . . . a great bench-racing story. The following story from Baja is from Don Moss.

"A cow, deer, or donkey had been hit by something in the night and was lying on the side of the road," he said. "The turkey vultures are the most common and visible animal I know in Baja, and there was a large flock of them going to work on this carcass. They always keep an eye out for approaching vehicles and fly off when it gets close.

"Most of them make their departure at right angles to traffic, but one in particular on this day decided to make what we assume was a career-ending decision to make a southbound departure in front of a very rapidly motivating Bronco.

"As they say, 'It's not the speed that kills, but the *difference* in speeds between two objects.'

"This fellow hit the front of the truck, rolled back on the hood, through the opening that used to be for a windshield, and into my lap!

"I was already busy with the steering part of this whole adventure but did take one hand off the wheel and handed our new passenger to my codriver, Cliff.

"We all know the hot potato game, but out of the corner of my eye, this was by far the hottest version I had ever seen while Cliff pushed our friend back out through the windshield opening in the 90-mph breeze."

But Wait, There's More!

If you race long enough, the stories keep piling up. This one deserved to be told here because sometimes the right answer is the most obvious. This was Don Moss's first-ever off-road race, and his innocence and common sense combined to provide a unique solution less than a mile into the 1,679-mile event.

"This story from the first race we ran came from the first mile of the 2000 Baja race," Don said. "Crew Chief Dave was my codriver for that first race. Before the start, we debated on whether to start the race with the hubs locked. We were rookies. We eventually decided to lock them. The course started in downtown Ensenada, right in front of the Riviera Convention Center. It makes a couple turns on the pavement, dives into the wash, and starts heading out of town.

"Like always, the wash magically filled up with water the night before the race. We got to the first water hole under the first bridge, and there was a couch floating in the middle of the pond with a hundred locals wildly encouraging the racers to hit the water with as much speed as possible.

"I stopped dead in the course while I decided what to do because I could see stalled racers lining the course on the other side. It finally occurred to me that the fans were all standing on dry ground. So, I mashed the gas and headed straight for them as they were all diving out of the way, and we continued on.

"We don't even bother with hubs anymore; the axle shafts are permanently splined to the front wheels at all times now."

compete in the rally deemed by those who were there as "The Happiest Race on Earth." Six of those were Broncos in three different categories trying to reach the end of the second annual peninsula trek. Four of them did.

The route was a copy of the previous year, starting in Mexicali and ending in La Paz three days later. Overnight stops were in the scenic Bahia de Los Angeles (Bay of L.A.), Loreto, and finally La Paz for the big party.

Steve Krieger II took a second-place finish in his class. In the Vintage class, there were three 1960s Broncos entered, but only one finished; Tito Tinoco brought home the big win. In the final class, Marco Tavares Gonzalez took second place, besting Feliciano Aldrete, who finished in a distant four place.

By the second year of NORRA's return, the Bronco's numbers increased. It set the stage for a bigger expansion over the next several years. (Photo Courtesy Trackside Photo)

See the windshield opening on the Moss brothers' Bronco? Do you think a full-grown turkey vulture can fit through there? Yes. Yes, it can. (Photo Courtesy Mike Ingalsbee)

Creative lines are a big part of off-road racing. Sometimes Mother Nature dictates an unorthodox racing line, and other times it is human inspired. (Photo Courtesy Moss Brothers Racing)

2012 NORRA Race

The amount of entries jumped to 99 for third annual Mexican 1000. The word was now firmly out, and the rally garnered a new title sponsor, General Tire. Eight Vintage Broncos came out for the party.

The year 2012 had some changes in store for the entire field. Still a three-day event, the course again started in Mexicali, but the finish moved down to the southern tip of the peninsula at San Jose del Cabo. Overnight stops were still in Bahia de Los Angeles and Loreto. Suddenly, Mike Pearlman and staff had a real happening on their hands. There was also an overhaul of the vehicle classes that further divided them by era and technology.

Michael Jakobson ran his bright orange No. 69 Bronco in the Vintage Open Truck class and took the last podium spot with a third-place finish. As the only Bronco entered in the six entry classes, it represented Blue Oval fans well.

Another podium finish went to Dean Wayman in the Vintage Open Truck with leaf springs class. Another orange Bronco, this time a late-1970s bodystyle with a half-cab look, took third against stiff competition.

The rest of the Broncos were entered in the 1997-and-earlier, 108-inch-wheelbase, 4x4 class (known as the VJ class). There was a lone flat-fender Willys Jeep versus six Broncos. It hardly seems fair.

The Devil Horse Cometh

After a few attempts, the Devil Horse Motorsports team of Boyd Jaynes scored its first victory at this event. Jaynes had one NORRA 1000 under his belt, but it did not work out well. In 2012, Jaynes teamed with Brian Godfrey, who was an off-road navigator with an excellent reputation and years of experience managing and navigating in trophy trucks. The pair tore up the peninsula with a 16-1/2-hour time after 3 days in the desert. This was not their last trip home with the big trophy.

Tino Tinoco, last year's winner, came home third in his class followed within 25 minutes of Chris Wilson and Sol Saltzmann, and Todd Zuercher took sixth place a few hours behind. Jason Elmblad was the seventh and final finisher in the class. That pesky Jeep weaseled its way into second place.

2013 NORRA Race

The rally really took off in 2013 with 148 entries, seven of which were Broncos. Six of those were pre-1977 Vintage class rigs. Again, in search of the perfect formula, the classes were juggled, sending most of the original Broncos into a pre-1977 Short-Wheelbase class.

James Gibbons in his 1990s Bronco took the win in the Evolution Division for short-wheelbase 4x4 vehicles.

Dean Wayman took advantage of the NORRA rules to build his Bronco with non-factory suspension, run in the Vintage Open Truck category, and perform well. (Photo Courtesy Trackside Photo)

Like a specter coming out of the foggy night, Cabello del Diablo *came looking for NORRA wins. (Photo Courtesy Boyd Jaynes)*

Andrew Norton and Todd Zuercher have been fixtures in the NORRA races almost since the beginning. Their first year together was in 2012, and they netted a top-five finish for their efforts. (Photo Courtesy Trackside Photo)

Carlos Tavares took second in the Evolution Short-Wheelbase 4x4 class for the 2013 edition. (Photo Courtesy Trackside Photo)

the pre-1977 Short-Wheelbase class, where three entries (all Broncos) battled for the win. The Jeeps must have been scared to come out.

Caballo Del Diablo means "horse of the devil" in Spanish, and it also happens to be the name of one of baddest Broncos on the NORRA entry list. World-renowned photographer Boyd Jaynes and Brian Godfrey laid waste to the field for the second year in a row in their 1968 Bronco. Chris Sullivan took the second spot, and Andrew Norton and Todd Zuercher filled the final podium spot in third.

In the Vintage division, Tom Webber in an early 1980s Bronco did not make it to the finish line with his Vintage Open Truck entry. Chris Wilson, in the same class, had issues and never made it to the start of the event. Carlos Tavares brought back out his later-model Bronco and took second in the Short-Wheelbase 1978-and-newer class.

Most of the action for vintage Bronco lovers was in

2014 NORRA Race

In 2014, a dozen vintage Ford Broncos came out to play. Starting in Ensenada, entries were headed south, crisscrossing the peninsula to Cabo four days later. The NORRA races were catching on with all types of off-road racers, new, old, legendary, and multigenerational. Established teams were rolling out long mothballed chassis. Old race Broncos were becoming highly prized.

After NORRA returned, other racing organizations followed with their own vintage classes. This Bronco, run by Tim and Brian Morris, is in the prestigious 2015 Mint 400 against vehicles from its own era. (Photo Courtesy Mike Ingalsbee)

This time, it was a podium spot for Norton and Zuercher against the other pre-1977 bobtails. (Photo Courtesy Track-side Photo)

Don Hatch took the big win in 2014, beating Norton and Jaynes who took second and third respectively. (Photo Courtesy Trackside Photo)

Long neglected in a wrecking yard in Barstow, California, the Pike family found an original Stroppe Bronco. They purchased it with the idea of donating it to Rod Hall, who was reestablishing the Off-Road Motorsports Hall of Fame. (Photo Courtesy Todd Zuercher)

Carlos Tavares was back with his 108-inch-wheelbase 4x4 and took second in class with a steady drive. Don Hatch took the pre-1977 class ahead of Andrew Norton by 2½ hours. Boyd Jaynes with special guest Brad Lovell brought home third after overcoming a broken driveline yolk and a broken transfer-case shifter.

It was a rough event for the Bronco field, as only 6 of the 12 starters finished the rally. That is the nature of Baja; it can be beautiful and treacherous all at the same time. At least it is scenic when you are broken in the desert.

The 2015 NORRA Race

In 2015, 10 Broncos came, and 8 saw the finish in Cabo. A total of 95 cars and trucks entered the rally.

The Return of Rod Hall

For the first time in 39 years, Rod Hall entered in a verified Bill Stroppe–built Ford Bronco. The story goes that longtime Bronco racers Gale and Matt Pike were in Barstow, California, checking out a long-neglected old

In its heyday, the Barstow Bronco flew the Stroppe team colors and was campaigned by two business owners out of Barstow, California. (Photo Courtesy MotorTrend and Petersen Museum Archive)

Newly restored and prepped, Rod Hall and his granddaughter Shelby returned to competing in a Bronco. The return was made sweeter by a second-place finish. (Photo Courtesy Trackside Photo)

race Bronco at a wrecking yard. It took several trips to bargain with the owner before he agreed to sell it.

It was verified to be a Bronco that Stroppe sold in the mid-1970s and was re-named the *Barstow Bronco* by Bob Jackson, a pharmacist, and his partner Myron Croel, who owned a water softener dealership in Barstow, California. The Bronco ran many races through the rest of the decade until 1980, when Jackson retired it and stored it at a wrecking yard.

There it sat for 20 years slowly returning to the earth when it was rescued from the relentless Mojave Desert. It was partially restored by Willie Stroppe and sat proudly in the Off-Road Motorsports Hall of Fame in Reno until Rod Hall's granddaughter Shelby talked Rod into entering it in this event.

On to Cabo

In the Vintage Open Truck class, Chris Wilson brought home a fifth place. Don Hatch in the Eversen Bronco was entered in the Ultra 4x4 class, and he brought home the win with his classic Bronco. All the other Broncos were entered in the pre-1978 108-inch-wheelbase class.

Boyd Jaynes and Brian Godfrey just seemed to have this NORRA thing down pat. The *Caballo Del Diablo* Bronco battled all the way down the Baja peninsula with the legend Rod Hall. In the end, old age and treachery did not win out over youth and skill, but it was close. Boyd Jaynes recalled, "For sure, racing in the same event as Rod was a thrill and surreal at the same time. As a

part-time amateur racer, to be lined up against a legend like Rod isn't something common in other formulas of motorsport. I feel fortunate to have shared a racecourse with him and to shake his hand at the finish line."

Andrew Norton and Todd Zuercher grabbed the final podium spot in their original Stroppe Bronco. Norton and Zuercher were brought together by a common love of the Bronco, in particular Stroppe-prepared Broncos. They spent years researching and plotting to purchase just such a historical specimen. A Bronco that was outfitted for sand-dune driving came on their radar. It was

The Everson Bronco has been a fixture at NORRA events for a long time. In 2015, with Don Hatch driving, he won the Ultra 4x4 class at the NORRA 1000.

Winning a straight-up duel with the legendary Rod Hall ranks right up there for Boyd Jaynes in his accomplishments. He and Brian Godfrey had a tough, close battle with Hall all the way down the peninsula. (Photo Courtesy Boyd Jaynes)

George Herman took third place in the hotly contested 2015 edition of the NORRA 1000. The Bronco George runs does double duty by also competing at King of the Hammers rock-crawling events. (Photo Courtesy Trackside Photo)

perfect: the cage was right, the engine bay was right, and the signature rocker-mounted exhaust was right. They had their bounty.

Over the next few years, the Bronco was refitted as a desert racer and returned as close as possible to the same condition it was in rolling out of Stroppe's shop.

Tim Mason, George Herman, and Scott Barnes picked up the remaining three positions in class. If you ask people who run these NORRA rally events, it truly is not all about where you finish but the adventures you have and the friends you make. The Bronco group is one of, if not *the* tightest-knit groups out there.

The 2016 NORRA Race

Things were exploding for Mike Pearlman, as 126 entries flooded his office on four wheels alone. Another 31 entered on two wheels. The event was becoming what every vintage racer hoped for: a fast-moving parade of legends moving southbound down the peninsula.

The Bronco contingent shrunk a little: only eight entered, and seven saw the finish line in Cabo. The Broncos might be old, but they are darned dependable. Another factor is the care that each one receives before, during, and after the event. Every one of the entries has a passion for the Ford Bronco and for the NORRA races.

Remember, It Is an Adventure

George Herman was the only Bronco that did not make the finish; his Bronco was out of the event after three of the nine stages. George ran a rock-crawler-style 1971 Ford Bronco that also saw double duty at the King of the Hammers events.

This was George's second NORRA race, and he remembered it well.

"About 180 miles into Day 1, when it was Ensenada to Bahia de Los Angeles, super long and tough, we were going way too fast and pushing too hard, and we broke an upper rear four-link," George said. "We got some help from locals, who helped by pushing my Bronco with his truck so that we were sitting over the rear axle again instead of having it two feet out to the driver's side. [We] got it centered, and then with some ratchet-strap magic, we made it another 80 miles to the highway where my all-volunteer crew was waiting with my trusty Miller Matic MIG welder and generator. [We] spent a couple hours getting it welded up to where the plan was to get to Bahia de Los Angeles and then really fix it."

After a nine-hour overnight fix and a quick breakfast, the team made its way to the start line for the days driving to Loreto.

"Other teams were pretty amazed at our determination and were super supportive," George continued. "We were the last to leave Bahia, but things were going well. We passed three other teams, got to our first team 5150 checkpoint and all the repairs looked good. We topped off the tanks and told the team we would see them after the silt beds.

"Well, we did see them, but not how we thought. The silt was really bad in 2016, and we were doing good about a half mile or less from getting through them and had now passed about 13 teams when we lost power, and my Bronco quit."

The 5150 crew retrieved the stricken Bronco with the help of the event sweep crew. While sitting out in the silt bed, George looked into why it just quit and found the answer. A broken air-cleaner plate and threaded rod allowed the engine to ingest about a cup of Baja's finest silt. The crew worked for a day on trying to resurrect the engine but to no avail. George's brother Paul was still running with his Bronco, so the team's attention turned to getting him to the finish.

If Baja racing was easy, anyone could do it. Even after all that trouble, the 5150 crew took the Bronco home, stripped it down to the frame and roll cage, and made plans to skip 2017 and return for 2018.

Meanwhile, in the Land of the Running

The course was the same as in 2015, which was five days and featured a total of nine stages. Overnight stops included Bahia de Los Angeles, Loreto, La Paz, and finishing in San Jose del Cabo.

Chris Wilson was back in his tricked-out 1966 Bronco fighting with the Vintage Open Trucks and again nailed

Precision driving and meticulous preparation has given Chris Wilson a lengthy resume of wins and high finishes. His 1966 Red Rocket Bronco has been upgraded with extended trailing arms and coilover suspension. (Photo Courtesy Chris Wilson)

Because it is the "Happiest Race on Earth," why not make special Mariachi driving suits? Boyd Jaynes and Brian Godfrey celebrate another win with the Devil Horse. (Photo Courtesy Boyd Jaynes)

Another podium finish awaited Norton and Zuercher after a herculean effort by the crew after a problematic first day. A dedicated crew can be the difference. (Photo Courtesy Trackside Photo)

a fourth-place finish in the competitive class. Wilson ran this class because he opted to change out the typical leaf spring rear suspension and go with a coilover setup and trailing arms. It obviously worked well because his Bronco was always competitive.

This was the year that NORRA rearranged how the classes worked, and it split up the Bronco entries into Vintage and Pioneer categories. The Pioneer category was for original Stroppe Broncos and had stipulations on tire size (33-inch maximum diameter) and shock absorbers (2 inch-diameter and no bypass or coilovers). The Vintage category trucks were allowed 35-inch tires and 2-1/2-inch-diameter shocks. Each class featured three Broncos.

Andrew Norton and Todd Zuercher finished third in Pioneer class. The team was plagued with flat tires, including double flat tires late at night on the first day. A bent track bar forced the team to stop on Mexico's Highway 1 and use a sledgehammer to straighten the bent piece. Hammered out somewhat straight, the damaged part cost the team time all the next day. Meanwhile, a crew member put in the drive of legends. He headed all the way back to Phoenix, Arizona, down two cylinders in his chase truck to swap trucks, get a new track bar, and then meet the team in Loreto to change the bad one.

Rod and Shelby Hall were back in the class, running the entire event without any penalty points over the five days, which was something that only one other team could say in the class. The 79-year-old made his 50th 1,000-mile race in Baja with this event. For their efforts, Rod and Shelby finished second place in their class.

Boyd Jaynes and Brian God-frey were at it again with the *Devil Horse* Bronco. This was the year that the pair unveiled a new driving suit decorated to look like members of a Mariachi band. The new driving suits were, quite possibly, the hit of the entire event.

The 1968 Bronco, immaculately prepared by the duo, was on point once again but not without some issues along the way, which was not unusual for a Baja rally. On the stage headed into Loreto, the front clip actually broke off the frame. The quick-thinking crew used ratchet straps that were stowed in the Bronco to reattach the clip. A secondary issue was overheating from the now-misaligned front clip. Luckily, it was not terminal, and they soldiered on.

It was the final day (the run from La Paz to San Jose del Cabo) when it almost all went wrong, Boyd Jaynes recalled.

"On the last day, last stage, 10 miles from the finish, we had a 40-plus-minute lead if I remember correctly, and we slid the Bronco into a tree, hitting the rear wheel and tire square on the face," he said. "The damage was a flat tire, bent rim, and a bent rear-end housing and U-bolts. We limped it in, hoping the bearings on the axle wouldn't smoke and seize. All of our competitors passed us while we changed the wheel, but we still managed to finish in time to maintain our lead and win the class."

Boyd Jaynes explained that the team did not want to embarrass the driver at this point. He just wanted to let everyone know it was not him.

In the Vintage Short-Wheelbase class, Roger and Brad Lovell took the win in a big way with three full hours in hand over the second-place finisher Randy Ludwig in his 1966 Bronco. The Lovells have raced in all types of off-road events from the King of Hammers races to running the desert in a spec truck (one step down from a trophy truck), and they honor their father by running vintage events in their 1968 Bronco.

The 2017 NORRA Race

By now, the NORRA organizers had their format down to a science. The five-day format was working well for all the teams. Mike Pearlman and his crew successfully opened a new pathway for vintage Broncos to storm

If you win enough races and present a clean racer, you too can be on display at the prestigious SEMA Show in Las Vegas. Lovell's win at the 2015 NORRA 1000 was one of those wins.

the deserts again. The Mint 400 and Best in the Desert racing series followed suit and now have Vintage classes in place as well.

This year saw the Bronco entries drop to just eight, which was spread over four classes. It seemed odd to have that many classes for the Broncos to fit into. However, when you consider the wide array of changes it went through from 1965–1996, there is a large performance envelope. Then, consider the modifications available in just suspension alone, including omitting the leaf springs and installing a coilover system. The need for the classes becomes clear.

The Bronco world was already aflutter because in January 2017 at the North American Auto Show, Ford officially announced the reintroduction of the Bronco after a 25-year hiatus of the brand. Intended for model-year 2021, the new Bronco would be a throwback in styling to the original so much so that the design chief, a proud owner of a 1976 Bronco, offered the use of his to be scanned digitally for the project.

Meanwhile, back in Baja California, some vintage Detroit iron was about to make the annual trek to the southern tip of the peninsula. A total of 146 four-wheel entries competed. The event was highlighted by Baja veteran Cameron Steele taking the win overall in his trophy truck. I mentioned this because in 2019 at the 52nd-annual 1,000-mile race, it was Steele's Desert Assassin team that built and ran the Bronco R program, which featured Shelby Hall as one of the drivers.

Roger and Brad Lovell repeated as the Vintage Short-Wheelbase 4x4 champions, conquering the course in 19 hours and 46 minutes once again over "Rapido"

Randy Ludwig by 1 hour and 10 minutes.

Notching yet another class win in the *Caballo Del Diablo* with Mariachi suits gleaming in the Baja sun was Boyd Jaynes and Brian Godfrey. Aside from a leaking oil cooler that was quickly patched, the Mariachis had a good run in the American Racing Wheel Bronco.

Dean Wayman in his 1978 Bronco took second place in the Legend Truck class. It was, at the very least, an all-Ford affair as he was beaten by Baja veteran Mark Stahl in an ex-Ivan Stewart F-Series pickup.

Jacob Davies ran a 1974 Bronco to the win in the Challenger 4x4 class, topping Rick "Hurricane" Johnson's 1969 Bronco.

The 2018 NORRA Race

For several years, the question among the Pioneer Bronco teams has been, "How to you stop the *Caballo Del Diablo*?"

Some muse that the flashy driving suits are just too intimidating, and there could be some truth to that. More than likely, it is immaculate preparation and their service crewman, Jose, who knows every road in Mexico, dirt or otherwise.

The year 2018 was not without its challenges for the Devil Horse crew. On Day 1, they arrived in San Felipe for the overnight stop with a broken exhaust that melted a motor mount. Day 2 was hot, and the crew added an extra fan to help keep things cool, but the engine saw 240°F a few times. Day 3 was cooler, thankfully, but there was deep silt to contend with, and the *Devil Horse* got stuck, requiring a tow from a friendly competitor. Day 4 was another hot day that ended with yet another broken motor mount. Luckily, the home stretch from La Paz to Cabo was free of drama, cementing their sixth class win.

It was another runner-up spot for the Bronco historians Andrew Norton and Todd Zuercher in their original Stroppe Bronco.

The Vintage Open Truck 4x4 class had a pair of Broncos. A bright yellow 1995 Bronco that was entered by Dave Moore brought home a fine third place in its class. Don Hatch in the 1966 Eversen Bronco was close behind in fourth place.

In the Vintage Short-Wheelbase 4x4 class was where the bulk of the Bronco roamed to. It was a repeat for Roger and Brad Lovell with a win by nine hours. Maybe repeat was too light of a term. It was a statement win. George Herman was second in class and was followed by Paul Herman in third.

Jacob Davies took the win in Challenger 4x4 over a Chevrolet truck to uphold the honor of the Blue Oval.

The 2019 NORRA Race

The largest entry of Ford Broncos to date gathered in Ensenada for the 2019 Mexican 1000 rally when 14 teams showed up. A slew of Broncos like that had not been seen in off-road racing since the days of Stroppe.

The event proved to be difficult with hot temperatures predicted along most of the route, and the silt was a factor with the dry winter that Baja had experienced. Off-road racing is not supposed to be easy, and while the NORRA group goes out of its way to make sure the vintage machinery can handle the demands, without some challenge, it would be a hollow victory at the finish.

The Bronco contingent was spread over seven classes that represented every era of the Bronco production period. From nearly stock to modified with the most modern of suspension technology, there was something for every fan of the Bronco.

In the Evolution pre-run truck category, David Jones was pitted against a field of seven other trucks. He brought home a third place in class in his 1996 model. In Vintage Open Truck 4x4 category, the 1966 Eversen Bronco of Don Hatch was able to come away with a third-place finish in class against a tough field. Scott Ulrich was fourth in his 1989 Bronco.

In the Vintage Open Truck with Rear Leaf Springs class, Dean Wayman was the fourth-place finisher. Jared Adame did not finish the event. The Vintage Open Truck class saw Bert Tjeenk take his modified 1983 Bronco to a sixth-place finish against a stacked field.

The Challenger 4x4 class saw two Broncos beat up on a lone Chevy Blazer to take first and second. Mark Van Leeuwarden in a 1983 Bronco ran a clean rally and beat out Baja Sur native Andrea Tomba in his 1987 Bronco. The Legend 4x4 class had two entries, and it was a Bronco versus Nissan pickup match-up. "Rapido" Randy Ludwig easily vanquished the Nissan by 4-1/2 hours to take yet another class win.

The Pioneer 4x4 class was the one that most of the Bronco enthusiasts watch because it was where the Stroppe-era Broncos ran. One of those was the beautiful 1972 model painted in tribute to *Big Oly* run by Chris Greenwood.

Andrea Tomba brought home second place in the Challenger 4x4 class. Tomba, a resident of Baja Sur, is a respected racer from the southern end of the peninsula. (Photo Courtesy Trackside Photo)

Bert Tjeenk spent some time mired in the sand and silt, which resulted in a sixth-place finish. However, he did finish, and that in and of itself is a victory in NORRA competition. (Photo Courtesy Trackside Photo)

Welcome to Baja, Rookie!

This was Chris's first desert race ever. Things started well the first few days, but they hit trouble at the end of day three. Chris remembered the incident.

"Unfortunately, about 5 miles from Comondú, we ended up going over a rise, and the steering got light," he said. "[I] probably overcorrected, and by the time we were steerable again, the Bronco was headed for a pile of rocks. The steering linkage and right front tire hit first, [and the] front bumper next. The Bronco pitched up on its nose and leaned over, landing on its side.

"We made sure the kill switch was off, hit the Stella warning button, and climbed out into the cactus patch we landed in—that crap goes right through boots. My codriver and I were okay, and [the vehicle was] not leaking fuel. As a matter of fact, we were not leaking anything, unbelievably."

A long night ensued, waiting for the chase crew and making the repairs they could on their own. Other teams stopped to make sure they had water and food. That was the best part of racing in Baja: the camaraderie. There was no sleep, lots of driving and wrenching, and determination to get to La Paz to start the penultimate day.

In the stage to La Paz, an innocent-looking mesquite tree branch entered past the brush guard, and the hearty branch stopped the fan blades and threw the fan belt, which damaged the radiator. Using one bottle of aluminum shavings and all the water they could beg or borrow,

and it sealed! Stopping at every opportunity for water, they pressed on through deep silt, seemingly endless rocky sections, and exhaustion. Just 18 miles from La Paz, the engine suffered irreparable damage. The final day, the team pushed the Bronco across the start line, onto the trailer, and headed for Cabo to celebrate with family and friends.

I added this story to highlight the fact that racing in the desert, especially in Baja California, is tough not only for new teams but also the experienced teams.

Lets get back to the Pioneer 4x4 class. Those merry Mariachis, the Caballo Del Diablo team, were unstoppable in pursuit of its seventh class win in nine attempts. Boyd Jaynes and Brian Godfrey rolled into Cabo as champions once again. Andrew Norton and Todd Zuercher took the second spot, finally enjoying a clean run down the peninsula. After years of accidents (some unavoidable and some self-inflicted) or mechanical breakdowns that took precious hours to repair, they were safely in Cabo without drama.

NORRA Takes a Break for the Worldwide Pandemic

The 2020 worldwide pandemic took away two attempts to run the Mexican 1000. Pearlman and his crew are pressing on with both of the 2021 events. The success of building a place for vintage racers gives NORRA a bright future.

The pandemic of 2020 had an adverse effect on NORRA's plan to run events that year. You could say the sun set on vintage off-road racing in 2020. (Photo Courtesy Mike Ingalsbee)

CHAPTER 8

THE NEXT-GENERATION
BRONCO RETURNS TO B A J A

Ford Motor Company and the United Auto Workers Union came together in 2016 to discuss reviving the Bronco nameplate. At the end of those meetings, it was decided that the Bronco would return as a midsized SUV. The Focus and C-Max production lines would move to Mexico, and the Michigan plant in Wayne (situated between Detroit and Ann Arbor) would retool for the new Ranger and Bronco.

Soon after those meetings, at the 2017 North American International Auto Show, the plan was revealed to bring back the Bronco in five years for the 2021 model year.

Prototypes were rolled out from time to time. Then, there was suddenly the odd spy picture in the media. This was really going to happen. The photos showed without a doubt that the body was styled after the first-generation Bronco with some obvious improvements such as aerodynamics. The design chief even volunteered his own

Previously, it worked well using the Bronco in off-road motorsports to show its toughness and versatility. Photos such as this from the 1968 National Four-Wheel Drive Grand Prix were used by various sponsors in marketing their products. As it was in the 1960s, so it is in the 2020s.
(Photo Courtesy Larry Minor)

Carrying the silhouette and drivetrain of its production brethren, the Bronco R was designed for Baja. Upgraded suspension, added safety equipment, and bigger wheels and tires are all that separate the two. (Photo Courtesy Justin W. Coffee)

1976 Bronco to be digitized for reference during the design process.

It Worked Before

If you go back to the beginning of the Bronco, Ford debuted the Bronco as a racer. In that instance, Bill Stroppe had time to build the vehicles and learn about the new Bronco. In 1965, there were simple mud races and club events where Stroppe was running the Bronco. Soon, proper desert racing evolved from these events, and the early Riverside Grand Prix short-course races ushered in the era of the Bronco in off-road competition.

Flash forward to June 2019. At the Ford Skunkworks, a team from Ford Performance started planning an assault on the Baja 1000 that was slated to start on November 17 of that same year. This is an extremely ambitious timetable for an assault on Baja, even for a team with the weight of the Ford Motor Company behind it.

The project was called the Bronco R Prototype, and being that off-road racing is so very specialized, experts were utilized to oversee the building of the project through from start to finish.

Geiser Brothers Design & Development was to build the truck. Cameron Steele and his Desert Assassins team know the Baja Peninsula from top to bottom, Pacific Ocean to the Gulf of California, better than possibly any other team and consulted on the build, put together a team of drivers, and executed the race strategy and pit stops.

The whole project was not only to introduce the new Bronco R Prototype, but to commemorate the epic and never repeated overall Mexican 1000 win by Larry Minor and Rod Hall in a four-wheel-drive vehicle.

The Bronco R

From the beginning, Ford mandated that the engine be stock (a 2.7L EcoBoost V-6) as well as the flappy paddle–actuated automatic transmission, transfer case, and front differential. The computer program remained so stock that the 105-mph speed limiter was left in place. The engine package boasted 335 hp and an impressive 380 ft-lbs of torque.

The prototype also had to be built off the Ford T6 body-on-frame chassis with some modifications for safety

The rear view of the Bronco R gives away some of its race breeding. Extensive roll cage work and oversized spare tires are visible as the Bronco R heads deeper into the wilds of the peninsula. (Photo Courtesy Justin W. Coffee)

equipment and suspension mounting. To ensure a finish in the race, some non-Ford parts were incorporated into the stock drivetrain. First was changing the rear differential to handle the expected 24 to 30 hours of constant pounding. Second was a racing exhaust system that was rerouted for maximum ground clearance.

The chassis featured four-wheel independent suspension dampened by custom-built Fox shocks that allowed 14 inches of wheel travel in the front and 18 inches in the rear built off a factory-based five-link system. Off-road racing tires from BFGoodrich that were 37 inches tall were mounted on special 17-inch beadlock wheels to handle the rigors of racing over every kind of terrain imaginable. A 70-gallon fuel cell gave the Bronco R a range of about 300 miles in race conditions.

The whole chassis was topped with a composite body that included a clamshell hood and roof.

The "R" in the letters on the grille is in red. This is exclusive to the prototype and denotes its special race breeding. (Photo Courtesy Justin W. Coffee)

The Race Before the Race

This accelerated timeline from the drawing board to actually starting the race was going to need maximum cooperation from every person involved. There are teams that work all year on a plan for this race, and that is with a vehicle already built and tested. However, for something like this, Ford had assembled the best people possible to make it a reality. Since the Desert Assassins had already been planning a multi-vehicle assault on the race, adding one more was not difficult. The real issue was getting the Bronco R built quickly and efficiently enough to allow for maximum testing before the race.

The race just to get to the starting line was a tough enough task, but there was another race as well. An updated reproduction of the famous *Baja Boot* was going to be entered in the same class as the Bronco R. This updated version of the famous original one driven and owned by Hollywood actor Steve McQueen was a prototype SUV like the Bronco R.

Cameron Glickenhaus, a builder of supercars, was behind the project. Glickenhaus purchased the original *Boot* at an auction. He was inspired to replicate it, update it, and offer it as a limited-production off-road supercar. Powered by a supercharged 6.2L C7 Corvette engine, the powerplant made 650 hp, which was nearly twice that of the Bronco. This, however, is off-road racing, and it takes a lot more than a big engine to win a race.

Shelby Hall was already a known talent in off-road racing having run with her grandfather in several NORRA 1000 events. She was coached by him as well. It made perfect sense to have her involved in the Bronco R Project from the start. (Photo Courtesy Kurt Scherbaum/The Lensman Photography)

The Drivers

This is the lineup that Ford and the Desert Assassins agreed upon to wheel the Bronco R. It is a powerful group of accomplished off-road racers.

Shelby Hall

If the name sounds familiar, it is because Shelby is the granddaughter of Rod Hall. Shelby is an accomplished racer in her own right, and she started navigating for her grandfather in 2012. After some time watching how to do it right (one race), Rod had her start to drive at the 2012 Baja 1000.

Shelby grew up off-road, working as the event director at Rod Hall Drive and as the administrator of the Off-Road Motorsports Hall of Fame. Already a veteran of quite a few off-road races in a utility terrain vehicle (UTV), she is considered an up-and-coming star in the sport.

In March 2019, three executives from Ford traveled to Reno, Nevada, to meet with Rod Hall. They came equipped with a virtual-reality unit to show the wheelchair-bound Hall the new Bronco and how they planned to pay homage to him when they debuted it to the public in October. Rod was thrilled with the presentation. Also present was his wife, Donna, and Shelby. After the presentation, Shelby took the time to write to Ford thanking them for involving her grandfather. Not long after, on June 14, Rod passed away.

Soon after that, an invitation arrived from Ford asking Shelby to travel to Detroit for a tour of Ford to record a message and have some meetings. It was at those meetings that Shelby was introduced to the Bronco R program and asked to drive part of the Baja 1000.

Cameron Steele

Mark Steele, Cameron (Cam) Steele's father, began racing off-road in 1971, and he made it a family-run team in limited-class race cars and Baja Bugs until the 1990s. His passion transferred to Cam, where it bloomed into a beautiful obsession.

Cam's accomplishments both in and out of a race car could fill a book this size. Just to hit on some high points, he is an overall winner of the 1,000-mile race in Baja, a class champion, member of the Off-Road Motorsports Hall of Fame, television personality, adventure travel tour guide, founder of the Desert Assassins off-road team, and Baja California's biggest promoter.

Although a listed driver in the Bronco R, Steele had his trophy truck ride to handle first, and he was not expected to drive the Bronco R in competition. However, in case something happened with his first obliga-tion, he wanted to be able to help if he could. Steering wheel in hand or not, this project could not have happened without him.

Johnny Campbell

There is no one like Johnny Campbell in off-road racing on two wheels. He has 11 overall wins in the 1,000-mile race in Baja as a rider and another six running the team. In 2001, he was the first privateer team finisher at the grueling Dakar Rally and earned an impressive eighth place overall. He has wins in every major off-road event and even took the navigator seat next to Robby Gordon in the Dakar Rally the year they won three stages.

Campbell's name is featured on accessories and parts for motorcycles. In building his own personal dynasty, Campbell is always looking to help groom the next generation of off-road racers and make sure they are trained on his team.

The years eventually catch up to motorcycle riders, and they eventually either manage a motorcycle team or convert to racing on four wheels. A motorcycle champion's innate ability to avoid obstacles at high speeds and drive with precision makes them sought after pilots when their time on two wheels is done.

Curt LeDuc

When Curt LeDuc was inducted into the Off-Road Motorsports Hall of Fame in 2015, he was described as "a self-made, grassroots champion, who has encompassed his love for the sport into a way of life."

Originally from Massachusetts, LeDuc started racing short-course off-road events in the East and Midwest. The Short-Course Off-Road Drivers Association (SODA) events in Crandon, Wisconsin, gave LeDuc his first championships in 1994 and 1996. By 1997, LeDuc was racing the desert-series events, running a factory team for Jeep with great success.

His talent as a designer, builder, and driver of off-road vehicles took him from the Midwest to Pikes Peak, Baja, and several campaigns in the world-famous Paris-Dakar Rally.

Curt is the namesake of his twice-yearly off-road swap meet in Southern California, which is a huge off-road happening.

Testing

Once the initial build was done at the Geiser Brothers shop in Phoenix, Arizona, the Bronco R was ready for the Desert Assassins to start testing. Time was getting short so the logical thing to do was to test around the Geiser Brothers shop in Arizona.

Still wearing some Nevada dust after a photo and testing session, the Bronco R Prototype was on display. Here it is at the tribute to Rod Hall at the 2019 SEMA Show in Las Vegas.

The accelerated test schedule showed some fixes that needed to happen under desert sky instead of in elaborate shops. Some wiring and fuse issues became apparent and were corrected. Then, some cooling issues necessitated some reengineering to increase airflow through the radiator. By the end of just shy of 1,000 miles of testing, the Desert Assassins felt confident in the machine and headed for Ensenada for technical inspection and pre-race festivities.

Whether the Weather

In the days leading up to the race, the Baja peninsula received an unusually large amount of rain. In fact, there was so much rain that many parts of the racecourse resembled Louisiana swampland. The organizers did everything they could to ensure the racecourse was passable, but time was not on their side. In a rare but not unprecedented decision, the organizers delayed the start of the race 24 hours. The rain subsided, which gave the racecourse a chance to drain and time for road crews to do damage control.

Much of the racecourse that teams spent weeks pre-running was now changed to a muddy mess that did not resemble what the racers pre-ran.

The Race Is On

After the 24-hour delay, the Bronco R was facing a truly unknown situation. How bad was the racecourse? How much damage would the faster classes do to the muddy roads before the Bronco R got to that point? Was the Bronco R tested thoroughly enough to finish the race? There were so many questions.

Word came back to the start about thick mud being responsible for getting faster vehicles stuck in precarious positions. They were blocking the road and causing massive backups. The Bronco R crew hoped that it would be cleared by the time they got to that point.

On Saturday, November 23, at the Riviera Cultural Center, where the race traditionally has a ceremonial start, it was finally time for the new Bronco R to get on its way. The Bronco R's 335 hp pushed it off the start line and into the famous wash leading out of Ensenada, which was lined with spectators to watch the entries fly off some man-made jumps before the real desert driving started.

It was not long into the race when the crew noticed that the Bronco R was sitting too low for the new conditions brought on by the extreme weather. The front end was hitting the ground in places where it should not have. This caused the drivers to slow down to try and save the truck and get to the finish. To finish was the goal. Even though there was competition within the class, Ford Motor Company just wanted the finish.

The Amazing Matomi Wash

Even though the pace was slowed, the team was running close to its ideal schedule coming off the Pacific coast and heading inland toward the mountains and the famous Mike's Sky Rancho. Out of the mountains now, the Bronco R was doing okay as it screamed across the Diablo Dry Lake bed, but ahead was the infamous Matomi Wash.

Finally doing what it was built for, the Bronco R corners hard on a lonely Baja dirt road. (Photo Courtesy Justin W. Coffee)

Matomi is a challenge to every vehicle in the race from motorcycle to trophy truck to those bone-stock VW Bugs that everyone cheers on. The course being "boulder strewn" is an understatement. Often, the rocks block your path, and you need to find a way around or over. Hard-core volunteers take their own 4x4 trucks in there with tow straps at the ready to help racers. However, the Bronco R would have an unusual (even for Baja) occurrence.

Making its way, the Bronco R got hung up on a boulder at about race mile 420. An impatient trophy truck driver went to drive up the side of the wash and tipped over, landing on the Bronco R. No real damage was done, but the trophy truck pinned the Bronco R, and the two teams had to wait until another truck came by to tow them out of the situation.

Traversing the rest of Matomi, the Bronco R hit a boulder and peeled the skid plate back, which was already beaten and weak from the pounding it had been taking all race due to the rain-packed dirt. As the skid plate peeled back, it punctured the transmission-cooler lines, which was a problem that did not become obvious until down the road.

The Beginning of the End

Shelby Hall was waiting at BFGoodrich Pit No. 4 at race mile 450 to take the Bronco around to race mile 580 and hand off the Bronco to Curt LeDuc to bring it home the last 200 miles. The damage from the Matomi Wash caused the team to repair the skid plate and transmission-cooler lines before Shelby could continue.

At race mile 580, Shelby brought the Bronco R into Pit No. 5 with a failed aftermarket radiator cooling fan motor that was causing overheating issues. She also reported that the transmission was starting to slip. Much time was lost replacing the cooling fan, and the Bronco R team was left with a conundrum. The northern loop of the racecourse was nearly 200 miles long, and over two-thirds of it was inaccessible to pit crews in the event that the Bronco R had more problems. Another issue was that it was already 8:30 p.m. on the second day, and it was questionable whether they could reach the finish in time to be an official finisher.

Calm heads prevailed, and Ford's Bronco R exited the race at that point. While tremendously disappointed, what Ford, Geiser Brothers, and the Desert Assassins accomplished in five months was amazing. Ford Motor Company wasted no time in letting the media know that they would be back in 2020 to finish the race.

2020 Rebelle Rally

The Rebelle Rally is a unique event because it is not a race, per se; it is an off-road navigation rally raid. There

Quick preparation is key to success at the Rebelle Rally. The day's route and maps are only released about 30 minutes prior to departure. Here, Shelby Hall and Penny Dale pour over the maps and plan for attacking the course. (Photo Courtesy Shelby Hall)

are no race cars (although you can run one as long it is street legal), no roll cages, no driving suits, no pit crews, no GPS, no cell phones, and most of all no Y chromosomes. This event is for women only.

So, what do you get to take along? A map, pencils, compass, ruler, plotter, and calculator. You also need a tent and sleeping bags because this 2,000-kilometer rally does not stop at hotels. The rally starts in Lake Tahoe and winds through Nevada and California ends eight days later at the Imperial Valley Sand Dunes near the Mexican border.

The rally organizers make this an all-inclusive event because who wants to have to haul eight days of food along? Meals are included, as are mechanics who are shared among all the teams. Bathroom and shower facilities are available at overnight stops, except for marathon legs. A marathon leg is basically two days back to back with limited overnight help. These legs end at a remote location without the luxuries of a hot meal (dehydrated meals are issued for teams), and there is no shower.

If It Is Not a Race, How Do You Win?

Since this is billed as a rally and not a race, it is about managing time, speed, and distance (TSD) sections and navigational waypoint sections to determine your score. Some days, the TSD legs are first; other days, they switch things around. You do not know what is coming until the checkpoint guide is issued in the morning. This leaves teams with 30 minutes to calculate the TSD legs and strategize on the waypoint legs.

Every team must make all the green checkpoints. The blue and black checkpoints are optional, as these are not as easy to find, but they score you more points. The black checkpoints are exceptionally hard to find. There is no marking on the land, and you record your coordinates and hope you found it. The black checkpoints score the most but take more time and effort to find.

Meet the Team

Ford saw the value in supporting the Rebelle Rally with its entry of three 2021 Ford Bronco Sport vehicles equipped with the Badlands package. The Broncos ran in the "X-Cross" class, which matched it with other two- or all-wheel-drive entries that did not come equipped with a 2-speed transfer case. This makes for good competition among Subaru Outbacks and Foresters, Toyota RAV4s, and Mitsubishi Outlanders.

2021 Ford Bronco Sport

Branded by Ford as the Bronco of small SUVs, this is not the larger Bronco that has been recently introduced. Call it the Bronco's little sibling. Based on the same platform as the Ford Escape, this has a myriad of extras that make it more off-road capable.

The Badlands-package Bronco has a 2.0L EcoBoost engine that pumps out 245 hp and 270 ft-lbs of torque. It is coupled with an 8-speed automatic transmission that features steering-wheel-mounted paddle shifters and a twin-clutch rear-drive unit with a differential lock.

The package rides on 17-inch wheels and all-terrain tires, which achieves clearance with the help of a factory installed 1-inch lift kit. The extra lift not only gives extra tire clearance but also helps achieve added ground clearance. It also comes with heavier-duty shock absorbers than the base models.

The interior and exterior features are like a wish list for those who want innovative features, including a 400-watt power inverter, slide-out table that can be used as a workbench, and room enough to stow two mountain bicycles.

All that aside, Ford knew it packed enough performance to make the Bronco Sport a contender in this kind of competition. The teams were also handpicked to achieve the best result possible, but the clear "A" team was that of Shelby Hall and Penny Dale, who were experienced off-roaders with racing and navigational skills as well as prior Rebelle experience.

After the 2019 Baja race with the Bronco R, Shelby thought that the new production Bronco would make a good vehicle for the Rebelle. She submitted a proposal to Ford for a single Bronco. Shelby had previous Rebelle experience, and her new relationship with Ford gave her the chance to run the event and feature the new Bronco.

By day, Penny Dale is a registered interior designer from Vancouver, British Columbia, and owner of Penny Dale Design. When she is not leading design projects of new or renovated properties, she likes to be off-road.

No stranger to adventure, Dale took on a nearly 28,000-mile journey from Vancouver, British Columbia, to Ushuaia, Tierra del Fuego, Argentina, in 2016. She began running the Rebelle in 2018 and is highly sought after for her navigational abilities.

Ford accepted Shelby's proposal with an addendum; it wanted three Bronco Sports to be entered. Two more Broncos were entered, and each pair was selected to complement the team overall.

Penny Dale (left) and Shelby Hall (right) teamed up in a Bronco Sport at the female-only Rebelle Rally. The pairing of these ladies and the Bronco Sport proved to be the winning combination against stiff competition. (Photo Courtesy Shelby Hall)

At the end of the rally, Team Ford Bronco Sport posed for a sunset photo on the dunes of the Imperial Valley. From left to right are Jovina Young, Penny Dale, Shelby Hall, Erica Martin, Betsy Anderson, and Elana Scherr. (Photo Courtesy Shelby Hall)

The scenery is one of the perks of running an event like this along the Sierra Nevada mountains. (Photo Courtesy Shelby Hall)

The "B" team consisted of a pair of off-road enthusiasts led by automotive writer Elana Scherr and Betsy Anderson. Both have Baja experience, and calling them a "B" team is almost a disservice to what they brought to Ford. Scherr is a contributor and columnist for *Car and Driver* magazine and a book author. This was her first Rebelle Rally. Anderson is a mechanical designer and has more than 20 years of off-road experience.

Then, there was a third team: Jovina Young and Erica Martin, who are a pair of Ford employees. Young is the brand manager of the Bronco Sport and a University of Michigan graduate. Martin is a marketing comms man-

The Bronco Sport performed flawlessly for seven days on the rally. It handled gravel roads, rocky trails, and miles of sand dunes with ease. (Photo Courtesy Shelby Hall)

ager for SUVs and has worked for Ford for most of her adult life. Both were able to go back to Detroit and speak firsthand about the capabilities of their newest small SUV.

On to Victory!

The road to the X-Cross Class win was not without its challenges. Shelby and Penny got to the end of day one in a tie with the Kia team. On Day 2, the Ford edged out the Kia and take the lead. On Day 3, a Mitsubishi edged Shelby and Penny, who actually hit more checkpoints than anyone, but one "wide miss" at a checkpoint cost them just enough to lose the day. However, they maintained a slight overall lead.

Day 4 was from Ridgecrest, California, to the Dumont Dunes. The ladies put together a great day, locating more checkpoints than anyone in the rally and extended their lead. This was also the first of the marathon days, so it was an excellent time to make a big move.

That move was almost wiped out on a disastrous Day 5 from the Dumont Dunes to the Johnson Valley. Late in the day, Shelby and Penny saw their lead disappear after running out of fuel prior to reaching base camp. It cost them a 35-point penalty and forfeiting the opportunity to earn any more points for the day. It seems that in an attempt to grab every possible checkpoint in the Dumont Dunes, the extra fuel consumption of sand-dune driving cost them mileage. With only two days left in the rally, it was time to have a big Day 6 from Johnson Valley to the Imperial Sand Dunes.

It is all business inside the Bronco Sport Badlands Edition. Ford put great faith into this team to take the win, which it did. The Ford employee entry gathered data about the functionality of the Bronco Sport. The media entry put the word out about the new platform. (Photo Courtesy Shelby Hall)

"Big" it was. The Ford Bronco Sport grabbed 27 points, the most of anyone that day, leaving them a manageable 24 points behind the leaders in a Mitsubishi, and the Kia was still uncomfortably close.

The last day in the dunes saw Shelby and Penny record a flawless day, distancing themselves from the Mitsubishi, which spent some time stuck in the dunes and needed a tow from a competitor. This caused the Mitsubishi to slip to third behind the consistent Kia.

To top off the event, competitors were asked at the end of the last day if they wanted to enter a special competition that would be revealed later. That competition turned out to be a tire-changing competition that Shelby and Penny won as well. It was a nice way to end the rally.

The 2020 Baja Race

After the 2019 debut of the Bronco R Prototype and its unfortunate early exit from the race, there were great hopes for its 2020 attempt at finishing the 900-mile loop. The team was back together again plus one: Ultra 4 Champion Jason Scherer. The extra mileage of this year's race (898 miles) and the unique layout of the course necessitated the extra driver.

Jason Scherer

Scherer is a multiple-time podium finisher in the grueling King of the Hammers competition, a finisher of the Mint 400, and a winner at the Brush Run race in Crandon, Wisconsin. It is considered by many to be a triple crown of sorts for off-road racing. With 18 years of off-road racing experience, he is known for his consistency and his ability to set up a race car.

COVID-19 Kills the Peninsula Run

The 2020 race was originally envisioned as a peninsula run to La Paz, which are normally scheduled every four years. Facing issues with the pandemic and social distancing, the organizers laid out a racecourse in a giant loop. Since loop-style races began in 1975, this was the longest loop run at 898.4 miles.

The Roughest Course Ever Seen

Those 898.4 miles were the biggest challenge anyone had seen in their Baja careers. The rains that made such an impact in 2019 and some ensuing storms the prior winter and spring left the terrain extra rutted, rocky, and silty.

After extensive pre-running expeditions, nearly every race team made comments about how this race would take longer than expected to finish. It also called for extra patience over the technical terrain. The typical feared spots on the course were extra difficult.

The Race

A total of 185 teams started the race, which was low for an annual Baja trek. The situation with the pandemic forced many teams to give this year a pass. In communicating with several Bronco teams that normally run the event, each one said that concerns over the pandemic and the health and safety of friends and loved ones overshadowed the call of Baja.

This left one Bronco in the event: the 2021 Bronco R Prototype. Curt LeDuc took the start, and at race mile 60, he handed the Bronco R over to Shelby Hall, who drove to race mile 200 after the Pacific Coast leg. LeDuc then hopped in a chase truck and followed Mexican Highway 1 to San Quentin to jump back in the Bronco R and drive to Valle de Trinidad, which was a very technical and demanding section.

At race mile 80, the Bronco R passed the *Boot*, which was pulled over with a tire issue. Shelby, who did not see the *Boot* pulled off, pushed the Bronco R to a 5-mile lead before the *Boot* got going again. As the Pacific rolled by on their right side, the *Boot* closed in at race mile 130 and passed the Bronco R. At this point, Shelby started to feel an irregularity in the steering system. It was nothing too drastic, but it was not normal, either.

At race mile 160, the *Boot* was pulled off again, letting Shelby into the lead again, but it was short lived, as by race mile 177, the *Boot* overtook the Bronco again. In San Quentin when Shelby brought the Bronco into the pit, she reported the steering issue. Looking at more than 150 rough miles with only one pit opportunity, the decision was made to replace the steering rack and pinion.

As the *Boot* moved out to a lead, the core mission for the Bronco R team was still to finish the race. With new steering installed, the Bronco went into the next section looking to make good time. Things went well until race mile 327 when the Bronco got involved in a big backup because of a stuck car in a narrow section. Some reports came that attempted to circumnavigate the traffic jam, but the Bronco R was stuck for a time.

After the jam cleared, the Bronco was underway again only to get 15 miles before the rear wheel bearing failed, necessitating a stop. The repair lasted more than 30 minutes.

After that, the Bronco continued largely trouble free through the rest of the course, but the purpose-built *Baja Boot* kept adding to its lead despite a double rollover late in the event.

After 32 hours, 31 minutes, and 21 seconds, the Bronco R returned to Ensenada as an official finisher of the longest continual off-road race in the world.

The race is a workout for every member of the team from the driver to the pit crew. It started at race mile 130 when the steering rack started to fail. No one gave up though, and it was satisfying to see the Bronco R accomplish its goal. (Photo Courtesy Justin W. Coffee)

With its lights on, the path ahead was treacherous in the evening hours of the race with dust obscuring vision and deep silt to traverse. (Photo Courtesy Justin W. Coffee)